INSIGHT GUIDE

AMSTERDAM

Ms. Brenda I. Sheldon
Unit 7
2800 S. University Blvd.
Denver, CO 80210

APA PUBLICATIONS
Part of the Langenscheidt Publishing Group

ABOUT THIS BOOK

Editorial

Project Editor
Zoë Ross
Managing Editor
Tom Le Bas
Editorial Director
Brian Bell

Distribution

UK & Ireland
GeoCenter International Ltd
The Viables Centre, Harrow Way
Basingstoke, Hants RG22 4BJ
Fax: (44) 1256 817988

United States
Langenscheidt Publishers, Inc.
46–35 54th Road, Maspeth, NY 11378
Fax: (718) 784 0640

Canada
Thomas Allen & Son Ltd
390 Steelcase Road East
Markham, Ontario L3R 1G2
Fax: (1) 905 475 6747

Australia
Universal Press
1 Waterloo Road
Macquarie Park, NSW 2113
Fax: (61) 2 9888 9074

New Zealand
Hema Maps New Zealand Ltd (HNZ)
Unit D, 24 Ra ORA Drive
East Tamaki, Auckland
Fax: (64) 9 273 6479

Worldwide
Apa Publications GmbH & Co.
Verlag KG (Singapore branch)
38 Joo Koon Road, Singapore 628990
Tel: (65) 6865 1600. Fax: (65) 6861 6438

Printing

Insight Print Services (Pte) Ltd
38 Joo Koon Road, Singapore 628990
Tel: (65) 6865 1600. Fax: (65) 6861 6438

©2002 Apa Publications GmbH & Co.
Verlag KG (Singapore branch)
All Rights Reserved
First Edition 1991
Third Edition 2000
Updated 2002

CONTACTING THE EDITORS
We would appreciate it if readers
would alert us to errors or out-
dated information by writing to:
**Insight Guides, P.O. Box 7910,
London SE1 1WE, England.**
Fax: (44) 20 7403 0290.
insight@apaguide.demon.co.uk
NO part of this book may be reproduced,
stored in a retrieval system or transmitted
in any form or means electronic, mech-
anical, photocopying, recording or otherwise, without prior written permission of
Apa Publications. Brief text quotations
with use of photographs are exempted
for book review purposes only. Information has been obtained from sources
believed to be reliable, but its accuracy
and completeness, and the opinions
based thereon, are not guaranteed.

www.insightguides.com

This guidebook combines the
interests and enthusiasms of
two of the world's best known information providers: Insight Guides,
whose titles have set the standard
for visual travel guides since 1970,
and Discovery Channel, the world's
premier source of non-fiction television programming.

The editors of Insight Guides provide both practical advice and general
understanding about a destination's history, culture, institutions and people. Discovery
Channel and its Web site,
www.discovery.com, help
millions of viewers
explore their world from
the comfort of their
own home and also
encourage them to
explore it first hand.

This fully updated
edition of *Insight: Amsterdam* is
carefully structured to convey an
understanding of Amsterdam and
its culture as well as to guide readers through its sights and activities:

◆ The **Features** section, indicated
by a yellow bar at the top of each
page, covers history and culture in a
series of informative essays.

◆ The main **Places** section, indicated
by a blue bar, is a complete guide to
all the sights and areas worth
visiting. Places of special
interest are coordinated by
number with the maps.

◆ The **Travel Tips** listings section, with an
orange bar, provides
a handy point of ref-
erence for informa-
tion on travel, hotels,
shops, restaurants
and more.

EXPLORE YOUR WORLD
Discovery
CHANNEL

Map Legend

▬ ▪ ▬	International Boundary
– – – –	Province Boundary
–▪– ▪ –	National Park/Reserve
– – – –	Ferry Route
Ⓜ	Metro
✈ ✈	Airport: International/ Regional
🚌	Bus Station
❶	Tourist Information
✉	Post Office
✝ ✝ ✝	Church/Ruins
✝	Monastery
☾	Mosque
✡	Synagogue
⌂ ⌂	Castle/Ruins
∴	Archaeological Site
∩	Cave
⌶	Statue/Monument
★	Place of Interest

The main places of interest in the Places section are coordinated by number with a full-colour map (e.g. ❶), and a symbol at the top of every right-hand page tells you where to find the map.

The contributors

This edition of *Insight Guide: Amsterdam* was comprehensively revised by **Zoë Ross**, a London-based editor, supervised by managing editor **Tom Le Bas** at Insight Guides. More recently, the book has been thoroughly fact-checked and updated by regular Insight Guides contributor **George McDonald**.

This edition's main author, **Joan Gannij**, moved to Amsterdam in 1987 as editor of *Master Chef*, an international magazine of food, wine and travel. Born on Amsterdam Avenue in New York City, she considers it her fate to end up in the Dutch city and is now the proud holder of two passports. As well as writing about Amsterdam, she works as a photojournalist and copywriter and is also a published poet and of late, a songwriter. In the last few years, she has been a contributor to the Insight Guides to Oslo and Bergen and, recently, the Netherlands. She has also been involved with *Insight Guide: Scandinavia*.

Gannij was assisted in her researches on the guide by **Frank Balleny**. Of English and Dutch parentage, Balleny spent the first five years of his career working all over the Netherlands as a specialist printer. A heavy industrial accident forced him to give up printing the written word, so he turned to writing and translating. His poetry has been published in Dutch and English, and he has written columns for a Utrecht newspaper, and a children's book.

The current edition builds on the excellent foundations created by the editors and writers of previous editions of the book, most notably **Christopher Catling**, editor of the original *Insight Guide: Amsterdam*. **Stuart Ridsdale** contributed much of the text of the original Places chapters, while **Tim Harper** and **Michael Gray** wrote the majority of the original Features text. **Joan Corcoran-Lonis** contributed the essay on Anne Frank.

Without the many stunning photographs this book would be a duller affair. The images of **Paul van Riel**, one of Insight's regular photographers, who has lived in the city all his life, have helped bring the book to life. Other photographers who have made valuable contributions include **Eddy Posthuma de Boer**, **George Wright**, **Christine Osborne**, **Lyle Lawson**, **Lesley Player** and **Michel Gotin**.

Thanks also go to **Sylvia Suddes** for proofreading this latest edition of *Insight Guide: Amsterdam* and to **Penny Phenix** for indexing it.

INSIGHT GUIDE
AMSTERDAM

CONTENTS

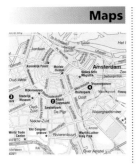

Amsterdam's ubiquitous gabled architecture

Travel Tips

Information panels

Insight on ...

Places

THE CHARACTER OF AMSTERDAM

Behind the tourist clichés is a cosmopolitan city with a village ambience and a remarkable breadth of culture

Amsterdam, the city of water and brick, is unique for the way it balances past and present. Perhaps no community has ever had such a glorious explosion of wealth and culture as Amsterdam during the 17th century, the city's Golden Age. While the legacy of that period is pervasive, the city is hardly devoted to worship of the past. Instead, modern Amsterdam, from the titillation of the Red Light District to the vitality of the contemporary arts, from the energy of the entrepreneurs in their small shops to the fast-growing immigrant fringes of the city, offers a range of experiences that are the result of a remarkable human heritage.

People either adore Amsterdam or abhor it. Which is why it is important to walk the less beaten paths away from the Red Light District and Damrak and discover the side streets adjacent to the canal circles, with their shops and friendly cafés. In strolling around Amsterdam – one of the best walking cities in the world – you are also reminded continually of how the city was built and how it thrives: on hard-headed business acumen and a sense of community that combines several qualities. Foremost among these, paradoxically, is the desire to be left alone and the willingness to leave others alone – that is, unless they need help. For while Amsterdam is, and always has been, a city of people pulling themselves up by their own bootstraps, it is also a city that believes in spreading its wealth. Money and comfort are important, but so is a happy, healthy society.

Amsterdam is intriguing in several respects. Largely because of its small size, in terms of both population and geography, it is intimate and accessible. It has the ambience of a cosmopolitan village rather than a European capital. English is becoming more and more of a second language; in fact many Amsterdammers speak at least three languages – few people plunge into conversation with strangers as readily as the Dutch – and this provides visitors with an opportunity to look beyond what they've read or heard about the city.

For Amsterdam, apparently so solid, as it sits astride its miles of canals, is really a city that is changing constantly. What's the latest trend in art? Where's the best place to go dancing *this* week? Who's saying what about the future of NATO and the EU? When is the next demonstration? How are the authorities getting along in their efforts to clean up the streets of hooligans, drug dealers and dog poop?

Amsterdam is a city of character and of characters. It is a free-wheeling city – so feel free. ❑

PRECEDING PAGES: reflections on Prinsengracht; De Silveren Spiegel restaurant and shop; food shops on Damstraat; carnival festivities on Dam Square.
LEFT: street theatre in the Rokin district.

JAARLYKSE OMMEGANK DER LEPROOZEN. OP

OPPERTIES MAANDAC OP GEHOUDE IN JAAR 1005

Decisive Dates

Early History (AD 1200–1500)

12th century AD First communities of herring fishermen settle on the banks of the Amstel.

circa **1220** The first Dam, or sluice, is built to hold back the tidal waters of the Zuiderzee.

1275 Floris V, Count of Holland, grants the people of "Amestelledamme" freedom from tolls on their goods; this is the first documentary record of Amsterdam.

1300 The Bishop of Utrecht grants Amsterdam official city status.

1334 Work begins on the Oude Kerk, Amsterdam's oldest church.

1350 Amsterdam becomes the export centre for local beers and an entrepôt for Baltic grain.

1395 The first city hall is built on Dam Square.

1452 Fire destroys many of Amsterdam's timber-and-thatch buildings. Laws ordain that new buildings shall be built of brick and tile.

1480 Walls are built to defend the city.

Religious Wars: 1500–1595

1519 As a result of war, treaties and marriage alliances, Amsterdam is part of the Spanish empire and nominally Catholic, but tolerant of Protestants (persecuted throughout Europe).

1535 Anabaptists invade the Town Hall to proclaim the Second Coming. The occupiers are arrested and executed. Catholicism is reimposed.

1566 The Iconoclasm *(Beeldenstorm)*. Calvinists protesting at the lack of religious freedom storm many of Amsterdam's churches.

1567 Philip II of Spain sends the Duke of Alva to restore Catholic control of Amsterdam. Many Protestants are executed or flee to England.

1572 The Dutch Revolt against Spanish rule begins in earnest, led by William of Orange.

1576 Amsterdam, loyal to Philip II, is besieged by Prince William's troops.

1578 Amsterdam capitulates to Prince William. Protestant exiles return to the city. Calvinists take over the churches and the reins of government in the peaceful Alteration *(Alteratie)* revolution.

1579 The seven northern provinces of the Netherlands sign the Treaty of Utrecht providing for mutual assistance in the event of attack. Protestant refugees from Antwerp, Amsterdam's trade rival, seek asylum in the city and help to lay the foundations for the Golden Age.

The Golden Age: 1595–1700

1595–97 Ships from Amsterdam sail east via the Cape of Good Hope to "discover" Indonesia.

1602 The Dutch East Indies Company is established to co-ordinate trade with the lands east of the Cape, financed by a public share flotation.

1609 The Bank of Amsterdam is formed, placing the city at the forefront of European finance. Hendrik Staets draws up the plan for the *Grachtengordel*, the three concentric canals ringing the city (work starts on the first section in 1613).

1621 The Dutch West Indies Company is founded and benefits from a monopoly on trade with the Americas and West Africa.

1626 Peter Minuit "buys" the island of Manhattan and founds the colony of Nieuw Amsterdam (taken by the English and renamed New York in 1664).

1632 The Athenaeum Illustre, the forerunner of Amsterdam University, is founded.

1642 Rembrandt paints *The Night Watch*.

1648 The Treaty of Münster recognises the northern provinces as an independent republic.

1650 Amsterdam now has a population of around 220,000, the largest city of the new republic.

1652 War with the English for maritime supremacy.

1685 Huguenot refugees flood into Amsterdam after the Revocation of the Edict of Nantes, reversing their rights to freedom of worship.

1688 William III of Holland is crowned as King of

England, having married Mary Stuart. William's wars against the French strain the Dutch economy and the republic's trade begins to decline.

CONSTITUTIONAL CHANGES: 1700–1900

1702 William III dies without an heir. Amsterdam and the northern provinces suffer further inroads to their trade when the Austrian Emperor Charles VI sets up a rival East Indies Company in Ostend.

1744 France invades the southern provinces.

1747 William IV is elected hereditary head of state of the seven northern provinces, now unified under one leader and called the United Provinces.

1751–88 The United Provinces are torn between conservative supporters of the House of Orange and liberal reformers, called Patriots.

1795 France invades Amsterdam and, in alliance with the Patriots, forms a National Assembly. The United Provinces are named the Batavian Republic.

1806 Napoleon reverses the constitutional reforms and establishes his brother, Louis, as King of the Netherlands, with Amsterdam as its capital.

1813 After the defeat of Napoleon, William VI is welcomed back to Amsterdam from exile.

1814 William VI is crowned King William I of the Netherlands.

1848 The new Dutch constitution comes into force, providing for a directly elected parliament.

1870–76 Socialist principles of government rapidly develop; improvements are made in education and public health, and the North Sea Canal revives Amsterdam's position as a port and shipbuilding centre.

WAR AND RADICALISM: 1900–2000

1914–20 The Netherlands remain neutral during World War I, but food shortages lead to strikes, riots and support for the Dutch Communist Party.

1928 Amsterdam hosts the Olympic Games.

1930s During the Great Depression, the city's unemployed work on job creation schemes, including the construction of the Amsterdamse Bos park.

1940 Germany ignores the neutrality of the Netherlands and invades on 10 May.

1941 400 Jews are rounded up in Amsterdam on 22 and 23 February. Dockworkers lead a two-day strike in protest at anti-Jewish measures.

1942 Anne Frank and family go into hiding.

PRECEDING PAGES: 17th-century Amsterdam as depicted by A. van Nieulandt.

LEFT: *Woman Spinning* by Van Heemskerck (1529).

RIGHT: J.R. Thorbecke, father of the Dutch constitution.

1945 After a bitter winter Amsterdam is liberated.

1963 Amsterdam's population reaches 868,000 and housing shortages lead to organised squats – occupations of empty buildings.

1965 The Provos, dedicated to shaking Dutch complacency, win representation on the city council.

1966 Protesters disrupt the wedding of Princess Beatrix and Claus von Amsberg with smoke bombs.

1975 Police battle with demonstrators over plans to demolish areas of Nieuwmarkt.

1986 Despite strong opposition the *Stopera* – Stadhuis and Opera – complex is completed.

1989 The government is defeated as its anti-vehicle laws are considered too soft.

1994 400th anniversary of the first tulip arriving in Amsterdam.

1997 The Eurotop conference of European leaders is held among much controversy; Amsterdam is named the fourth "Tourist City" of Europe.

1998 The first Gay Games attract thousands of visitors; the pedestrianised Museumplein opens.

2000 The Rijksmuseum celebrates its 200th anniversary. Passenger Terminal Amsterdam opens for cruise liners.

2002 Crown Prince Willem Alexander weds Argentinian Máxima Zorreguieta at the city's Nieuwe Kerk; and the world's first same-sex marriage with an identical legal status to heterosexual marriage takes place in Amsterdam. ❏

VILLAGE IN THE BOGS

It began as a tiny fishing community, but ingenious building methods

and craftsmanship soon turned Amsterdam into a thriving city

The herring fishermen who established a community at the mouth of the Amstel River in the 12th century must have struggled to survive. As elsewhere along the North Sea coast, they pieced their huts together on top of mounds anchored by wooden stakes and piled up the mounds with seaweed and anything else dredged from the tidal flats that couldn't be put to a better use. Along with a few craftsmen, these early settlers had to devise a more reliable existence than living at the whim of the unpredictable tides that surged in from the Zuiderzee.

Yet the Amstel community grew, and the scattered huts became rows of timber-framed houses built on top of the dykes by the river. Three of the old dykes are still visible today as Warmoesstraat, Nieuwendijk and Kalverstraat.

Damming the tides

With the excess soil from digging drainage canals, the level of the houses was raised about 70 cm (27 inches) above Normal Amsterdam Level (NAP). NAP is the standard "zero" measurement for the nation, not sea level – in Amsterdam and the whole of western Holland, sea level would mean knee-deep or even neck-deep in water. Examples of the NAP, showing how so much of the Netherlands is below sea level and what happened when the country was devastated by the flood tides of 1953, can be seen in a permanent exhibition in the Town Hall *(see page 206).*

The first dam, intended to hold back the highest tides, was built around 1220, most likely near the present Centraal Station or further up Damrak. It is likely to have been nothing more than a sluice gate across the mouth of the Amstel. The gate would halt the inundation from the large tides and at low tide could be opened to allow the Amstel River to flow into the sea.

LEFT: *The Mill at Wijk bij Duurstede* by Jacob Ruysdael (1670), now in the Rikjsmuseum.
RIGHT: *The Noorderkerk*, A. Beerstraten (1644).

By 1275, the peat bogs surrounding the hamlet known then as "Amestelledamme" had gradually attracted farmers, refugees and tradesmen who bolstered the population to the point where it might, generously, be called a town; even so, it was still very small by comparison with higher, drier European capitals.

From burg to city

According to a contemporary woodcut, the forerunner of the Oude Kerk (Old Church) had been erected near the site of today's church, on Oudekerksplein, along with about 600 houses. Surrounding the little burg was a moat, the remnants of which can be traced in the Oudezijds Voorburgwal and the Nieuwezijds Voorburgwal canals; the latter was not filled in until 1884, some 600 years after it was first dug.

Amestelledamme, or Amstelredam (it did not become Amsterdam until the mid-16th century), then began making great strides – quickly enough, in fact, to find itself the prize in a battle for provincial fiefdoms between the

Bishop of Utrecht and the Count of Holland towards the end of the 13th century. In the first recorded reference to the city, Count Floris V granted the people of Amsterdam freedom from paying tolls on goods shipped along the waterways of Holland. As the city's trading status grew, the count was trying to curry favour with residents who technically fell under the domain of the Bishop of Utrecht.

To a point, Floris was successful. But the local nobles did not want to be anybody's pawn. Led by Gijsbrecht van Amstel, a group of city barons ambushed and murdered the count in 1296. Gijsbrecht was later turned into

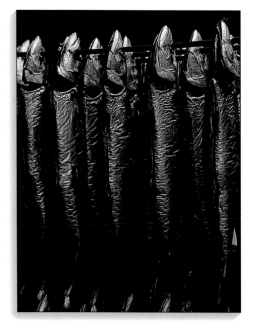

a hero of a classic 17th-century play by Joost van den Vondel, affectionately known as the "Shakespeare of the Netherlands".

In 1300, Amsterdam was officially granted city status, receiving its charter from the Bishop of Utrecht. By this time the conflict between the bishop and the counts of Holland had been resolved; in typical medieval fashion, the heir of the assassinated Count Floris V defeated the old bishop and installed his brother as the new Bishop of Utrecht. When this bishop died, the Count of Holland cleverly inherited his brother's fiefdom, including the whole of the city of Amsterdam and the surrounding Amstelland.

A city of canals

The weirs and drainage ditches that had kept residents dry were proving an obstacle for the shipping that the city was attracting, and the canals were equally restrictive for population growth. Locks were constructed to enable smaller vessels to move into the city, where they often sold their wares from the canalside. Shops sprang up alongside the dykes and on the approaches to the big dam (Damrak). An agricultural market and town square evolved around the Waag (Weigh House) on the present-day Dam Square, which lasted until the King of the Netherlands removed it for blocking his view in 1808.

Expansion would prove to be an eternal dilemma for the growing port. The first solution was to widen the tops of the dykes and embankments to enable them to become the main streets. Next, rows of warehouses and homes were extended over the water. Narrow alleys and tiny canals connected the principal canals to the Amstel. The next step was to dig more canals parallel to the dykes on either side of the river. This symmetrical process led to more pairs of canals on both the old and new sides.

This process was repeated throughout the 15th century. Following popular urban planning practices of the day, an encircling series of canals and walls was built. The city boundary can still be traced; the squat turret at the Nieuwmarkt is one of the best remnants of the old wall.

Built on piles

Residents of Amsterdam had also become ingenious builders. The soft, porous top soil, usually a mixture of sand, peat and clay, meant that the buildings needed deep foundations to keep them from sinking. Long pine tree trunks, almost like modern pilings, were imported from Germany and Scandinavia to anchor the foundations. They had to be driven up to 12 metres (40 ft) through the sand into firmer soil. The same practice is still followed today. Long rear annexes took advantage of every inch of soil.

By 1500, Amsterdam was the largest city in the Netherlands and 50 years later had a population of 30,000 people. In the crowded conditions, with timber the predominant construction material, fires were inevitable. After a series of infernos in the mid-1400s, one of the earliest fire codes in history was adopted. New façades had to be built of stone or brick and roofs had to be of slate or tile. Thatch was prohibited.

Fuelling all this growth was commerce, particularly with the coastal towns of the Baltic. Salt became crucial for cod and herring fishermen, who, by gutting and salting their catch, could preserve it and stay longer at sea. Salt came from Portugal, and Amsterdam was the perfect halfway point between southern Europe and the Baltic, especially since the city benefited from the favourable tax status granted by its benefactor, the murdered Count of Holland.

TAX DODGES

Homes were taxed according to the width of their façades, traditionally designed with large windows. Warehouses and homes were therefore often narrow at the front but extended at the rear.

rose up in protest at the conditions under which they worked. Several times during the 15th century entire groups of labourers would protest by leaving the town *en masse*, giving new meaning to the word "strike".

Amsterdam's beer trade was equally vital to the medieval economy, especially since water at that time was of dubious quality. The Count gave Amsterdam the sole right to import large quantities of hop beer from Hamburg. Eventually, Dutch brewers in Haarlem,

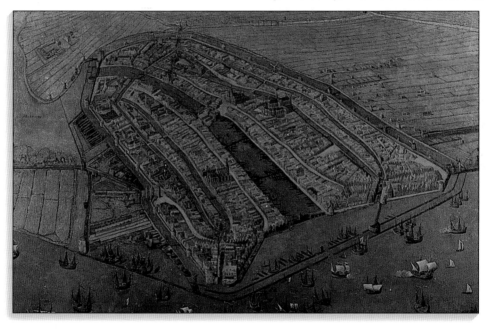

The wool and beer trade

Clothing sweatshops were well established in Amsterdam, according to city records, as much as 600 years ago. Wool from England initially went to workshops in Leiden and Haarlem. Increasingly through the 1500s Amsterdam manufactured quality cloth and eventually became the leading wool centre in the country.

Though the city grew prosperous on this trade, not everyone benefited equally. According to one city historian, the oppressed workers

LEFT: herrings, the basis of Amsterdam's early wealth.
ABOVE: Cornelius Anthoniszoon's well-known 1538 map of Amsterdam.

Gouda, Delft and Amsterdam abandoned their own grout-flavoured brew and began making a similar style of stronger-flavoured hop beer. These local breweries proved so successful that they were soon exporting their products through the free port of Amsterdam.

Grain for beer and bread also passed through the Baltic to Amsterdam. Spices, pitch, fur, timber and iron ore kept city warehouses full, and the principle of *entrepôt* was born. This meant that goods entering the city but ultimately destined for another port could be stored without incurring tolls, taxes or duty. This principle, maintained through the centuries, still exists today in the form of bonded warehouses. ❑

PROTESTANTS AND ICONOCLASTS

From the 16th to the 18th centuries, Amsterdam alternated between Catholic and Protestant leanings, eventually emerging as a uniquely tolerant city

Amsterdam in the 16th century was a veritable pot-pourri of religious convictions. Even so, not everyone could practise their beliefs openly and the fine line between religious orthodoxy and heresy was often drawn along political, rather than religious, grounds.

It wasn't always this way. Until the turbulent 1500s, Amsterdam's population was 98 percent Catholic. The city even had its own miraculous host, housed in a healing shrine that soon turned Amsterdam into an important destination for pilgrims.

City of miracles

The so-called Miracle of the Host occurred in 1345 when a dying man was given his last communion rites, but he was not able to keep the host down. The man's vomit was thrown on the fire, as was customary in those days, but the host refused to burn. A small shrine was built on the site of this miracle and over the ensuing years other magical acts were attributed to the host.

A century later, when the chapel burned down, the host was again miraculously spared. This only served to confirm the special properties of the host and the whole of Amsterdam, swelled by pilgrims from further afield, would turn out for the annual procession in which the sacred relic was carried around the city for veneration.

Interrupted for centuries by the Reformation, the *Stille Omgang* (Silent Procession) was revived once again in the 19th century, but it was conducted in silence and at midnight so as not to offend the non-Catholic residents of what was still officially a Protestant city. Today the silent night-time procession, held from Saturday to Sunday between 12 and 22 March each year, still attracts thousands of worshippers from Amsterdam and beyond.

LEFT: late 19th-century painting by Hugo Vogel of Luther nailing his 95 Theses on Wittenburg Cathedral.
RIGHT: the religious reformer John Calvin.

The 15th-century church built on the site of the miracle at the Nieuwzijds Voorburgwal, however, did not survive. It became Protestant after the Reformation and continued this way until 1908, when the Catholics wanted to buy the old building. Protestants refused to sell and the church was ultimately destroyed.

Reform and uprising

Erasmus of Rotterdam was the first of the religious reformers to challenge the established church when he claimed man was the ideal creation rather than the root of sin, as depicted by Adam. But Spanish and Catholic dominance of northern Europe really began to fragment after the Augustinian monk Martin Luther nailed his 95 points, condemning church abuses, to the chapel door of Wittenburg Castle in 1517. Luther's translation of the Bible was first published in the Netherlands.

However, more popular in Amsterdam were the teachings of a French Protestant theologian, John Calvin, which leaned heavily on the doctrine of predestination. The Catholic Church urged strong punishment on the heretical followers of Calvin, but little was done in Amsterdam. The civic fathers were not going to shatter their prosperous co-existence with the Calvinists at the behest of Catholic bishops based in Brussels who, technically, held pastoral authority over the Netherlands.

This lax attitude was blamed for the Anabaptist uprising of 1535. These early Protestant charismatics were followers of a

ICONOCLASTIC LEGACY

Many churches in the Netherlands were never restored after the Calvinist uprising. Their plain interiors remain as evidence today of the violent destruction of icons during the 16th century.

Strict Catholics quickly replaced the apparently unvigilant leaders who had allowed the Town Hall to be stormed and a period of anti-Protestant repression followed. But naturally when something is forbidden, curiosity to discover more about it increases exponentially. Calvinism was no exception; it soon gained support from many wealthy city merchants, including several liberal Catholic burgomasters, who felt that the city was being administered through corrupt measures and complained to

furrier named Melchior Hofmann, who imagined himself to be a Doomsday prophet. In May that year, about 40 "Melchiorieten" who had worked themselves up into a religious frenzy tore off their clothes and stormed the Town Hall, imitating an earlier coup attempt in Münster. The revolt, which was intended to shock Amsterdammers into renouncing their worldly ways, succeeded briefly only because it was an annual Catholic feast day – the civic guards and officials were, as one record put it, "far gone in drink". The next day the guards retook the Town Hall. Many rioters were executed on Dam Square and their heads placed on pikes at the city gates.

Margaret of Palma, Regentess of the Netherlands. A famine in 1565 in which many Protestants suffered only exacerbated the situation.

Summer of discontent

By the 1560s, Protestant services were being held outside the city gates and out of the jurisdiction of the Catholic police. Religious tensions boiled over in the summer of 1566. In another episode of copycat violence, this time with inspiration from Antwerp, a mob of Amsterdam Calvinists smashed their way through the altars and statuary of the Oude Kerk, a protest which became known as the "Iconoclasm". In the following months the rioters also turned their destructive attentions to the city's priories, hitting the wine cellars when they ran out of works of religious art to break upstairs.

Again, in typical Amsterdam fashion, the city fathers chose to placate rather than confront the situation. In return for profitable peace they allowed the Calvinists to hold services openly in one of the Franciscan churches they had earlier looted. The Protestants accepted their lot and were quietened for a while.

NEW RELIGIONS

Migrants quadrupled Amsterdam's population to 220,000 between 1600–50. Portuguese and German synagogues appeared alongside German Lutheran and French Walloon and Huguenot churches.

to switch allegiance to the Protestant Prince William of Orange, leader of the Dutch revolt against Spain. Only in 1578, when it was obvious that the Spanish were in retreat and William's forces surrounded Amsterdam, did the city prudently and swiftly change sides.

What followed is politely known as "the Alteration". The United Provinces were formed against Spain and all Catholic city officials were peacefully replaced with good Protestant merchants. Overnight the city's

Change of fortunes

But the vandalism had not gone unnoticed: it earned Amsterdam the harsh attention of King Philip II of Spain. The northern front of the Eighty Years' War extended as far as Amsterdam shortly thereafter. Repression at the orders of the Iron Duke, Fernando Alvarez de Toledo, was ruthless – some 12,000 rebels from the recent raids were sentenced to death. Unlike the majority of the Netherlands, however, Amsterdam remained loyally Catholic, choosing not

LEFT: the Anabaptist uprising of 1535.
ABOVE: Anabaptists, portrayed as licentious communists in contemporary engravings.

churches became Calvinist. Wealthy Calvinist merchants fled from Catholic southern Holland and the southern provinces of the Low Countries (modern Belgium) – still under Spanish rule – and moved to Amsterdam. As Amsterdam grew into a major trading capital, many of these men were to finance the Dutch merchant fleets and trading companies that fuelled the expansion *(see page 223)*.

Although part of the agreement of the formation of the United Provinces was to allow freedom of belief, this was not yet translated into freedom of worship, largely in fear that Catholicism and Spanish sympathies were too closely interlinked. Many of the more devout

Amsterdammers remained Catholic, however, and with this reversal in their fortunes it was they who now had to worship secretly and quietly, in barns or in the hidden attics of city homes. While traces do remain of other attic churches, only one, the Amstelkring, is today completely preserved, and serves as a museum *(see page 137)*.

An unofficial "pacification" evolved by 1630 under which the Catholic minority was quietly tolerated but barred from public office. The attic churches then became an open secret, even though for the next 200 years Catholic worship was officially prohibited. Police in search of

bribes often "raided" services. Still fearful of papal influence, however, the authorities would not yet allow any of the Catholic churches to become "visible".

Once the Catholic threat was removed, however, it wasn't long before the Calvinist principle of "freedom of conscience" evolved into an ethos of religious tolerance, for which the Amsterdam city fathers became widely damned – or praised, depending on your point of view. Pragmatic citizens were now in a position to choose their religion at the time of marriage, often influenced by the power of different denominations to offer a secure guild job or large dowry.

A free press

Preoccupied with commerce, Amsterdam was practically the only city in Europe to have no form of censorship on publications. The city pastor even published a book denouncing his own church for its superstitious belief in witches and black magic. The church dismissed him, but the city burgomasters continued to pay his salary and held the official position vacant until his death.

This freedom of conscience was not without economic benefits. Over the next century, Amsterdam became a haven for intellectuals unable to work in their native land because of their religious beliefs, including philosophers such as René Descartes and John Locke. Writers and, symbiotically, Amsterdam printers used the city's liberal ethos to create publishing empires, the remnants of which are still important to the city's economy.

By the time aftershocks from the French Revolution hit Amsterdam in 1796, the religious make-up of the city clearly reflected the previous two centuries of tolerance. Only 22 percent of the population was now Catholic, compared to 98 percent three hundred years previously. The largest group was now Calvinist (50 percent), and there were also sizeable Lutheran (16 percent) and Jewish (12 percent) communities. Already the city had developed a mixed character and was shortly to change again, as migrants arrived from far-flung parts of the mighty Dutch empire *(see page 41)*. ❏

ANTI-SEMITIC RULES

While the liberal climate of 17th-century Amsterdam resulted in the tolerance of Catholics, non-Christians had an altogether more difficult time. Portuguese Sephardic and High German Ashkenazic Jews enjoyed good relations with officialdom but they suffered economic discrimination. Citizenship had to be purchased anew each generation and could not be inherited. Intermarriage with non-Jewish citizens was prohibited by religious and city law. With the exception of surgeons, brokers, printers and booksellers, Jews were prohibited from guild membership. This left street trading and diamond cutting, which had no guilds, as the preserve of the Jews.

LEFT: the secret attic church that is now the Amstelkring Museum.
RIGHT: Nieuwe Kerk interior in the 17th century.

ART AND THE GOLDEN AGE

The term "Golden Age" was first used by a city mayor, inspired by the Greeks, and although art went into decline after 1675 the era's mystique continued for centuries

Amsterdam now regards itself as Europe's fourth city, behind London, Paris and Rome. But during the 17th century, Amsterdam was pre-eminent. Then, as now, it was much smaller than its rivals. Nevertheless, during that brief shining moment in history known as the Golden Age of the Netherlands, it was very much the commercial and cultural capital of Europe.

The rapid growth of the Dutch trading empire provided the prosperity at home that led to an unprecedented period of development in art, architecture and many related crafts. Besides the paintings of the Dutch Masters and the attendant "Little Masters", Amsterdam was the focus for developments in silver, porcelain, furniture, engraving, printing and various skills related to building. Sculptors such as Artus Quellinus and Rombout Verhulst also made their mark but sculpture was never as popular in Amsterdam as it was in the Italian Renaissance cities, perhaps because there were no princes to commission grand stone monuments in the hope of keeping their family name alive through the ages.

New realism

Art historians credit the Dutch artists of the Golden Age with launching the era of realism in painting, particularly with their landscapes and seascapes – as well as what one critic whimsically called "cowscapes", after the detailed portraits that some farmers commissioned of their favourite bulls and cows, often complete with a fresh cowpat beneath the animal's hindquarters.

Frans Hals (1580–1666) is regarded as the founder of the Dutch School of realistic painting. Often called "the first modern painter", he introduced to fine art the emotion of the moment, a glance or a grimace that might be seen anywhere on the streets but nowhere in the posed, stilted portraiture that had been seen in the past *(see page 186)*.

Throughout his short life, Jan Vermeer (1623–75) lived and worked only in Delft *(see page 252)*. Although only 30 works of his are known, he (along with Rembrandt and Van Gogh) is regarded as one of the Great Dutch

Masters in the history of the Netherlands. However, he did not achieve fame as an artist of great stature until the late 19th century, when a French writer and critic singled him out for his techniques in painting, use of light and talent for creating illusions. Most of his works are painted in bright tints that produce clearly defined forms, thus creating a strong feeling of reality. His *View of Delft*, for example, looks astonishingly vivid, as if a colour photograph had been reproduced.

Despite his limited output, Vermeer's œuvre had great diversity. Like many of his contemporaries, he began painting Biblical and mythological themes, then concentrated primarily on

LEFT: Rembrandt's house on Jodenbreestraat.
RIGHT: detail of Rembrandt's most famous work, *The Night Watch*, in the Rijksmuseum.

cityscapes as well as composed interiors featuring one or more figures – often young ladies or noblemen. These figures tend to be absorbed in their activities, as in *The Lady Writing a Letter with her Maid* or *Young Woman with a Water Pitcher*.

Gerard de Lairesse (1641–1711), another student of Rembrandt, was known as "the Dutch Raphael". Unlike Rembrandt, his work was more defined in line, colour and use of light. Ten years after painting what many consider his masterpiece, *The Banquet of Antony and Cleopatra*, de Lairesse went blind. However he continued to lecture on the principles of art.

Among those less well known today but extremely influential in 17th-century Amsterdam, was Jan van Goyen of Leiden (1596–1656), who led the way in making landscapes the whole purpose of the painting instead of a mere background.

Rembrandt's rise

Few, however, would doubt that the Golden Age painter with the greatest reputation, then as now, was Rembrandt van Rijn (1606–69) who started painting in his native Leiden but spent his most productive years living and working in Amsterdam. More than three centuries after his

ART FOR ALL

Did art become so popular in Amsterdam because it was home to so many good artists, or did Amsterdam produce so many good artists because art was so popular? In either case, the wealth of the middle classes allowed the Dutch to indulge their love of art. For the first time, ordinary citizens could afford to commission and buy paintings.

Instead of being tied to a few rich patrons who demanded grand religious and historical works, artists in Amsterdam were able to sell to the highest bidder. It was the first truly open market for art. And the Dutch buyers, as much interested in their own enjoyment as in posterity, commissioned paintings of themselves, their friends, their families, their homes, their shops, their ships, their farms and even their prize cattle. Bankers, bakers and even common farmers had paintings on their walls.

Certainly the Dutch appreciated art, but the middle-class families of 17th-century Amsterdam also had down-to-earth reasons for collecting paintings. A painting allowed them to display their success to their neighbours without being seen as trying too hard, and paintings, along with ceramics and silver, were a hedge against inflation.

As one critic has pointed out, the Dutch fledgling art market exploited "the need for sound investment and conspicuous display in a rapidly expanding economy".

death, Rembrandt remains the most deeply loved of all the great masters of painting, his face so familiar to us from the self-portraits painted at every stage in his life, yet still so mysterious. Indeed, there are certainly few artists of the 17th century so popular that they are known familiarly by their first name.

Like other leading members of the Dutch School, he broke new ground in realism. One of his most daring, and most costly, paintings was his 1642 masterpiece *De Nachtwacht (The*

THE SIMPLE LIFE

The critic Eugene Frometin once commented: "Dutch painting was not, and could not be, anything but the portrait of Holland, its external image, faithful, exact, complete, lifelike, without any adornment."

The Night Watch condemned Rembrandt – who up to that point had been extremely popular and grown quite rich – to a period of relative obscurity. Fewer commissions meant that he could no longer support his extravagant (and, in that way, un-Dutch) lifestyle. He was forced into bankruptcy and out of his fine house at Jodenbreestraat 4–6, where he lived from 1639 until 1658.

The house was completely refurbished in 1999 and has been restored as it was when Rembrandt originally lived there. At

Night Watch), a study of the members of one of Amsterdam's volunteer civic guards. The large painting now has pride of place in the Rijksmuseum *(see page 189)*, but was apparently ill received at the time because it was regarded as too casual and haphazard; in particular, critics did not like the fact that not all the faces of the guards could be seen clearly, demonstrating an insensitivity to factors which modern critics most admire – Rembrandt's realism in creating a crowded scene.

LEFT: two works by Jan Vermeer, *The Letter* and *Head of a Girl*.
ABOVE: *The Young Bull* by Paulus Potter.

first the museum had simply been a receptacle for Rembrandt's drawings and etchings, but a new museum wing now houses these precious artefacts, creating the opportunity to restore the residence to its pre-museum role and thus give an impression of the artist's life as well as his work *(see page 207)*. Also recommended, even for those who are not art aficionados, are Rembrandt's often ruthless self-portraits, reflecting his moods and the process of ageing as he moved inexorably towards frailty and senility.

In his recent book, *Rembrandt's Eyes*, scholar Simon Schama writes: "Like Shakespeare, the facts of his life are difficult to come by: the Leiden miller's son who briefly found fame in Amsterdam, whose genius was fitfully recognised by his contemporaries, who fell into bankruptcy and died of poverty... there is probably no painter around whose life more legends have grown up, nor to whom more unlikely pictures have been attributed (a process now undergoing rigorous reversal)."

Practical value

According to historians, Dutch art went into decline some time after 1675. Sales of pictures gradually stagnated and after 1700, their popularity took a turn for the worse. Many critics say that the quality of the paintings diminished.

The so-called "Nederlandish" painting reached its zenith with Rubens in Antwerp around the 1620s and then in about 1650 in Amsterdam. This was halfway through the century, after the Eighty Years' War, when Dutch trade was flourishing and purses were full. Although the term Golden Age originally referred in classical writing to a period in Greek history in which the idyllic, natural simplicity of people was as yet uncorrupted by the artificiality of civilisation, a former Amsterdam mayor (Joan Huydecoper) borrowed the term and the rest, as they say, is history. Looking back at the heyday of the painters and poets in the mid-17th century, Huydecoper reflected: "Those days were a golden age for art, and golden apples – which are now scarcely to be found, what with dangerous roads and grinding labour – in that blissful time dropped ripe into the mouths of the happy artists."

But as art declined the Dutch love of everyday beauty did not. The modern Dutch disdain for self-aggrandisement has its roots deep in the 17th century – even during the Golden Age, the emphasis was on enjoying a comfortable life, not on ostentation. The quality of goods, of workmanship and artistic talent was highly valued but the Dutch liked to be able to show the symbols of their prosperity in belongings and property that had practical value and could be used in everyday life.

In this way, people could show their wealth without being accused of putting on special airs. Their salt shakers, for instance, were typically silver and often carried luxuriant floral designs. Plates, beakers and knife handles were engraved. The walls of the formal reception rooms might be covered in hand-tooled leather, and the veneering and marquetry, often renderings of floral patterns, were of a quality that has rarely, if ever, been excelled.

Far-sighted plan

The ultimate lasting expression of the Golden Age in Amsterdam is the city itself, particularly the 17th-century design and construction of the concentric rings of canals linked by radial canals – a model much studied and admired by other cities. It is doubtful whether such a project could have been planned, much less completed, without the medieval-style city-state administration that prevailed in Amsterdam.

Because Amsterdam was its own master in the loose alliance with other Dutch city-states, known as the United Provinces, the commercial middle classes were the city's driving force. They had no ruling monarchy over them and the other provinces had little say over the internal affairs of the city. Consequently, the usual vetoes were absent for such an ambitious and far-sighted project as the expansion of the city by building the three new canal rings outside the old 1481 city walls: Herengracht, Keizersgracht and Prinsengracht *(see page 155)*.

Designed by Hendrick Staets, the municipal carpenter, the Herengracht is 3.5 km (2¼ miles) long, the Keizersgracht 4 km (2½ miles) and the Prinsengracht 4.5 km (2¾ miles). The three ring canals were built 2.1 metres (7 ft) deep and 25 metres (82 ft) wide to accommodate four lanes of medium-sized ships 6 metres (20 ft) wide. Ships frequently moored directly in front of a merchant's home and the cargo was unloaded directly into the fourth-storey storeroom/warehouse via the crane-hooks that still survive in the gables of most canal-house façades.

The combined 25 km (16 miles) of quayside on the three main canals provided enough space for some 4,000 ships to be moored at once,

TREE SURGERY

Dutch elm disease got its name not because the disease originated in the Netherlands, but because the most comprehensive studies have been done there.

The straight-sided sections of the large canals made it easier to lay out regular building plots for the fine houses, but precluded the sweeping canal vistas of cities such as Venice, Pisa and St Petersburg.

Many commentators have remarked on the fact that the physical layout of the ring canals means that they must be "enjoyed as scenes of individual vignettes", and that the only real way to get an idea of the massive scale of the design is simply to walk all the canals and their numerous side streets.

which resulted in a forest of masts that often obscured the views from the houses. The most prestigious residences were all to be built on the three main ring canals, while smaller homes and shops would be fitted in along the radial canals. The Jordaan area was constructed from 1612 to provide accommodation for local artisans and small factories, which included sugar refineries, potteries, print works, ropeworks and glass factories, among others (see page 158).

LEFT: frieze detail from the Royal Palace.
ABOVE: Golden Age splendour on show in the Museum Van Loon.

Further diminishing the potential grandeur of the design were the thousands of trees planted along the 11-metre (36-ft) wide quays on either side of the three main canals. Originally, the quays were planted with elm trees and those that survive are diligently looked after by municipal tree surgeons.

This town plan, which has effectively left modern Amsterdam perched on 90 islands linked by 500 bridges, also provided the model for future municipal zoning. The city paid for the construction of the canals, which took most of the 17th century to complete, by selling off canalside housing plots. Owners of the houses had to agree to conform to a set of strict rules, including a requirement to pay for maintenance of the quayside and footpath that lay in front of their homes.

Although a few exceptions were made for some of the most influential and wealthy residents, especially the six "Magnificat" families, most of the canalside lots were sold with 30 metres (100 ft) of canal frontage. Canny property speculators sometimes bought two adjacent plots and then re-sold them as three 20-metre (67-ft) plots.

> ### CITY COLOUR
>
> To this day, doors and railings of the houses along and around the Grachtengordel must be painted "Amsterdam green", a rich dark green which is similar to the colour of the water in the canals.

Uniform style

Zoning laws also limited how deep the houses could be, and insisted on a certain amount of clearance between the backs of houses on adjacent canals. Other rules specified that certain types of brick and stone should be used in the construction, and left only minor opportunity in the façades and gables for owners to express their individuality – sometimes these were embellished with flourishes or a sculptural relief to indicate the owner's occupation, such as cannons on a gunmaker's home. The result is a city of essentially similar buildings, but with distinctive decorative elements. "Architectural good manners", today's critics call it.

Golden Age monuments

The Trippenhuis, on Kloveniersburgwal, is an example of one of the very few Amsterdam houses that can be said to rival the palaces of Venice. It was built in 1662 by Justus Vingboons who, along with brother Philips, designed many of the big canal houses, often marked by their trademark pilaster gables. Across the street from the palatial Trippenhuis is the narrowest house in Amsterdam. According to the story, the Trip family coachman was overheard complaining that he wished he could afford a canal house even if it was only as wide as the door of his master's home; so they built him exactly that at No. 26 – a house that is just over 1 metre (3 ft) across *(see page 148)*.

The wealth of the Golden Age also produced most of Amsterdam's best-known public buildings and monuments, particularly the churches. The most prominent building, of course, is the Town Hall, now the Royal Palace, completed on Dam Square in 1662 *(see page 129)*. Jacob van Campen, a Haarlem painter and architect, was given the job of designing the grandest town hall in all of Europe, and he did – but only after managing to overcome the enormous technical difficulties of putting a building of such a size on what was virtual swampland.

The building was eventually constructed on 13,659 pilings dug 18 metres (60 ft) deep; virtually every Amsterdammer knows the number of pilings because of a formula, drilled into them at school, that goes: "Take the number of days in a year and add a 1 at the beginning and a 9 at the end."

Modern critics still marvel at the wealth of decoration on the Royal Palace. There are a number of specifics for visitors to note, including the plan of the building, constructed around two courtyards, with a huge central hall. The bronze gates are fitted with gunports for muskets, and the narrow staircases and hidden entrances were designed to allow officials to defend the building easily against mob attack. On top, the weathervane represents one of the thousands of Dutch merchant ships that roamed the world and came home laden with riches. ❑

LEFT: cloisonné spice jar from the East Indies.
RIGHT: *Street in Delft* by Jan Vermeer.

EMPIRE BUILDERS

Amsterdam used its shipping prowess to sail the world during the 17th and 18th centuries, setting up Dutch colonies across the globe in the process

The Golden Age of the Netherlands, which spanned most of the 17th century, is today best known for its art and architecture. But the Golden Age would probably never have occurred, and certainly would not have carried the same sheen, without the extraordinary boom in world trade that paved the way for Holland to become the financial and artistic hub of Europe. The increase in trade provided immediate benefits in the form of unprecedented wealth, particularly in Amsterdam. It also established the far-flung Dutch empire, extending from South America and the Caribbean to the Far East.

War with Spain

The Dutch Empire grew out of the 80-year conflict with Spain, beginning with the 1568 revolt against Spanish rule led by William of Orange, whom the Dutch revere as the father of their country. The 1579 Treaty of Utrecht created the United Provinces, which provided the foundation for the modern Netherlands, a loose alliance of seven northern provinces – as distinct from the southern provinces, which had remained subject to Spain and evolved into modern Belgium and Luxembourg.

The decades of strife with Spain are commonly characterised as arising out of a religious dispute – the result of the refusal by Dutch Calvinists to allow Philip II of Spain to impose Catholicism on them as part of his anti-heresy Inquisition. But there were – as there always seem to be with the Dutch – underlying economic factors. Spain not only wanted to control religion but also wanted centralised control of the Dutch economy. In the face of attempts to limit their religious freedoms and restrain their economy, the Dutch reacted in typical hard-headed fashion. They outlawed Catholicism and did everything they could to

expand their economy, which included competing with Spain for trade and colonisation across the globe.

The first Dutch ships landed in the East Indies (now Indonesia) in 1595, and the East Indies Company (VOC) was formed in 1602 with a government-guaranteed monopoly on all

trade east of the Cape of Good Hope *(see page 18)*. In an innovative move for that time, the East Indies Company sold shares, in effect allowing any daring Dutch investor to help finance voyages and reap the profits. This gave a much broader section of Dutch society a personal interest in the spread of the empire.

Spices and profits

In 1611, by which time the United Provinces had supplanted Portugal as the leading spice importer in Europe, the East Indies Company paid a dividend of 162 percent. Annual dividends for the next several decades typically ranged between 12 and 50 percent – a tidy little

PRECEDING PAGES: Amsterdam's flower market, around 1670, by G.A. Berckheyde.
LEFT: Neptune in the Scheepvaarthuis.
RIGHT: Oost Indisch Huis (East Indies House).

return that certainly helped to build and furnish quite a few of the imposing canalside houses still standing today.

Dutch ships ranged as far as China and Japan. Occasional shiploads of Ming porcelain, arriving in Amsterdam, caused great excitement along the docks and the strong demand led to the foundation of a domestic pottery industry that made Delft famous *(see page 252)*.

Eventually, the eastern Dutch empire included parts of Ceylon (now Sri Lanka),

the capture of the Mexican silver fleet in 1628. But the company, virtually an organisation of sanctioned pirates, was never as financially successful as its East Indies counterpart.

Nonetheless, the Dutch holdings eventually expanded to include Tobago, Cayenne, Bonaire, Curaçao, St Eustatius, St Martin, the Dutch Antilles, Aruba and Dutch Guyana (now Suriname). Trading settlements were also established, or taken over from the Spanish and Portuguese, in Venezuela and Brazil.

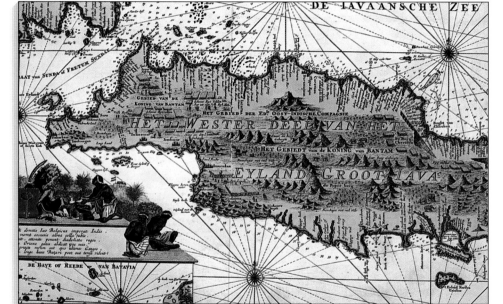

Tasmania and South Africa, but the heart of the company – and of the whole empire – was the Dutch East Indies. The East Indies totalled nearly 8,000 islands stretching over 4,800 km (3,000 miles) and included many of the islands of modern Indonesia: Bali, Timor, Java, Sumatra, Borneo and Western New Guinea.

The West Indies Company (WIC) was founded as the 1609–21 truce with Spain, the only formal break in the decades of war, came to an end. The West Indies Company was modelled on its East Indies predecessor, except that making a profit was secondary to fighting the Spanish. The WIC's captains won some famous victories over the old enemy, notably

Trade and finance

At home, the Bank of Amsterdam was formed in 1609 and quickly established fiscal policies that made the city the financial centre of Europe. Mortgages and loans, almost impossible to obtain in most other capitals, were readily available in Amsterdam, and at interest rates of 3 to 4 percent compared with 6 percent in London or Paris. The Amsterdam Stock Exchange, founded in 1611, is one of the oldest in the world.

Accounts of Amsterdam at the height of the Golden Age describe a bustling city – the population grew from 40,000 to 200,000 during the 17th century – with business being conducted everywhere. There were no major universities, however, nor were there huge cathedrals or meeting places, except those used for commercial purposes. Dam Square, in the shadow of the imposing Town Hall (now the Royal Palace), was the main public space in the city, but it was partially given over to a weighing house and a fish market. The major buildings seemed to be warehouses, where Dutch traders stockpiled their goods, often until they had created scarcity in the market and could then drive prices up. Smaller ships sailed up the canals, and goods were winched off the decks into the attic-storehouses in the canal-side houses of the merchant owners.

numbers of African slaves to work the colonial Caribbean sugar plantations.

The Dutch did not impose slavery in the East Indies, but nonetheless ruthlessly exploited both the people and natural resources. When the European spice market collapsed in the early 18th century, the Dutch successfully introduced coffee, which remains a key Indonesian crop today, but then proceeded to wring a higher and higher percentage of the profits out of the islands.

The United Provinces became an independent republic as part of the Treaty of Münster in 1648. The treaty was part of the Peace of West-

The decline

The empire was not destined to last, however. The home-loving Dutch were never very good colonists. They liked to arrive, conduct their trade and then go back to their native provinces rather than settle in faraway countries. As a result, they never put down the roots that were the key to the longer-surviving European colonies in the New World. The failure of Dutch farmers to settle the West Indies is one of the reasons cited for the importation of untold

LEFT: the Dutch East Indies as shown on a 17th-century map.
ABOVE: *Amsterdam Harbour* by W. van der Velde.

COSMOPOLITAN CITY

As the empire spread and the streets of commerce became ever busier, Amsterdam became Europe's most cosmopolitan city. Besides the Dutch themselves, with their widely varying manner of regional dress and speech, the harbour and the shopping streets were suddenly crowded with Germans, Poles, Hungarians, French, Spanish, Muscovites, Persians, Turks and Indians, all coming to buy and sell in this thriving city. As the empire expanded across the globe and the Dutch intermarried and took on natives as partners and employees, so the ethnic mix grew to include Malays, Arabs, Chinese, Papuans, Caribs, Creoles and Africans.

phalia, which ended the Thirty Years' War, the wide-ranging conflict that had diverted the attention and resources of other European powers while the Dutch were quietly building up their empire. Peace among the other powers, however, allowed them to turn their attention towards the traders (and pirates) of Amsterdam for the first time in decades.

England wasted little time in initiating the first of several wars with the Dutch (1652–4) that resulted in the loss of significant chunks of East Indies trade. In the West Indies, war with Portugal also cost the Dutch their holdings in Brazil.

By the mid-17th century, the lustre of the Golden Age was fading. The Zuiderzee had begun silting up and it became difficult for ships to reach the Amsterdam docks. Perhaps more significantly, many of the citizens living in their fancy new canal houses no longer wanted ships sailing up to their front doors and unloading cargoes into the attic.

Gentrification

The second and third generations of the merchant families did not share their ancestors' zest for chasing the guilder to the ends of the earth. As the concentric canal design neared

NEW YORK

Another war with England erupted in 1664 over the New Netherlands in America and its harbour at Nieuw Amsterdam (now New York). New Netherlands was founded in 1612, but there was no permanent settlement at Nieuw Amsterdam, the capital of the colony, until 1625. By 1626, when Peter Minuit, the Dutch governor, "bought" Manhattan Island from its American Indian inhabitants for the proverbial $24-worth of beads, the population was still fewer than 300. After the English seized the colony in 1664 and renamed it New York, the Dutch gave up claims on the New Netherlands in exchange for English promises not to take Dutch Guyana.

completion *(see page 155)*, the monied classes in Amsterdam seemed more interested in spending money than in gathering more. The merchant fleet was depleted, the national debt grew and peasants who had been wearing leather shoes for years went back to making wooden ones.

The Dutch, nevertheless, managed to hold on to a good part of their empire when the Netherlands emerged from French rule at the end of the Napoleonic era *(see page 19)*. Trade in important colonial products such as tin, quinine, coffee, timber and rubber remained an integral part of the Dutch economy until the outbreak of World War II.

Independence and migration

After World War II, the East Indies came out of Japanese occupation with a new determination to seek independence. So much so that Dutch nationals who had suffered the horrors of Japanese internment camps during the war (many didn't survive) found themselves re-interned by the Indonesians during the conflicts that were to follow in 1945–9. The Dutch decided that "the East Indies must be liberated from the tyranny of the collaborators Sukarno and Hatta and their followers."

Sukarno was the charismatic voice of students and activists seeking independence

Since Suharto took power in 1969, the Netherlands and Indonesia have conducted a long-distance love affair highlighted by cultural exchanges. Anyone visiting Amsterdam today will see the consequences, from the many citizens with island ancestry to the innumerable Indonesian restaurants *(see page 98)*.

Several of the smaller Caribbean islands remain part of the Dutch realm, but the western colonies have had much less cultural impact on modern Amsterdam – perhaps because of slavery, lower profits and disinterested rule. By the time Suriname gained independence in 1975, Dutch roots were so shallow that many of

from the Netherlands. In 1945–9 there were many violent outbursts which did not go entirely unsupported by the US, Britain and Europe. The Dutch wanted to let Indonesia go gently and set up an interim board before independence. Sukarno and his followers had other ideas: they renounced not only the interim board but also its Indonesian members. The conflict dragged on until 27 December 1949 when Dutch sovereignty had been transferred and Sukarno became Indonesia's first president.

LEFT: Dutch troops in Indonesia before independence.
ABOVE: the first Indonesia president, Sukarno (left) and his successor, Suharto.

Suriname's educated and professional classes were Javanese, trained in the East Indies and moved in by the Dutch to work as managers.

At independence, 150,000 of Suriname's estimated population of 400,000 exercised their right of immigration to the Netherlands. Though many of them were middle-class and have become a valued part of Dutch society, they are frequently blamed for involvement in drugs and other crimes and have not assimilated as well as the Indonesians *(see page 84)*.

The Dutch are not overly caught up in history, but the rise and fall of the empire certainly helps to explain the modern city of Amsterdam and its ethnic-cultural diversity. ❑

THE WAR YEARS

Occupied by the Nazis during World War II, Amsterdam suffered badly,
experiencing famine and the devastation of its Jewish community

Despite remaining neutral during World War I, the Netherlands suffered severe food shortages, exacerbated by a large influx of refugees. Far worse was to come. After a brief period of prosperity in the 1920s, during which time Amsterdam hosted the Olympic Games, the city was hit by the global economic depression of the 1930s. With Europe heading back into war, the Netherlands hoped to retain their neutral status, but this time it was not to last; on May 10 1940, German air and ground units invaded, plunging the nation into the darkest chapter in its history.

The Jews in Amsterdam

The first Jews came to Amsterdam in the 16th century, fleeing from persecution in Portugal. The Netherlands had a reputation for tolerance but the Dutch, also excellent businessmen, were aware that many of the Portuguese Jews were rich and would bring their money and vital trade connections with them to the north. Less affluent Jews ended up in ghettos, poor but safe, for a few centuries at least *(see page 213)*.

One of the relics of rich Portuguese Jewish life in Amsterdam is the beautifully restored Pinto family house *(see page 146)*, located near Rembrandt's home in Jodenbreestraat. Rembrandt chose to live in a Jewish neighbourhood because he found the ambience colourful and stimulating, but he was given to violent dislikes and Pinto, a successful banker, became a target. Amsterdam city records chart a bizarre court case when Rembrandt, who always lived beyond his means, bought a great deal of expensive wood for repairs to his house and charged it to Pinto. The judge ruled that, as Pinto's name was on the bill, Pinto must pay.

Apart from this trivial incident, and a degree of economic discrimination *(see page 28)*, records show that the Jews lived peacefully in the city and the Dutch seemed to hold no dislike or fear towards them. Therefore the revulsion felt by the Dutch when the first Nazi deportation of 425 terrified Jewish men and youths from occupied Amsterdam got under way was great. The Nazis started with the men; women and children followed.

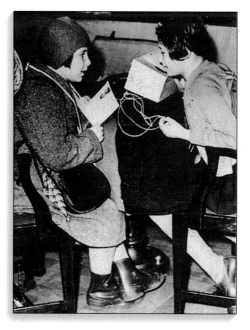

The Occupation begins

Amsterdam's Raadhuisstraat, a street leading to the city's Dam Square, was lined with hundreds of silent Amsterdammers when the German convoy drove in during the first weeks of May 1940. One tenth of the population – the Jews – stayed at home.

The crowd watched the Germans arrive in their lovely city with fascinated horror. Many had read the red-bordered proclamation of power issued by the country's new ruler, Dr Arthur Seyss-Inquart, which was displayed around the city. The message was friendly in tone. "I have today taken over civilian authority in the Netherlands… The magnanimity of

---

PRECEDING PAGES: Bickersgracht in 1893.
LEFT: the Nazis enter Amsterdam in May 1940 as part of the German Occupation.
RIGHT: Jewish refugees.

the Führer and the efficiency of German soldiers has permitted civil life to be restored quickly. I intend to allow all Dutch law and general administration to go on as usual."

Some people watching the triumphant arrival of the Germans that day actually allowed themselves to believe the message and these glimmerings of hope anaesthetised their sense of foreboding. But the city's Jews knew better; especially the 25,000 German Jews who had fled the country of their birth to Amsterdam to escape German persecution in the 1930s. They now had their backs to the North Sea, with nowhere left to go. All possible escape routes were cut off, all hope abandoned. It was merely a question of how long it would take the Führer's evil tentacles to reach them.

They did not have long to wait, but the Nazis had other details to arrange before the attack on the Jews could get under way. A number of people unfortunate enough to be on Nazi blacklists had to be rounded up, many of them political activists. The Dutch Nazi party (NSB) was coming into its own, with many of its members, black-shirted louts and rednecks, being promoted to executive positions. The party had already, with great efficiency, prepared lists of "troublemakers" for the perusal of their Ger-

THE ROYAL FAMILY IN EXILE

Prince Bernhard had been ordered by his mother-in-law, Queen Wilhelmina, to accompany his wife and two daughters to Canada via Britain. He was reluctant to do so as he wanted to remain with his people. Wilhelmina was adamant: the royal blood-line must be protected. The prince, a fervent Nazi-hater, agreed to go on the condition that he be allowed to return to Britain, where he was made head of the Dutch free forces. The shy, lonely Princess Juliana, meanwhile, began coping alone in Canada, looking after the two young princesses. The eldest, Beatrix, became Queen of the Netherlands when Queen Juliana abdicated for her daughter in 1980.

man overlords. It was a perfect opportunity for settling old scores – the playground bullies had taken over.

Soon certain new signs became a familiar part of the city scene. For Amsterdammers the long drawn-out agony of tension and rumour was over. German army traffic signs went up, Nazi newspapers appeared on the streets, sold by the hated Dutch NSB members, German marching songs, accompanied by hectoring German voices and the sound of marching jackboots, were heard everywhere. But Dr Seyss-Inquart continued his efforts to convince Amsterdammers that the Führer had sent his troops to watch over them like a kind father figure. As yet nothing ghastly had been seen to happen, and many people still hoped that their lives would continue as usual.

Then, on 29 June 1940, the Dutch showed that, though they may have abandoned any thought of taking direct action against the occupiers, they had not abandoned hope. Thousands of people took to the streets wearing white carnations. It did not take the Germans long to realise what was going on. It was Prince Bernhard's birthday. The Dutch were copying one of his discerning vanities as a symbol of passive resistance – he always wore a white carnation in the buttonhole of his tweeds.

were rounded up and herded into Jonas Daniël Meijerplein in the Jewish quarter. Photographs in the Jewish Historical Museum show them staring straight ahead, hands above their heads, faces full of terror *(see page 208)*. They were kept in the square for hours before being moved into transport trucks lined up beside the Portuguese Synagogue. The trucks drove off; there was one survivor.

Protest strike

Today a statue of a burly Amsterdam docker stands on the square commemorating what happened two days later. News of the deportation

Anti-Jewish measures

In Amsterdam the noose was tightening for the Jews. From July 1940, the Germans started to issue more and more restrictive proclamations. Jews could not be employed in the Civil Service and those who already were must be sacked. Jews could not enter cinemas or travel on public transport and all firms owned by Jews must be reported for registration.

On 22 and 23 February 1941, the Germans made their move – 425 Jewish men and youths

LEFT: Seyss-Inquart, Nazi ruler of the Netherlands.
ABOVE: the *razzia* (round-up) by the Nazis of Jewish youths and men in February 1941.

of the men spread around the city and from 25 to 26 February there was a general strike led by the city's dockers. It was Amsterdam's first open gesture of rebellion, as revulsion for the occupiers began to conquer collective fear.

The Germans, at first stunned by this show of defiance, quickly moved to stamp it out. German police patrolled the streets arresting hundreds and shooting nine people dead. Notices were posted ordering everyone back to work. The text, which was signed by General Friedrich Christiansen, read as follows: "There will be no meetings or gatherings of any kind, nor any political party activity. Anyone disobeying will be proceeded against under

German military law. Hereafter anyone who strikes, or who agitates for strikes, will receive up to fifteen years and, if the defence industry is involved, death." On 15 March three members of the strike committee and 15 resistance members were executed.

People slowly went back to work, morale temporarily boosted by the fact that Amsterdammers had openly dared to resist tyranny. But the euphoria did not last long, as the everyday, mind-destroying *ennui* of the Nazi occupation began to sink in. There were no more posters urging

BRAVERY REMEMBERED

The two-day dockworkers' strike in 1941 has gone down in Dutch history as Amsterdam's "day beyond praise".

By now Jews were being forced to wear the yellow Star of David, six-pointed, black-bordered and bearing the word "*Jood*" (Jew). Most wore it proudly. Even more restrictions were being introduced: Jews could not use the public parks, could not own telephones nor use public ones. A curfew was introduced: Jews had to be indoors from 8pm to 6am and were not allowed to have visitors at home.

More and more Jews were being "transported" – the euphemism for train transport to

the Dutch to learn to "trust" their German friends. The kid glove was revealed to be covering a steel fist, and it was being used against the Jews with the utmost force.

The nightmare begins

Jews watched in horror as the stories they had heard of Nazi brutality in the German ghettos became reality on their own streets. The sight of pathetic groups of people, the men clutching suitcases or knapsacks, the women carrying infants, toddlers clinging to their coats, being hustled along by the military or plain-clothes police, became an everyday reality that Amsterdam people were powerless to prevent.

Westerbork camp in the province of Drente, close to the German border. The trains to Westerbork were normal passenger trains in every respect, except that they were locked from the outside.

One woman survivor told how, after months of claustrophobic terror in Amsterdam, she remembered enjoying the journey through the countryside to Drente. That is where any enjoyment would have ended, because Westerbork was a transit camp for Auschwitz; from there the long journey east was made, not in passenger trains but in locked cattle trucks; the railway line ended in front of the gates of the camp where the real horror began.

As it started to dawn on the Jews that they were only being cooped up in the city for identification and processing in preparation for the cattle trains to the slaughterhouse, some lucky ones were able to "dive" *(onderduiken)* – to disappear into hiding.

Of course, to do this you needed to have very brave friends because anyone caught harbouring Jews was shot without question. Many non-Jews on the German "wanted list", including members of the resistance, also "dived".

Humanity's two sides

Organisation of those volunteers willing to take fugitives and to provide their food – which was now only available with coupons – lay in the hands of an extraordinarily brave group of people with networks extending throughout the city and surrounding countryside. There were betrayals, too, with catastrophic results, as in the case of the now famous Frank family in Amsterdam *(see page 163)*. Humans under duress can display the most extraordinary courage and valour, but the horrible chaos of war can also produce monsters.

The Frank family decided to "dive" in July 1942, after receiving a card calling up their 16-year-old daughter Margot for work in Westerbork. They had been planning to go into hiding for some time – in a concealed apartment behind Mr Frank's Prinsengracht office (an *achterhuis* or "house at the back").

Anne Frank was then 13, already a clever and natural writer. But the unnatural ambience of eight people (four others joined the family) being incarcerated in a small room for two years, living in fear of German discovery, brought out her true genius. Her diary is variously a wonderfully sane, funny and perceptive book, and, at the same time, dreadfully sad.

Moreover, Anne's story reflects the best and the worst in human behaviour. The best were the people who looked after the Frank family when they were in hiding, her father's two partners, known as Koophuis and Kraler, and the two office girls, Miep and Elli, who came to work each day to give the impression that nothing had changed, even though they were terrified of what would happen if the fugitives were

found. Then there was the greengrocer round the corner on Leliegracht, one of the city's 105 who supplied "divers" and did not ask any questions when Miep turned up regularly to shop for provisions to feed eight.

Whoever tipped off the police epitomises human nature at its worst. At the beginning of August 1944, the Germans led the family away. Only Mr Frank survived. Anne's last diary entry, written three days before her capture, read: "I keep on trying to find a way of becoming what I would so like to be, and what I could be, if… there weren't any other people living in the world."

LEFT: the first Jewish deportations to concentration camps.

RIGHT: excerpt from Anne Frank's diary.

AN EYEWITNESS ACCOUNT

One Amsterdam man recalls watching a Jewish deportation: "On a beautiful autumn day... a group of prisoners passed by, mainly women and children, who had been hiding in a nearby house. They were Jews. I heard later the owner had been shot. One little girl stopped to pick up a leaf. I heard her mother sob in fear as she called to the child. One of the guards butted her in the back with his rifle when she paused to wait for the infant who was about three years old. As they crossed over a bridge I saw the child give the leaf to its mother… Then they were gone and silence returned to the canal. That was the moment I stopped believing in God."

Anne Frank finally died of hunger and disease in Bergen-Belsen, as did her sister. So much life was turned into a sad bundle in dirty rags, huddled on the bare boards of the bunk nearest the door, through which icy winds blew each time it opened.

The Hunger Winter

The long-suffering Amsterdam population became host to yet another cruel enemy in the winter of 1944–5: starvation and extreme cold. The "Hunger Winter" claimed at least 20,000 lives, a large

proportion of which were Amsterdammers. The causes lay in Nazi reprisals, requisitioning, broken transport links and the cold.

The Dutch government (exiled in London) called for a national railway strike in September 1944 thus reducing enemy troop movement in preparation for the ill-fated Allied operation "Market Garden" in Arnhem. The Germans, insisting that the Dutch were only delaying their own food supplies, retaliated by banning all food transport to the west, which included Amsterdam. The ban was lifted on 8 November but was of little relief. Food transport on a scale to prevent starvation had become virtually impossible: food depots in the harbours had

> ### STARVING CHOICES
>
> During the famine, the term "*dakhaas*" came into being, which referred to the stray cats that now ended up on the dinner table. Tulip bulbs were also commonly eaten.

been "requisitioned" by the Germans (including depots in the north and east). The 30,000-strong striking railwaymen had gone into hiding with financial aid from London. Barge skippers were afraid to take on any cargo. In November a small fleet was allowed to operate with guarantees of German requisition immunity. This too was of limited relief because on 23 December a big freeze began, making transport impossible.

Coal was also scarce. North and South Holland were cut off from liberated Limburg and the coal mines. Power stations became dependant on German coal so domestic gas and electricity supplies were cut off in October. Apart from German interests the only institutions to receive fuel were some power stations, bakers, soup kitchens and hospitals. By 11 April 1945 the last power station had ceased operating.

Amsterdammers found themselves involved in unthinkable situations to survive. To get just a few potatoes people would cycle on bicycles with wooden tyres (the Nazis had confiscated all rubber) many miles and barter goods or services with farmers at extortionate rates. The journey home would often result in the food being taken by German soldiers. Any combustible material was looted, trees were chopped down and empty houses were ransacked. Wood had become so scarce that the dead were buried in coffins made out of paper.

With the Canadians approaching from the west, the Germans blew up the sluices at IJmuiden, from where the North Sea Canal runs into Amsterdam. Suddenly there was water rapidly rising around the city, the sewerage system broke down and a plague of rats ensued.

Then at last came salvation, with Allied planes dropping food parcels. Hitler was dead, the Germans were on the run and the Canadians were in the city. The war was over – almost. Two days after the German surrender on 7 May a handful of Nazis opened fire on Dam Square killing 19 and injuring 117 people. For Amsterdam, a long period of reconstruction lay ahead, but war wounds, physical or emotional, take years to heal. Sadly, some still weep. ❑

LEFT: the famine of The Hunger Winter, the final winter of World War II, which claimed 20,000 lives.
RIGHT: Jewish memorial on Waterlooplein.

לזכרון לוחמי המחתרת
בשנות ת"ש-תש"ה

TER HERINNERING AAN HET VERZET
VAN DE JOODSE BURGERS
GEVALLEN IN 1940 – 1945
5700 – 5705

MODERN AMSTERDAM

Today's city is renowned for its freewheeling attitudes, from liberal views on sex and drugs to radical politics and arty expressionism

In a city that has, over the centuries, become the home to political and religious refugees it is not surprising that Amsterdam has been witness to all forms of social paradoxes and ironies. To the newcomer this manifests itself in a freedom of expression that is seldom encountered in other European nations and it may seem that Amsterdam is a city that flourishes in a state of random chaos. Choices abound everywhere, whether it's a question of food, sexual orientation, cultural activities, drugs, alcohol, politics or the colour of one's socks.

Any society that can maintain so much freedom of choice and fiercely defend that privilege has to be fairly organised and therein lies the paradox, because on the street there is little to indicate a sense of order. On a short walk one may encounter the graffiti of some street urchin or the finer artworks of Fabrice that now adorn numerous public buildings which would otherwise remain drab affairs.

This is the charm of Amsterdam in the new millennium: a place where visitors may admire 17th-century façades while strolling along a street with Postmodern litter bins and "New Age" benches. Surprise becomes routine.

Protest on every front

Since the mid 1960s, Amsterdam has acquired a reputation for trying to see just how far individual liberties can be allowed to go before society in general is harmed. These experiments have produced memorable newsreel footage, such as the demonstrations of the late 1960s against autocratic university administrations or the two-day battle in August 1970 when police fought with hippies who had been living on Dam Square and scaring the tourists away.

In the 1970s, soft drugs became rampant and effectively legal for personal use, and the Red Light District expanded, both as a centre for sex and for those same tourists. Dutch feminists, the *"Dolle Mina's"* (Mad Minnies),

PRECEDING PAGES: floating coffeeshop.
LEFT AND RIGHT: city centre graffiti.

marched against anti-abortion laws under the slogan *"Baas in eigen buik"* ("Boss of your own belly"). Beards and long hair were permitted for policemen and soldiers. While the rest of the Netherlands celebrated on the day that Queen Beatrix was inaugurated as head of state in 1980, squatters in Amsterdam rioted

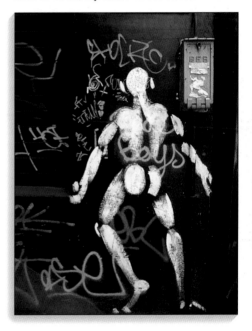

over the lack of adequate housing in the city.

Fourteen years earlier, the wedding between Beatrix and Claus von Amsberg was marred when young protesters threw smoke bombs at the wedding carriage. Many of the protesters said they were anarchists, but the newspapers called them "provocateurs" – or Provos, for short. Active over the next several years, the fully committed Provos probably never numbered more than a few dozen people, but they had many spontaneous sympathisers who readily joined in with the mass street "happenings". They protested against all manner of local and national government policies as well as against other popular institutions and cultures, from art to marriage, that they considered to be part of "The Establishment".

The Provos did, however, achieve some notable political successes. Several members of the group, together with members of a splinter group known as the Kabouters, or "gnomes", were actually elected to the Municipal Council, where they smoked cannabis during meetings and put forward endless zany proposals, such as the planting of rooftop gardens on all city buses.

WITTY PROTEST
In protesting, the Provos usually employed whimsical humour. When police showed up at a happening brandishing batons, the Provos waved sticks of rhubarb back at them.

Sex for sale

Prostitution is not strictly legal in Amsterdam; streetwalkers and hookers soliciting in bars can still be arrested, though brothels were legalised in 1990. The majority of prostitutes who perch in the windows of their "sitting rooms" do so because of Amsterdam's long-held belief that what people do in their own homes is their own business – whether inviting Catholic neighbours in for a forbidden Mass in the 17th century, or inviting strangers in for

One Provo proposal that sounded wonderful in theory but failed miserably in practice was the so-called "White Bike" programme, under which the city was supposed to provide hundreds or maybe even thousands of white bicycles and distribute them around Amsterdam. The idea was that the bikes belonged to no one and could be used by anyone. If you needed a ride, you simply grabbed the nearest white bike, rode to your destination and left it there for the use of someone else. Unfortunately, the experiment lasted only a few days – the amount of time it took for drug addicts to steal the bikes, paint them a different colour and then sell them for money to buy drugs.

commercial fornication in the 21st century.

The concept of a legalised Red Light District is nothing new to modern Amsterdam. The English consul in the mid-17th century complained about the Amsterdam music-houses patronised by "lewd people of both sexes" and there was an exchange, modelled on the stock exchange, that operated for prostitutes during the evening.

Prostitutes even then lived and worked without harassment, in an area just south of today's Red Light District (see page 150). If prostitutes strayed out of the area, where they paid rent to the local bailiff, the bailiff sent his drum-and-flute guard to track them down. The musician-policemen would play loudly outside the house where the prostitute was ensconced until she returned to the designated area.

The drugs problem

Besides prostitution, drugs represent Amsterdam's best-known, out-in-the-open "sin". International reports have focused on the clinics where registered addicts get their daily fixes to the marijuana coffeeshops that have menus listing the different types of grass and hash available that day. Those who don't want to smoke it might try some "space cookies" or THC-laced chocolate cake with their coffee, carrot juice or milk shakes.

Contrary to popular belief, *all* drugs are illegal, be they soft or hard, but in reality the police would never pursue anyone with less than 30g (1oz) of soft drugs unless they thought the person was dealing. The authorities sanctioned the use of cannabis in the 1960s, but since 1988 pressure from other European countries has led them to impose tougher penalties on traffickers, and ecstasy has been upgraded from a soft drug to a class "A" drug under the opium law. During 1991–2 the police launched a major operation which succeeded in reducing registered "coffeeshops" from 750 to 250 in number. A registered "coffeeshop" now has to display a green and white licence plate in its window, may not hold more than 500g (1 lb) of soft drugs in stock, may not sell more than 5g (0.1oz) per deal and the lower age limit is 18.

Many citizens of Amsterdam have mixed feelings about the merits of legalising drugs, but nonetheless defend registration and medical support for heroin addicts. Amsterdammers reluctantly concede their city's status as a world drugs capital, but usually blame drug-related crimes – one of the highest rates in Europe – on non-registered addicts from other countries. They also argue that things would be worse without the controls that registration imposes on perhaps one quarter of the city's estimated 8,000 addicts – a number that hasn't changed in years, according to officials.

Efforts to clean up the illegal drug trade, in part by deporting the estimated half of Amsterdam's addicts who were not Dutch citizens,

have not proved to be a notable success. At the same time, most Amsterdam residents and return visitors would agree that there are still more addicts than there were 20 years ago, but not as many as 10 years ago.

Mixed reputation

Most people come to Amsterdam aware of its reputation for sex, drugs and rock 'n' roll. That reputation, to the dismay of some but the applause of many, has changed in recent years due to efforts to clean up aspects of the city – including pornography, drugs and graffiti – and to improve its overall image.

LEFT: advertisement for a transvestite club.
RIGHT: "space cakes" (mixed with marijuana) for sale in one of Amsterdam's parks.

Conversely, in relation to people's perception of the drug situation, many people would say that crime is still worse than 20 years ago, but has improved in the past decade or so. Certainly the official crime statistics have dropped for much of central Amsterdam, and there is no doubt that the area around Centraal Station is now cleaner and safer than it once was. A police station set up in 1999 appears to have displaced the criminals on the main square to the rear of the railway station.

Amsterdam, ever the victim of its own infamous tolerance has, since 1999, undertaken measures to curb certain behaviour that at best

the graffiti that disfigures so many buildings are the most visible annoyance that results from living in a *laissez-faire* society.

But even as they redecorate their canal houses or search out the newest and best in Mexican food or sushi, the new middle class of Amsterdam still carries a burden of civic and social concern. Nowhere in Europe, or perhaps in the world, is public sentiment stronger on issues such as the environment or nuclear weapons. Such is the depth of commitment on environmental issues that the long-popular centre-right coalition government, led by the Christian Democrats, was finally brought down

was antisocial and at worst offensive; dogs defecating on pavements and men urinating in public. That Amsterdam is a city of canals can never be an excuse for a man to relieve himself just anywhere, but until recently that's what used to happen. Now any male caught in the act of urinating in the open is liable for a hefty fine, as are dog owners who cannot control the whereabouts of their dog's motions.

New concerns

For many of Amsterdam's upright young citizens, however, the days of free drugs and free love have faded as they face new concerns over their career, home and family. To many of them

in 1989 for proposing vehicle pollution rules that were not considered tough enough.

In June 1997 yuppies and elders alike took to the streets to vent their disapproval of the EC heads of state meetings in the city. The media had dubbed it the "Eurotop" meetings, but it didn't take long before banners with the words "*EU rot op*" started to appear, which translates as a well-known obscenity. A demonstration was planned but the police redirected the crowds back to Dam Square where they tore up a floral display in the shape of the EU flag. In keeping with the Dutch tradition of recycling, many of the plants were gathered up and given to good homes.

Experiments and exploitation

A prominent example of the way in which the Dutch deal with current problems is the attitude towards euthanasia. In 2002, the Netherlands became the first country in the world to legalise regulated euthanasia. Doctors can now follow specified procedures for assisting terminally ill patients in ending their lives – sometimes with a lethal injection but more often by giving them a potion of fast-acting poison.

Patients must undergo extensive counselling, including sessions with consultant physicians brought in to advise on each case. The doctor directly involved, typically the long-time

atives, friends and social workers can refer cases to government-financed centres staffed by doctors who sweep the entire family straight into intensive counselling. Experts believe that the system, started in 1972 and now operating throughout the Netherlands, helps to stop the abuse and helps the child recover without necessarily breaking up the family or sending anyone to jail.

Despite their reputation for tolerance, the Dutch will sometimes admit that they have let things go too far. A good example is the child pornography that began to be circulated in the 1960s and boomed after Sweden out-

family physician, often helps the patient and surviving relatives to plan a brief, simple ceremony for administering the poison. Doctor-assisted death has become very popular – studies estimate that doctors assist in as many as one in eight deaths in Amsterdam.

Another example of how social concerns have been subject to far-sighted and liberal experimentation is the programme for dealing with child sex abuse. The Confidential Doctor Service is a programme whereby teachers, rel-

lawed it in 1980, followed by Denmark in 1982. Soon after the US Customs Service had branded Amsterdam "the 1984 version of Sodom and Gomorrah" and the British media had made similar accusations, Dutch officials moved in to shut off the trade in material showing children in sexual acts. Legislation was passed outlawing the production and circulation of child pornography, but US officials still complained that it was too lenient: those who break the law receive only a three-month jail sentence compared with up to 10 years in the US, and only pictures of children performing sexual acts were outlawed, instead of all child nudity.

LEFT: Provos launch the White Bike programme.
ABOVE: colourfully painted trams brighten up the streets of the city.

Housing problems

While the grandest of the big old canal houses have been given over to business, Amsterdam continues to suffer from a severe housing shortage that has plagued the city since World War II. Part of the reason is immigration, much of it from former colonies such as Indonesia and Suriname, and part of it is due to the resettlement, legal or otherwise, of workers from countries such as Turkey and Morocco *(see page 84)*. Another factor is the remarkably low rents, sustained by government subsidies. For those who can find a flat, the rent is likely to be the lowest of any northern European capital.

One ramification of the housing shortage, which affects up to one in 50 Amsterdam families, is that adult children remain at home with their parents much longer than either they or the parents might like. Another effect over the years has been the spread of illegal squatting *(see page 80)*, sometimes by well-meaning but poor people who try to improve the property, but as often as not by people who devote more of their energy to drugs and crime than to home decoration. There have been conflicts between junkies and non-addict squatters that have even led to pleading for assistance from their mutual enemies, the police.

Concerned property owners may now call upon the services of the anti-squatters office who keep a record of trustworthy "housesitters". The housesitters promise to live in a property for a minimal rent thus preventing any potential squatters moving in. There is an 18-month waiting list to be a housesitter, which gives some indication of how serious the threat of squatters is taken.

Another reason for the crackdown has been the damage the squats and squatters were doing to the city's image among the 1.6 million tourists – twice the local population – who visit each year. A related factor may be Amsterdam's desire to host the Olympic Games; the city's most recent bids have failed and some people say that this is because members of the International Olympic Committee do not think that Amsterdam is the sort of place to bring wholesome young competitors.

Most of the squatters have indeed been displaced, but at a cost. Their rowdy protests, stink-bombs in tourist areas and graffiti focused even more attention on Amsterdam's problems. In some parts of the city, the crime and vandalism got so bad that area residents formed vigilante groups called the "*Stadswacht*", along the lines of the 17th-century civic guards. Crime has led to occasional strikes by night bus dri-

This is equally true of the music that is played in the clubs that open at an hour when many other European capitals are tucked in for the night, and even of the way that Amsterdam clubbers dance. In terms of choreography, Amsterdam has been a hot space for modern and jazz dance developments, whether home-grown or imported by the best of the world's troupes.

But the avant garde in the postwar Netherlands is best seen in popular artists. The Van Gogh-inspired Expressionism of the first half of the 20th century gave way to a more questioning, vivid, witty but sometimes cynical style. Instead of expressing something, some local

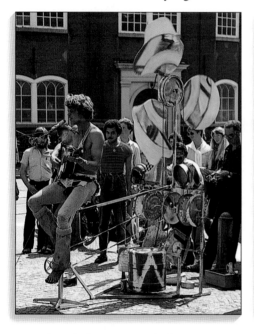

vers, though they were mollified somewhat when the city authorities installed emergency buttons for calling the police.

Vanguard

Some of Amsterdam's social liberalism may have dimmed, but the city still prides itself on being at the cutting edge of art. Since World War II, Amsterdam has become more than a cultural centre with avant garde aspects. Instead, it is now the centre for the avant garde.

LEFT: avant garde fashion in the Vondelpark.
ABOVE: one-man band.
RIGHT: Fabiola, one of the city's colourful characters.

artists avoided expressing anything; others suggested that everything and anything could be art. Others again created an updated version of the realistic style of the old Dutch School, but combined with the distinct influences of modern art *(see page 105)*.

A high percentage of Amsterdammers today, as in the 17th century, seem to have an interest in art. There was much good-natured grumbling when they heard how much government money had gone into spurious art-school projects. But the grumbling would take an ugly turn if the opportunity for such folly was withdrawn, for modern Amsterdam is a city of all kinds for all kinds. ❑

WORKING IN THE CITY

Although many of the major Dutch companies have moved out to the suburbs in recent years, Amsterdam remains a hub of small-scale commercial activity

The working force of Amsterdam has changed in recent years. The industrial dinosaurs have moved to less cramped quarters or faded away. The monumental city banks and their high-tech followers have relocated to the new business parks southeast of the city. The financial market-makers downtown have rebounded strongly to fill the city-centre gaps. Schiphol Airport is relocating old tenants to make room for more profitable new ones. And, perhaps most noticeably, the area inside the canals is being colonised by successful, often self-employed people and multitudes of small commercial enterprises.

This influx has halted a 20-year population slide and fuelled an economic boom that the city should enjoy well into the 21st century. But today's employees are not merely yesterday's factory workers in new suits. Education and income levels have risen, resulting in an explosion of up-market shops and restaurants to serve the needs of workers with new affluence and expectations.

Constraints

As industry retooled in the late 1970s, the limitations of a 17th-century city surrounded by water became painfully obvious. Parking and transportation difficulties still head the list of every Amsterdammer's complaints. Narrow canalside streets are frequently blocked for hours by delivery lorries. The beautiful but problematic historic buildings cannot be safely expanded or legally demolished to create much-needed new office space.

As a consequence the big concerns moved out of the city centre. Shipbuilding, traditionally centred along the IJ and on the north island of Amsterdam, was the first to go. Traces of these old activities still lingered on until the early 1980s when KNSM, the last

remaining shipping company, moved to Rotterdam. The Mobil Oil refinery and Ford assembly plant left Amsterdam about the same time. By 1985 some 75,000 people, nearly a quarter of the city's workforce, were unemployed. Most of these people were semi-skilled machinists and labourers, unprepared and untrained to participate in the technical revolution that was taking place around them.

Adding insult to injury, one of Amsterdam's oldest established businesses, the brewer Heineken, finally decided to move out to Zoeterwoude in 1986. Long a subject of neighbourhood complaints, the 100-year-old beermaker decided that worldwide transportation of its famous nectar would be much easier once its delivery lorries moved out of central Amsterdam. For the sake of thousands of thirsty pilgrims, the old brewery building remains open for tours *(see page 179)*. Residents rather miss the company now that it has gone but console themselves by saying that

---

PRECEDING PAGES: making wooden clogs at the Clara Maria cheese farm in Amsterdam.
LEFT: Amsterdam's World Trade Centre.
RIGHT: 1950s advertising for the Dutch firm, Philips.

at least Heineken is in the Netherlands; it has not been bought by the Americans or Japanese.

Unemployment in the city is down since the worst days of the mid-1980s and still declining, but many of the former shipyard, refinery and assembly plant workers remain on the dole. One government incentive scheme generally known as "Melkert" jobs, after the minister who put it into operation, has in recent years aided some who became entrapped in the jobless syndrome. The idea was to get people back to work for a minimum

PAYING TAX

The excellent Dutch welfare system is supported by one of Europe's highest tax systems: the basic rate is 37.5 percent.

Foreign input

A curious twist, however, is the lack of skilled hands for the local building trades. Most often the people seen working on scaffolding in Amsterdam are likely to be from the rural province of Friesland, or from Britain or Ireland.

There are distinct advantages for employers to hire foreign labour, the main reason being that whilst the employer is responsible for paying all social premiums they often design the contracts in such a way that the employee can never get a

wage, thus building up work experience and better prospects on the job market. The scheme has met with mixed success. Since the dole payment is extremely generous and some people like their Melkert job so much, they abandon all ambition – a good example being a carpenter who works in one of the city's museums; he can use their workshops to do "work on the side". Supplementing a minimum wage this way leaves no incentive to work elsewhere. It remains a sad fact of modern living that many of these men, especially if they are middle-aged or older, are likely to be jobless until they reach retirement age and then disappear from statistical view altogether.

permanent position. Although there is legislation to prevent this sort of exploitation the employees are seldom aware of their rights and the employer can wash his hands of any further responsibility. It was a sad state of affairs some years ago when foreign aircraft technicians working on contracts for Fokker were unwittingly denying local workers the chance of a permanent position.

In the ever tougher webs of commercialism it is becoming harder and harder to get a permanent contract. Often only a renewable contract is on offer. Of course this sort of practice is great news for the *uitzendburos,* or temping agencies, that have mushroomed in the last few years. Temping agencies have always existed, but never before have there been so many specialising in specific professions.

Fortunately the catastrophic changes in the job market and the migration of people have not weakened the city's economic base. In fact, the residents shrug off the upheaval. Historically, they quickly point out, the city has always had a commercial base and not an industrial one. This very observation contributes to the long-standing rivalry between Amsterdammers and Rotterdammers, the latter proudly proclaiming that their sons are born wearing shirts with rolled up sleeves – an obvi-

ural Dutch facility for language and the generally high education and productivity levels of the workforce.

Many companies have already answered the siren call. Some have taken up space in the new docklands regeneration scheme. The whole of the 15-km (10-mile) stretch of waterway that runs behind Centraal Station and northwest to the North Sea is the site of a €500 million (£315 million/US$475 million) project that will eventually include conference centres, 20,000 housing units, museums, marinas and parks. Space for a smaller harbour, plus rail- and airport-related businesses

ous reference to the industrial and manufacturing capacity of the biggest harbour in the world *(see page 253)*.

The municipal government of Amsterdam, faced with a potential collapse in revenue from big businesses, has aggressively courted American, Swiss and Japanese multinational companies eager to establish European headquarters and participate in the single European market. The city is pushing, in particular, its multiport advantage combined with the nat-

LEFT: Amsterdam and its surroundings are well serviced by a modern railway network.
ABOVE: Amsterdam's Schiphol Airport.

POINT OF ARRIVAL

The facilities around Schiphol Airport southwest of the city have improved markedly in recent years and transport-related companies are now the second-largest employers in the area. Schiphol is one of the fastest-growing airports in Europe as more and more companies from central Holland relocate to be near Amsterdam's major sea, rail and air terminals. It is also regularly voted as the favourite airport among business travellers and tourists alike, for its modern, well laid-out terminals, easy-to-follow directions and facilities such as shops and restaurants. Its links with the city centre are also excellent *(see page 264)*.

will also be included. Already an impressive new terminal has opened in the harbour, with a capacity for 2,500 cruise-ship passengers *(see page 222).*

Greenfield sites

Shrewdly the city also began creating new residential and commercial space in the southeast, an area already well served by public transport. Neighbouring farmland was annexed and marshes were drained and filled. Cramped companies were so eager to move out of the

STADIUM STATUS

The Amsterdam ArenA in the suburb of Duivendrecht opened in 1996 as one of the most high-tech stadiums in Europe. It is home to Ajax football team.

Netherlands' *Yellow Pages,* have fled central Amsterdam to relocate here. Some of the national dailies also moved to Wibautstraat to the east of the city and a stroll down Nieuwezijds Voorburg-wal reveals a string of grandiose, ghost-like buildings, not unlike those in Fleet Street, where the old printing presses used to be. Some downtown cafés and restaurants were hit hard as long-standing customers vanished, and city old-timers complain that the daytime pace is no longer so exciting.

city that the usual incentives such as tax breaks and property deals were not needed.

The big banks, such as ABN, AMRO and ING, were among the first to move and their computer support services were quick to follow. The country's major teaching hospital, Amsterdam University's Academic Medical Centre, also moved to the area, taking with it a host of other medical research companies.

The only representatives of the industrial sector are the large printers. Even they have taken advantage of the technological revolution – probably more so than anyone. As in London's Fleet Street, some of the city's daily newspapers and major publishers, such as the

Commuting

Not everyone who works in Amsterdam lives there. In fact, almost half of the workers in the southeast business parks come from outside the Amsterdam area.

About 150,000 people a day come in and out of the city to work. But, despite one of the most efficient public transport systems in the world, thousands of people insist on clogging up the motorways each morning. People continue to drive because public transport routes and schedules lag behind worker demand and no one likes to cross muddy fields or construction sites to get to a bus or train stop. In addition, for older workers, travelling to and from work in the company car is still a status symbol of privileged suburban living.

Most Dutch people also use the excuse that rail travel is too expensive. Thanks to government policy, however, travelling by train is now becoming a more viable proposition. Since the proposed introduction of tolls on certain motorway routes people are starting to reconsider their options.

To further encourage regular travel on public transport, some companies offer a travel allowance to their employees, as well as bicycles. Yet probably the greatest incentive of all, apart from tax concessions on season tickets,

30 percent of the workforce. Another constant is tourism. The 1.6 million yearly visitors are the city's cash cow, contributing about €750 million (£470 million/US$715 million) to the local economy.

The liberal and tolerant reputation of the city has also made it a mecca for the country's intellectuals and artists. "Everyone with brains is coming into the city," a business editor for *De Telegraaf* proclaimed. The same goes for nearly every other branch of creative activity. The influx of highly educated people has created a positive boom in what economists call "informal economic activity" and self-employment.

is the off-peak rail pass; with 40 percent discount on all rail travel, given the option of flexi-time an Amsterdam worker can enjoy a relatively quiet and efficient journey to and from work.

Employment trends

The largest single employer is the government. When staff from two universities and the large social service programmes are included, civil servants total more than 120,000 people, or

Astonishingly, 12,000 Amsterdammers are freelance. One labour economist estimates that as much as one third of all business and economic activity in the city comes from the self-employed and their businesses.

As a result, every canalside house seems to contain the basement or studio of an architect or graphic artist. They obviously enjoy their high profile. Curtains and blinds are never drawn because the brightly lit studio is an advertisement for the values and affinities of the occupants – every item of furniture, every plant and picture is carefully chosen to make a statement to passersby. Media types and advertisers also compete for passing attention.

LEFT: the high-tech Amsterdam ArenA stadium, to the south of the city centre.
ABOVE: selling bric-a-brac.

Art and commerce

Actors, writers and musicians regard Amsterdam as their natural habitat *(see page 86)*. The city has more than 50 theatres and 175 stages; it is home to two symphony orchestras, in addition to the national ballet and dance theatre. Experimental, nouvelle, avant garde or simply modern; there are 150 art galleries in Amsterdam and this does not include the craftsmen whose studios clutter the Jordaan, or the 170 antiques shops *(see page 169)*. For these artists, artisans and dealers, there is nowhere else to live and work – at least not in the Netherlands. Their influence on the character

and spirit of the city is clearly visible and their value immeasurable.

Also inescapable is the aroma of commerce that flavours everything. The increased demand from newly affluent residents and tourists has fuelled an explosion of shops, and a walk through the city gives an impression that the official figure of 10,000 retail outlets is a conservative estimate. In addition there are 26 markets selling everything from sex toys and marijuana pipes to fruit and vegetables.

This however has given some small shop owners cause for concern over the future character of city. When the rents go up, it forces out the marginal businesses such as antiquarian bookshops, traditional grocers and specialist retailers trading on slim margins. Those same shops are what give Amsterdam's side streets their enviable charm. If this trend continues, one bookshop owner explained, all you will end up with are multinational chains.

The city's small shops contribute to the quality of life that Amsterdammers universally adore. The older generation still refer to "my butcher" or "my baker", shops that they have used since childhood, and no glitzy emporium is going to shake their loyalty. And the younger generation seem to have inherited this view.

Local pride

They may have political disagreements with the city government or contretemps with the climate, but almost no Amsterdammer would ever want to live anywhere else. Inner city residents have a deep affection for their town, unlike residents of some other national capitals where a litany of complaints always seems to precede faint praise.

This attitude is visible in the workplace. It is hard to find someone to answer the telephone after 5pm as most people have gone home. Holidays are taken seriously and involve months of preparation. The average office worker gets 25 holiday days a year, an eternity compared with the 10-day average in the USA. "The quality of life is most important here", a resident explained. "People don't feel they need to stay late to further their careers. Even company presidents leave at five o'clock." ❑

SHOPPING HOURS

Amsterdam has strict laws on shop opening hours, which are in keeping with its "leisure before work" attitude. Most shops open only from 9am to 6pm (or 9pm on Thursdays), and are closed on Sunday and often Monday too. Sunday remains a day for pleasure and social activity, not business. Only in the heavily touristed areas, such as Kalverstraat *(see page 134)* do shops operate a seven-day week policy.

There are, however, a number of "night shops" *(avondwinkels)* which open until about 1am for emergency essentials, although their convenience pushes prices up far higher than the average store.

LEFT: knighted for a donation.
RIGHT: the flea market in Waterlooplein, the former Jewish quarter.

LIVING IN THE CITY

Housing shortages and immigrant problems may blight city life for some residents,

but few would deny Amsterdam still offers a lively mix of art and culture

Housing in Amsterdam is about more than just the construction or conservation of buildings. Housing policy is one of the city's most visible social engineering tools. To the relief of residents, the city abandoned the practice of clearing whole neighbourhoods of tenants in order to restore or redevelop certain areas, a practice that earned it so many enemies in the 1970s. The approach now is to restore decaying streets house by house, rather than tract by tract, thereby preserving the social fabric of the area.

By creating more and better urban housing, the municipal government hopes to keep Amsterdam as a living, residential city, with the well-heeled ensconced cheek by jowl with the less well-off. Since 1950, 143,400 new apartment units have been built for low- and middle-income tenants. Up to 1970, however, 90 percent of this was built on annexed suburban land. Today, 25 percent is directed towards the city centre.

Renewal

The goal has been to boost the inner-city population to 725,000, still 155,000 less than the peak of 1964, but in line with what planners call the "compact city" plan. This way the city escapes becoming the "Venice of the North" – the most dreadful epithet you could attach to Amsterdam, whether you are talking to a city planner or a resident. Both see the Italian city as a slough of stagnant canals whose residents and businesses have fled to higher ground, abandoning the city to the tourist hordes. Whilst this goal has been more or less realised, it is worth mentioning that new developments on the old shipping harbours (Java and KNSM islands) are completed, shifting the emphasis of the original plan.

Municipal government can exert this kind of social influence because it owns about 70 per-

cent of the land in the city. Amsterdam is unusual in that only a small percentage of homes are owner-occupied, although in the past 10 years a growing amount of interest has led to more home-owners. In 2002 home-ownership had increased by nearly 10 percent in the previous five years. The rest, about 350,000 units,

is rental property. The city owns outright about 40 percent of this total. Much of the large residential area beyond the inner canal ring is held in leasing arrangements, under which the city sells long-term rights to land developers, who in turn build or restore the housing and rent out the units.

Shortages

In both these cases, units are set aside for a variety of income levels. Rents, compared with New York, London or Paris, are surprisingly affordable – but bound to continue rising since developers cannot renovate up-market apartments fast enough for the moneyed profession-

---

PRECEDING PAGES: downtown street scene.
LEFT: street parties are spontaneous events.
RIGHT: dressed up for the Queen's Day festival.

als craving to move back into the city. Amsterdam is probably unique in Europe for having an upper-class housing shortage.

Housing – whether in fashionable Jordaan or in Bijlmermeer tower blocks – is allocated by means of waiting lists. You could get into one of the suburban housing projects tomorrow if you are not fussy about where you live; but if you want to live in the centre, you could wait at least six years. The waiting list policy greatly disturbs some residents and contributes to racial friction in the outwardly tranquil city. Newcomers to the city, most visibly foreign immigrants and their families, move to the top of the

re-renting city apartments from middlemen, or from tenants willing to move out in return for some financial incentive. Demands for "key money" – the fee paid to the resident or "broker" for a technically illegal sublet – are not unusual. The "key money" for a three-room apartment in the city might be as much as €500, or three months' rent, before they are allowed to move in. "Key money" remains an illegal practice in Amsterdam but it's difficult to avoid if you are desperate to find a place to live.

About half of the city's housing and most of the inner canalside property is owned privately or by quasi-private housing corporations, many

list. Lifelong Amsterdammers complain of receiving second-class treatment.

If you prefer to rent in the private sector, competition is ruthless. The fact of urban life is that you will never find a good property unless you know someone who knows of one. When asked how they found their present abode, everyone, from squatters to penthouse dwellers, will just flash a conspiratorial smile. One honest revelation came from a woman who admitted that her tip-off came from her mother – who happens to work in a hospital for long-stay and terminally ill patients.

The less well-connected are often forced to resort to underhand measures, subletting or

of which have benefited from city financing for restoration. In the past 10 years, many stately canalside homes and old warehouses have been converted into offices and studios to meet demand from the professional and artistic classes. Once renovated, the spacious and airy 17th-century buildings, often still with their original brick and beams decorating the interior, will sell for between €500,000 and €1 million. Again, however, this is a bargain compared to almost anywhere else in Europe.

Squatters

Some of the well-to-do residents of these newly restored buildings formerly occupied them as squatters. In the early 1970s squatting was a popular form of existence for young people and students, many of whom were looking for cheap housing in the city centre and were willing to work hard to renovate dilapidated buildings. The exodus of many businesses from the city centre at that time had left scores of buildings unoccupied and the city without funds to renovate them.

It was easy enough to establish a squat. The first thing you had to do was change the locks

SQUATTING STYLE

The squatters have even left an architectural legacy: most city development projects now incorporate large, communal living spaces into their floorplans.

banners usually announced the presence of a squat, and a few can still be seen around the city today, urging people to step back from their comfortable bourgeois lives, even if just for a moment.

Today it is hard to find anyone over 30 who does not claim to have squatted during that romantic and heady period of counter-culture and people power. In those days, there were well-organised squatters' advisory offices in operation, which offered lists of vacant houses and city development plans, as well as

and take the boards off the windows. Then, provided that the abandoned building was not scheduled for imminent renovation, it took a legal crowbar to dislodge you.

Not to be confused with homeless people or vagrants, the squatters were often students from one of Amsterdam's two universities. They were also greatly instrumental in transforming neighbourhoods from forgotten "ghost towns" into lively areas with their own subculture of trendy cafés, shops and cinemas. Enormous

---

LEFT: desirable properties on the junction of Keizersgracht and Brouwersgracht.
ABOVE: apartment blocks in Bijlmermeer.

expertise in carrying out title searches.

By the early 1980s, however, this idealistic situation more or less came to an end. The city authorities started to erode the substantial public support that existed for the squatters by building more inner-city housing and converting the "illegal" squats into legal rent-paying ones. During the period that these houses were being renovated, squatters were supposed to be relocated into alternative accommodation at the city's expense – this was often easier said than done. Violent protests often broke out at eviction time.

Even so, the new policy has proved to be largely effective. Squatters and city officials estimate that today only a dozen or so large buildings in the city are still occupied by squatters and maybe another 50 smaller houses, and most of these are privately owned properties. Few city-owned buildings are still used as squats today and it is unlikely to be very long before the last wave of controversial eviction proceedings is implemented.

Houseboat living

Many visitors to Amsterdam, seduced by the city's beautiful canals, dream of sailing back

CANALSIDE STAYS

To gain a different perspective of Amsterdam, tourists can rent out houseboats for long or short stays in the Netherlands *(see page 267).*

Even so, many people are seduced by living on the water. "After one week, I knew I would never move back to a flat," was the typical reaction of one convert to life afloat. The attractions of canal-boat living are even greater now that the conditions of the waterways have improved, the result of a 10-year clean-up campaign. Now only the houseboats themselves are allowed to flush directly into the canals. Ducks, swans and fish have returned as sea water is pumped in nightly through the city locks.

one day and mooring alongside Prinsengracht. Forget it. Amsterdam's generous public housing system ends at the shore. The number of canal-side moorings is fixed at 2,600. About 5,000 people live on floating concrete slabs, converted canal barges and the occasional genuine sea-going vessel.

Moorings are fixed and sold like conventional building plots, so you cannot sail off on whim for a sunnier pier. A quiet spot behind Westerkerk can cost €20,000 (£12,500 or US$19,000), and that does not include the boat. When expenses are totalled, residents estimate that houseboat living is no cheaper than a conventional apartment.

The canal boats, such an integral part of the Amsterdam scene, lack nothing in basic amenities except storage space. Some owners, though, have resolved this problem by installing storage bins below the floor. Usually gas-heated, they are also warm through the winter months.

Many people take maximum advantage of their floating domicile. Roofs and decks quickly get converted into porches and balconies as soon as the sunshine appears. Others have sailboats tied up alongside for leisure use. Depending on location, it can take less than an hour to reach the open waters of the IJsselmeer.

The Jordaan

Fashionable among bohemian artists and artisans, the Jordaan district is a warren of streets, 2 km (1¼ miles) long and 500 metres (550 yards) wide, which has its origins in a zig-zag series of polders and ditches dug in the mid-1600s *(see page 158)*.

In previous centuries the Jordaan was home to thousands of poor, working-class families. In 1890, 85,000 people were crammed into this area, four times the present population. Then, as now, more than 90 percent of the 11,000 apartments had no more than three rooms. In the early 1970s, private developers acted faster and bid higher than the city authorities for many of the area's 700 listed, historic buildings and converted them into attractive, up-market apartments and studios. As a result, city housing initiatives, designed to accommodate long-time residents and senior citizens, have scarcely gained a toehold in the area.

Traditionally, the Jordaan was home to clothing factories, breweries, distilleries and other small industrial firms. Under the development plan for the area these "nuisance" activities have been relocated and the district has received yet another new lease of life as industrial buildings have been converted into flats, shops, studios and cosy brown cafés *(see page 102)* to serve the changing needs of the area's residents.

Despite all this trend towards renovation, many of the old buildings of the Jordaan are considered beyond salvation and are now being rebuilt completely. Residents sigh with resigned frustration at the piecemeal construction that has been clogging up their narrow streets for more than 10 years. It could have been worse, they shrug, referring to the city's ill-fated plan to run a second subway line through the neighbourhood. Faced with that prospect, old timers as well as new arrivals cannot help but be happy that their beloved neighbourhood is now being carefully preserved. On balance they consider a few cement lorries and a bit of noise pollution a small price to pay in return.

LEFT: houseboat living.
RIGHT: the city's hundreds of cafés and restaurants open their terraces in the summer months.

OLD PEOPLE'S HOMES

One of the charms of the Jordaan are the *hofjes*, the almshouses built around courtyards during the 17th century. Many are still residential, so explore quietly.

Bijlmermeer

At the other end of the scale, modern Bijlmermeer appears, at least when viewed from the elevated Metro platform, to be a jewel made up of new, clean, high-tech business parks. But behind the ultra-modern, corporate façades and plazas, an open-air shopping centre snakes its way back to a honeycomb of concrete high-rises for which Bijlmermeer is infamous. The atmosphere may be futuristic, but at the same time it is alienating and impersonal.

This 1960s experiment in social planning, designed to provide housing for some 50,000 people, was an expensive lesson for the city fathers, and they are still paying. Today it has one of the highest crime rates and concentration of drug-related problems in the Netherlands. Needless to say, they don't build them like this any more.

The problem with Bijlmermeer, one city official said bluntly, is that the people for whom it was originally built never wanted to live there. They preferred to stay in the shabbier parts of the city where they remained immersed in the street life, local cafés and markets, and paid cheaper rents.

Immigrants in Amsterdam

In the run-up to Surinamese independence in 1975, many immigrants moved to Amsterdam and were steered towards the vacant housing units of Bijlmermeer. Now the area's 35,000 Surinamese residents make up the second-largest Surinamese "city" in the world. The Dutch-speaking Surinamese also make up the largest proportion of the city's immigrants – 5 percent – and, as a former Dutch colony, they are granted the same

rights as Dutch-born citizens. Connections with their South American home are still strong, however. The shops, planted under overpasses, sell native staples and one grocery doubles as a Surinamese travel agency-cum-freight office.

Other concentrations of immigrant communities are found all round the fringes of the old city and they make up an increasingly visible and fast-growing part of Amsterdam's population – nearly 25 percent in total. Half of the children in Amsterdam schools are from non-Dutch families.

An estimated 35,000 residents are Turkish and Moroccan guest workers "imported" to the Netherlands in the 1960s to take on jobs that Dutch people wouldn't do. Government inducements to

get them to return home – usually offering a portion of their pension or unemployment benefit – go uncollected. After living for 20 years in the Netherlands, most understandably have no desire to return to lower standards of living at home.

Many live in the city housing projects on the eastern and western fringes. The first-generation immigrants, especially those from Muslim countries, remain very close knit and have not integrated well. Language is the biggest barrier, but so is the highly modern culture. The liberal, often agnostic or atheistic Dutch are seen as frosty and godless.

The children of immigrants have generally integrated better than their parents. Social activities, such as sports, are popular and racially mixed. Dutch boys have even picked up the Arab custom of going around the room with a quick handshake for everyone when they enter. Many of the girls have not been so fortunate. Muslim boys are quick to take advantage of Amsterdam's liberal social life, but their sisters are often trapped at home by traditional parents. When allowed out they must be accompanied by a vigilant younger brother. As a result of vastly unequal opportunities, some teenage girls are driven to attempt suicide.

"De Pijp", a highly compact housing area south of Frederiksplein, is a working-class neighbourhood where Turks, Moroccans, Surinamese, Indians and Dutch mix better than they do in other areas of the city (see page 233). Perhaps it is because they are all near the same income level or because they share common interests; most residents are young and just starting families in the squat, brick apartment buildings; most of them like living where they do. The area's colourful grocers, butchers and restaurants cater to all tastes and act as the glue that holds the area together.

The area of Dapperplein, just east of Artis Zoo, is similar in income and racial make-up to "De Pijp". Its market, the city's second largest, is a sprawling and colourful economic magnet for the east side of the city.

Despite occasional racial conflicts, Amsterdam remains a comparatively harmonious mix of cultures. The traditionally liberal attitude of the Dutch results in thousands of requests for asylum in the Netherlands every year from troubled areas around the globe – requests that at least until now have usually been met with more sympathy than elsewhere in Europe. ❏

LEFT: one of the many foreign residents who have made Amsterdam their home.

Disaster and rebirth

At precisely 44 seconds after 6.35pm on 4 October 1992 Bijlmermeer was to change forever. Cargo flight El Al 1862 crashed into a corner of the high-rise flats. The 747 jumbo jet claimed an official death toll of 43 and sparked off a series of enquiries that compromised government ministers and state security. The jet had been carrying depleted uranium, although initially it was strenuously denied that there were any dangerous chemicals or toxins on board. Most disturbing of all, at the scene of the crash numerous figures in white protective suits were seen by police and survivors. They were thought to be rescue workers but their identity was never revealed and it is now a popular belief that these figures were members of the Israeli secret service, the MOSSAD. Investigations later revealed that the flight recorder had been tampered with and that apart from the uranium there were six containers of highly toxic substances on board at the time of the crash.

The initial impact of the crash had far reaching effects – the mayor went to the scene immediately and the queen appeared the next day. But by the time the rescue workers had finished their work and some semblance of order had been returned, another revelation occurred: it was found that a lot of the local residents involved in the crash were illegal immigrants. Almost certainly out of mercy, they were granted Dutch citizenship.

After the crash the damaged building was completely demolished, so by a cruel twist of fate some could view this as an improvement. Local residents created a beautiful makeshift memorial on the exposed site. This was later replaced with an official monument and a memorial service is now held every year.

Perhaps it took such an horrendous catastrophe to re-highlight the social problems of this district and, while there are certainly no plans to build upon the memorial site, Bijlmermeer has enjoyed more positive attention in recent years. Police and community workers have been working hard to reduce crime and many initiatives have been undertaken to make it an altogether more livable place. In keeping with this new image the council and larger companies are now involved with a new development that will include residential, industrial and recreational sites. The railway station is being expanded and is also undergoing a major facelift which will include a boulevard some 600 metres by 70 metres (2000 by 230 ft) linking the residential and work areas. Apart from the Amsterdam ArenA (home to Ajax football club and museum, opened in 1996) and the Amsterdam Poort (a modern shopping centre), Bijlmermeer will be enjoying substantial additional investment in the coming years, including a large cinema complex and several theatres.

However, there remains an element of racial tension. Many of the city's Surinamese and Guyanese immigrants like it here, provided that they live in a building that doesn't have too much crime. Many live with extended families or have relatives living nearby. Moving out is not the priority it is for other residents. Unemployment is high and those residents who are working are embarrassed and resentful of those taking advantage of generous welfare benefits, giving the community a bad name.

The thousands of skilled employees and professionals who work in the neighbouring high-tech buildings do not live in the area. They commute elsewhere at 5pm. ❑

RIGHT: shopping for groceries at the Albert Cuypmarkt.

Performance Arts

The arts have always been an important element of life in Amsterdam, and although in recent years much of the state funding has been cut back for public art projects, there is still a wealth of arts to be seen.

Amsterdam calls itself the "Capital of Inspiration", and indeed it is an inspiring destination that will stimulate all the senses. There is no other city in Europe that hosts so many international festivals during the summer months when music, dance and theatre performances are held in

parks, squares and historic concert halls, as well as on the water *(see page 91)*. There are hundreds to choose from, language is no barrier and some even offer free admission.

The Vondelpark, for example, offers its open-air concert series on an annual basis, from the end of May to the end of August. A tradition since 1974, this popular series presents performances in a large, half-moon shaped "bandstand" in the afternoon and evening, Wednesday through to Sunday. A wide selection of jazz, classical, pop and world music is presented, along with the occasional comedian, cabaret artist or dance performers. The highlight of the season, however, is the special concert featuring the Royal Concertgebouw Orches-

tra which is held in the large pasture in the centre of the park *(see page 232)*.

Throughout the year, Amsterdam's various cultural institutions present a variety of performances in music, dance and theatre. Again, the Royal Concertgebouw Orchestra, under the leadership of conductor Riccardo Chailly, is renowned for its repertoire of masterpieces by the great composers as well as more contemporary music from the 21st century. During the summer months, the Robeco series hosts a popular festival in both the large and small halls of the Concertgebouw, featuring the music of the great composers performed by some of today's finest musicians. Free "surprise" lunchtime concerts are offered on Wednesdays from 12.30–1pm *(see page 198)*.

The Beurs van Berlage in Damrak, Amsterdam's former stock exchange *(see page 135)*, is the home of the Netherlands Philharmonic and the Dutch Chamber Orchestras. The unique red-brick Classical building by H.P. Berlage dates from 1903 and is considered one of the most important historic monuments in Dutch architecture. Concerts are held in two different halls praised for their acoustics, one made completely of glass.

The Muziektheater (also known as the "Stopera", because the grandiose building houses both the Amsterdam City Hall [Stadhuis] and de Nederlands Opera) presents many international events throughout the year, including those of its resident companies, the Nederlands Opera and Nederlands Dans Theater *(see page 206)*.

The Carré Theatre along the Amstel River is more than 100 years old. The theatre once hosted the famous Circus of Oscar Carré and these days is the venue for many musical theatre productions (some in English) as well as staging concerts by many pop artists such as Randy Newman, Marianne Faithfull and Lou Reed *(see page 181)*.

The elegant Stadsschouwburg (Municipal Theatre), a porticoed red- brick building which dates from 1894, offers theatre, music and dance performances throughout the year and during June is the main venue of the Holland Festival, which features a wide range of productions, including opera, theatre and dance *(see page 92)*.

Just across the street on Leidseplein is the famous spot where street musicians, mime artists and fire-eaters have performed for decades. The traditional form of busking is still prevalent throughout the city, but many café owners are no longer as receptive to having their terraces forcibly given over to entertainment – perhaps because some of the less talented street performers started to harass more than entertain, braying old blues tunes just to be paid for going away. Some clever street vagabonds even began emulating mime artists by standing still on a cardboard box, hands outstretched in the hope of a few coins. The joy remains in encountering the traditional buskers, sincere and dedicated to sharing their talents. One of the best places to do this is in the passage under the Rijksmuseum where one can encounter a spirited violinist, several steel drum players or a traditionally costumed Tibetan horn player. Besides Leidseplein, the square in front of Centraal Station remains a prime spot for buskers, from Russian jazz musicians and gypsy violinists, to magicians, puppeteers, *a capella* choirs or a quartet of chamber musicians.

The most traditional form of busking takes the form of ornately decorated barrel-organs which are driven to strategic points all over the city. Their carnival-sounding music, from classical pieces to more popular songs, creates a nostalgic soundtrack in these modern times. Small oval brass tins are shaken vigorously literally under one's nose to receive a donation of small coins. This is not just for the benefit of the tourists – it is a charming tradition that needs support.

There is also still the rare performance artist who walks the streets, creating delight and surprise among the passers-by. Fabiola, who refers to himself as a "living artwork of no gender" has done this for many years with creative costumes that give an "other world" impression of a fashion diva from outer space. Encountering him unexpectedly immediately puts a smile on one's face.

Besides the traditional arts and the street happenings, Amsterdam has a variety of venues where less expensive, if not free, performances are offered. The Amsterdam Music Conservatory on Van Baerlestraat, opposite the Stedelijk Museum, offers free concerts by their students most evenings from 7.30pm. One can hear a variety of instruments from a range of periods. The IJsbreker, along the Amstel, is a café/concert hall which specialises in performances of new music by local and international guests.

There are also many music venues which offer jazz and blues, comedy, world music and alternative cinema. The Bimhuis is a jazz club which hosts local musicians as well as those of international repute such as Steve Lacey and Charles McPherson *(see page 278).* There are a dozen Irish pubs in the city which have live music on certain days of the week. Winston Kingdom in Warmoesstraat began as an alternative space with poetry readings and music performances. The hotel/café now has an art gallery, in addition to its performance space and attracts a mixed public of post-punk and avant garde.

Many local museums also offer concerts and lectures, including the Allard Pierson *(see page 134)* and Tropenmuseum *(see page 235).* The Westergasfabriek (the former Gas Company at the

WesterPark) is now the site of a cinema featuring Dutch films, theatre. gallery and concert hall. They host many cultural happenings throughout the year and the West Pacific is a very good café/restaurant with reasonable prices and a popular disco at weekends. There are also many new art galleries throughout the city and innumerable "surprise" cultural events which are sometimes announced at the last moment.

The Uitbureau at Leidseplein 26 has an information centre and booking office, and publishes the *Uitkrant,* a free monthly magazine listing events throughout the city *(see page 262).* Although it is in Dutch, it is fairly easy to read in terms of events, dates and venues. ❑

LEFT: Peruvian street musician.
RIGHT: live performance in a jazz bar.

FESTIVALS

No other European city holds as many summer festivals as Amsterdam, but the rest of the year is lively as well, from the Sint Nicolaas parade to Queen's Day

Amsterdam is a festive city with a number of popular festivals held throughout the year. The Dutch like to celebrate at the drop of a hat, whether it's the appearance of the sun or in the rare winter when the canals freeze over and they take to the ice on skates.

Winter celebrations

The celebrations begin on *Oudejaarsavond*; what we know as New Year's Eve. On the days preceding 31 December the city becomes crowded with visitors from all over Europe who come for the Amsterdam experience. Many of them come from warmer climates in southern Europe and roam the streets forlornly wrapped in layers of clothing trying to find reasonably priced lodging for this time of year.

Amsterdam's New Year is ushered in by the consumption of large quantities of currant-filled doughnuts (*oliebollen* or oil balls) and the launching of fireworks to chase away the evil spirits of the old year. The Chinese quarter *(see page 146)* in the heart of the Red Light District is renowned as the centre of attraction for firework displays which are both colourful and noisy. Huge strings of firecrackers are suspended from the upper floors of buildings and ignited from the bottom causing thunderous crescendos followed by applause from the crowds. In recent years, the public has participated more directly, setting off fireworks in neighbourhoods throughout the city. So when the clock strikes twelve, there is an unrelenting hour's worth of noise and brightly lit skies. After 1am, which the police have designated as the end of festivities, the streets are covered with red debris and the air is thick with smoke.

Even during the mildest of winters there is a great deal of talk about whether or not the canals will freeze. When they do, it is a time of national contentment. The nation mobilises, delves into cupboards to dust off seldom-used

skates and certain canals of the city become a network of silver thoroughfares packed with woolly-hatted skaters, hot chocolate vendors and enthusiastic spectators. The most recent severe freezes occurred in 1997 and for an unprecedented two years in a row in 1985 and 1986, and before that in 1963. During the big

freeze the main event is the *Elfstedentocht*, a gruelling race on skates between 11 towns in the province of Friesland. The entire Amsterdam population, if not competing or spectating by the side of the ice, is glued to the television set with hot cocoa permanently ready on the stove. Those who prefer to be active are skating in the Amsterdamse Bos or in Vondelpark.

Koninginnedag

Koninginnedag (**Queen's Day**) is on 30 April. Although events in commemoration of the former queen's birthday (the current queen's birthday is seasonally unfavourable) take place throughout the Netherlands, they take on a

---

PRECEDING PAGES: street musicians in Dam Square.
LEFT: concert on Prinsengracht.
RIGHT: celebrating Queen's Day.

particularly chaotic form in Amsterdam with more than 500,000 in attendance. The day is one of unbridled commercial fever, the result of a decree stating that anyone can sell anything, within the bounds of legality.

The initial idea was to create a day on which children could sell their handicrafts and play their instruments to passersby, but the spirit of enterprise pervades both old and young nowadays. The entire city becomes a cross between a junk sale and a carnival from the night before when sellers

> ### PATRIOTIC HUE
> Orange is the colour of Queen's Day (to commemorate the House of Orange), with banners, body painting and the Dutch flag flying everywhere.

begin setting up their pitch on the prime sites. Thousands of stalls selling old ships' tackle, second-hand bric-a-brac and handmade items – along with people challenging all-comers at chess, egg throwing contests at people dressed in costume and various food vendors selling everything from kebabs to Vietnamese *loempias* – form aisles along the pavements for the throngs of slightly perplexed visitors. During the day, Vondelpark, the Dam, the Jordaan and Leidseplein become the prime spots to soak up the atmosphere.

As the afternoon progresses a giant street party develops in the city centre. A solid jam of beer-drinking humans provides the audience

for live bands which play on stages outside the bars. By 7pm, the late shift of merry-makers witnesses the surreal sight of convoys of water-jetting sweeper lorries which clear the streets of rubbish ready for the next day. Trams and buses start operating again and the streets return to normal. By the next day, the only memory is the collective hangover of the celebrants.

Summer celebrations

Founded in 1947, the **Holland Festival** runs throughout June and is the biggest dance, drama and music festival in the Netherlands. This often rather highbrow carnival of the arts is an international crowd-puller and encompasses performances held at numerous venues throughout the city, mainly at the Stadsschouwburg in Leidseplein *(see page 170)*.

The **Uitmarkt**, held at the end of August in Museumplein, is a three-day fair in preparation for Holland's new cultural season. Groups of theatre, music, dance and video artists from across the country flock to the city to present short performances.

Around the second week of September the Jordaan begins 10 days of merriment. Accordion groups and vocalists perform traditional folk music. Food stalls and stages are set up around the cafés. A less raucous affair is the flower parade, on the first Saturday in September, when decorated floats and costumed attendants proceed from Aalsmeer *(see page 255)* to the heart of the city.

Sint Nicolaas

On the second or third Saturday of November, Sint Nicolaas arrives "from Spain", proceeding up Prins Hendrikkade to the city centre. Looking rather like Father Christmas, but wearing a bishop's mitre, the saint greets the crowds of children.

A parade through the streets heralds the build up to St Nicolaas' Eve; children put out their shoes for the saint and wake up to find them filled with marzipan cakes in a variety of fanciful shapes. On 5 December the children receive more substantial presents. ❑

LEFT: at the festival of Sint Nicolaas, which takes place in mid-November.

Gay Amsterdam

Homosexuality in Amsterdam, male or female, is an issue, but it is an issue in the most positive sense of the word. Amsterdam affords a freedom to gay people that is almost unparalleled in other major European cities – little wonder that the city is often referred to as "the gay capital of Europe".

With at least 35 gay bars (including two lesbian cafés), 14 gay or gay-friendly hotels and at least three gay discos, it is easy to speak of the "gay city quarters". There are three main areas where gays of all ages congregate in the many diverse bars and restaurants catering to the leather, denim and regular gay populace. In the heart of the city in the Warmoesstraat area there are six bars, a cinema (with darkroom), several gay sex shops and gay lodgings/hotels. Secondly, behind Rembrandtplein on and around the Amstel there are 10 bars, a disco, a gay "escort club" and gay-friendly jewellers. This is by far the most famous quarter for visiting and local gays. Lastly, there are four bars, a disco and three gay-friendly shops in Reguliersdwarsstraat.

Most, if not all shops are "gay-friendly" but some shop-owners pride themselves on their gay roots and are annotated in the Amsterdam Columbia Fun Map, a free map made by and for gay people, widely available at all gay outlets and a must for all gay visitors (see page 261). It is worth mentioning that in Kerkstraat and around Leidseplein there are also numerous gay bars, restaurants and hotels, but these tend to be frequented by slightly older clients and offer a quieter and more relaxed atmosphere, although the area does have some discos and a leather bar. Surprisingly, the demand for lesbian-orientated bars seems, by comparison, minimal, although they do exist.

The gay community didn't always enjoy the same freedom it now has – in the 1970s the placing of wreaths on Remembrance Day for homosexual victims at the war memorial on Dam Square was forbidden. During World War II the Nazi administration forced gays to wear pink stars sewn onto their clothes and many suffered the same fate in concentration camps as other Nazi victims (Jews, gypsies, handicapped and subversives). In 1988, in response to this ban and the fact that many gay

soldiers were omitted from official rolls of honour, a Homo monument built of pink granite was erected to the side of the Westerkerk. Although initially founded to commemorate gay war victims, it now also functions as a memorial to Aids victims and gay people the world over who are discriminated against because of their sexual orientation. Today, the ban on wreaths at Dam Square on Remembrance Day has also been lifted.

The greatest annual gay event in Amsterdam is undoubtedly the Gay Pride celebration. It takes place every first weekend in August. On the Friday bands play in the streets of the above-mentioned gay quarters. Saturday is the highlight of this

spectacle, with a colourful carnival parade on the water. There are boats of all descriptions, dressed up like their crew in costumes ranging from mild avant garde to the blatantly bizarre and unashamed. This visual orgy of colour and form is enjoyed by all, gay or straight, young or old.

Any gay visitor to Amsterdam would be more than well advised to visit the national gay and lesbian organisation, the COC. Founded in 1946 for the specific needs of homosexuals, this non-profit-making outfit now serves a dual role in the gay community – to provide a meeting place for kindred spirits and to stand up for the rights, privileges and interests of homosexuals, bisexuals and transgenders (see page 261). ❑

RIGHT: Amsterdam is known as the "gay capital" of Europe.

FOOD AND DRINK

*Amsterdam is a gastronome's delight, with its wholesome local dishes
complemented by an ethnic variety that spans the cuisines of the world*

These days, when it comes to dining out in Amsterdam, it is possible to dine out in almost any language. And just as the Dutch explorers once brought back spices from around the world, innovative restaurateurs are seeking inspiration in fusion cuisine, combining east with west. In terms of spots to choose from, thanks to the proliferation of ethnic restaurants one can experience the delights of such varied (and often exotic) cuisines as Vietnamese, Ethiopian, Thai, Turkish, Spanish, Greek, Portuguese, Tibetan and Polish. Of course there are also traditional French, Italian, Japanese and Chinese restaurants, from the fanciest with two Michelin stars down to the most humble pizzeria.

Choose the ambience according to your mood. The basic Dutch *eetcafé* is usually favoured by locals who come for the *dagschotel* or daily special, which offers a choice of meat, fish or vegetarian main course, served with vegetables and chips. Some of these locals have a menu as well. Otherwise, the sky's the limit for the adventurous diner. There are sushi bars with revolving lines of food; arty environments where diners recline the whole evening; authentic *tapas* or *dim sum* in the heart of the Red Light District; a cosy retreat on a pier in the harbour. There are restaurants that specialise in fish, vegetarian fare and kosher cooking, as well as the local pancake house.

Large, pancakes are popular, whether sweet or savoury, and offer a variety of fillings from apple and Grand Marnier to a creamy mushroom and beef ragout. *Poffertjes* are sold from tents set up on the Dam and around town from crystal-chandeliered, mirrored pavilions. They are mini pancakes eaten with large quantities of sugar and butter. Both large and mini pancakes are quite delicious when topped with thick sugar and butter.

PRECEDING PAGES: a brown café: for regulars, a home away from home.
LEFT: herring consumption the traditional way.
RIGHT: an *eetcafé* provides straightforward cuisine.

Dutch favourites

For many years the Dutch kitchen was synonymous with potatoes, cabbage, bread, cheese, potatoes, herring, endive and more potatoes, with some sausage thrown in for good measure. Just look at any of the Old Master paintings with the family gathered round a sumptuous

meal or a still life with a bountiful buffet, especially Van Gogh's portrait of the *Potato Eaters* (*see page 193*).

Because the Dutch prefer to eat their national dishes at home, there have not been that many restaurants in the Netherlands which exclusively offer Dutch specialities. However, Amsterdam favourites such as Dorrius, Haesje Claes, De Blauwe Hollander and De Poort all take pride in serving most of the traditional dishes such as *hutspot met klapstuk* (hodgepodge with meat, carrots and potatoes), *stamppot van zuurkool en worst* (sauerkraut mashed with potatoes and sausage), *erwten* (pea) soup and *bruine bonen* (brown bean) soup all year round. At the renowned d' Vijff Vlieghen (Five Flies) restaurant, the diverse menu is based on the "new Dutch cuisine", which features fresh local produce prepared seasonally from traditional recipes with a light touch in terms of fat content.

Severe Dutch winter weather at one time necessitated large, hearty meals rich in fats and carbohydrates to provide energy and keep in body heat. Life is now more amenable so vast meals are a thing of the past and thick pea soups and mashed vegetable dishes omit the extra fat for the weight-conscious. The most traditional winter dish, still popular among the

Your hotel will most likely include breakfast with the price of your room. This comprises a plate of cheese and meats, a cooked egg, and a bread basket (with butter and jam), which holds a variety of breads, from pre-cut white to heavy, black rye and perhaps wholewheat, raisin and seed bread. A spiced cake, *ontbijtkoek* or *peperkoek*, often eaten with butter, is also included. Coffee or tea gets you going for the day. The *koffietafel* (coffee table) lunch which is served in homes and in office canteens includes a variety of breads, cheeses and meats. The drink of choice is usually milk or *karnemelk* (buttermilk). It has only been in

older generation, is *boerenkool-stamppot met worst* (cabbage mashed with potatoes and served with smoked sausage). There is a Dutch saying that *boerenkool* ("farmers' cabbage", otherwise known as kale) is best when taken from the ground after the first frost. Meanwhile, other specialities of the Dutch kitchen include white asparagus served with ham and chopped egg (in May and June), smoked eel, special puddings *(vla)* with whipped cream, pancakes and herring, known as "the poor man's oyster". But young people tend to prefer McDonald's, which has in recent years, along with other fast-food chains, become a visible part of the national foodscape.

recent years that the Dutch have started leaving the office to have business lunches. More restaurants are starting to offer lunches for workers on the run, and some cafés are starting to open before 10am to offer breakfast.

Colonial cuisine

When in Amsterdam, you must experience Indonesian food. Usually it is the unsophisticated, plainly furnished restaurants that serve the most interesting and authentic dishes. Restaurants such as these are often family-run, with mother or grandmother presiding over the kitchens and preparing dishes that are unique to a particular village or island in Indonesia.

The menu is often extremely simple: some offer smaller variations of the more tourist-orientated *rijsttafel* and nothing else, which gives you a plate of rice with two or three small samplings of vegetables and meat. Some *rijsttafels* come with 15, 25, 30 or more side dishes of meat, vegetables, refreshing fruits and garnishes. When the *rijsttafel* is served, a hotplate is placed on the table to keep the separate bowls of food warm. You are then served from a large bowl of rice, which can be replenished. Gone are the days when a multitude of dishes was brought to the table by a procession of white-clad waiters, each bearing a single dish.

The *rijsttafel* is eaten by arranging the rice on your plate then placing a small portion of each dish around the edge, lastly filling in the centre. Typical dishes include vegetables in coconut milk, chicken, lamb or goat skewers served with satay, fried bananas and fish and meat prepared in various ways. The dishes themselves are usually spicy rather than hot, but beware of the small saucers of red *sambal*, likely to destroy your tastebuds for the rest of the meal. Beer or tea is the ideal beverage.

Another cuisine unique to the Netherlands is that of Suriname (a former Dutch colony in South America), which offers a spicy mixture of Creole and Indian. This is considered a kind of soul food with hearty curries and typical dishes such as peanut soup and *pom*, a kind of sweet potato, served with roti bread.

Eating on the run

If you fancy something quick to eat on the run, there is a wide variety of options, from the *broodje* (filled bread roll) shop to the Vietnamese *loempia* (spring roll) vendor, pizza slices, or the Middle Eastern takeaway stand that sells *shoarma* (roasted pork or lamb in a pitta bread) or *falafel*.

Broodjes can be bought in most bakeries or in special *Broodjeszaken*, filled with a variety of cheeses, meats and salads. Croissants have now started overtaking the *broodje* as a snack food, and are sold filled with cheese or ham.

LEFT: satay and peanut sauce *(sambal)* in an Indonesian restaurant.
RIGHT: traditional Dutch pancakes.

> ### WHERE TO GO
>
> A *rijsttafel* should be experienced but not at the overpriced "tourist traps" around the Dam or Leidseplein. Choose local favourites such as Tempo Doeloe, Speciaal or Kantjil en de Tijger.

Some Dutch people now seem to favour the "wall food" snack bars such as Febo, which sell their wares from a coin-operated *automatiek*, where cooks place the food (from behind) in small compartments with glass doors. A *kroket* is long, round and filled with stew; it tastes better with mustard or eaten in a roll. A *nasibal* is ball-shaped and stuffed with spiced fried rice. A long type of sausage, twice as long as a *kroket* and with very questionable stuffing, is a *frikandel kroket*.

You should definitely also try the most popular snack: the Belgian-style *patat* (chips or *frites*) which were famously satirised by the John Travolta character in the film *Pulp Fiction* because of the Dutch habit of eating them with a tiny fork and dipping them into mayonnaise rather than the usual British and American custom of using tomato ketchup. These excellent potatoes bear no relation to their fast-food counterparts and really should be sampled, ideally at a stand with a queue and a sign saying "*Belgian Patat Frîtes*".

The next most popular snack is herring, eaten raw or salted, with plenty of chopped onion, either picked up by the tail and dropped whole into the mouth, or, more often, eaten with a fork from a small plate. Herring stalls are a feature of Dutch life, especially in May when everyone wants to try the mild *nieuwe groene haring* – the first green herring of the season. These stalls or wagons attract a variety of clients, many of whom eat it the traditional way, holding it aloft by the tail between thumb and forefinger of the right hand, head lifted, mouth open and swallow! Others may prefer a *broodje haring*, slices of herring in a soft roll or

just herring slices on their own. Whatever way you choose, chopped onions are *de rigueur*. If you prefer another sort of fish, the stalls also sell smoked salmon, smoked eel and two varieties of succulent Dutch shrimp, the *Noordse* or *Hollands garnalen*, the North Sea's finest.

Light meals

If you get hungry while in a café, before the dinner hour, try a plate of *borrelhapjes* (snacks) like *kroketten* (meat or shrimp croquettes) or *bitterballen*, balls of meat coated with breadcrumbs which are deep-fried and served with mustard. Be sure to let them cool before taking a bite because the inside is notoriously hot

> ### RAISE YOUR GLASS
>
> A favourite New Year drink called *Bisschopswijn* (Bishop's Wine) may have been named after St Nicolaas. This mulled wine is used for a Dutch toast – *Gezondheid* (Your health!) or *Proost*.

and the Dutch always get a perverse pleasure watching foreign guests innocently tuck into them. Plates of cheese, olives or nuts are other options to enjoy with your "happy hour". Late at night a *tosti*, or grilled cheese sandwich, often combined with a slice of ham, usually hits the spot and helps temper a potential hangover.

As for sweets, the most popular with adults and children are liquorice drops *(dropjes)* made of gum and laurel. Available in various flavours and shapes (sweet or salty, animals or coins), they may be bought either in packets or singly. The colours are predominantly black or brown and for most visitors they remain an acquired taste.

What to drink

Many people drink beer, especially Pils, a light beer, though the favoured drink is jenever or Dutch gin, made from distilled malt wine with juniper berries. At about 5pm people drop into their local café for a *borrel*: a small glass of either the colourless *jonge* (young) jenever, less creamy than the *oude* (old), which has a pale yellow colour and a noticeably heavier, muskier flavour. The Dutch are famous for their liqueurs and fruit brandies, although these are now losing popularity to imported drinks such as Campari. Beer, mineral water and wine are drunk with meals. *Spa Rood* (Spa red) is sparkling mineral water, while *Spa Blauw* (Spa blue) is the still variety. Most wines in bars are not so drinkable, but are steadily improving, depending on whether the bar is attached to an *eetcafé* (where one can also dine).

Coffee can be considered the Dutch national drink and *koffiedrinken* is the national pastime. A cup of strong coffee, or a *bakkie*, is usually served black. *Espresso* is a popular alternative and *koffie verkeerd*, or "wrong coffee" is a popular choice, a kind of café au lait served with a lot of steamed milk and a little coffee for flavouring.

Hot chocolate is mostly a winter drink and when people go skating, private stands are set up on the ice with large urns on stoves. ❏

LEFT: Dutch cheese in the village of Volendam, just outside Amsterdam.
RIGHT: Café Hoppe at Spui.

BROWN CAFES, GRAND CAFES AND HASH CAFES

Amsterdam is big on cafés, and half the fun for visitors lies in wandering in and discovering for themselves their unique personalities

Amsterdam has a long café tradition. Some claim that the first bar, euphemistically called café, opened its doors in the 13th century, when two men and a dog in a boat drifted ashore on the marshy banks of the (then) river IJ. By the 17th century, there were countless taverns in Amsterdam, which slowly and surely would extend to other cities. Dutch cafés have as much cultural value as museums and a visit to one is essential for the true flavour of the city.

Traditional brown cafés (so-called because walls and ceilings have turned brown from age and smoke) are identified by dark, cosy, wooden interiors. The only audible sound is the buzz of lively conversation and the tinkle of glasses being rinsed. Coffee is generally brewed, not machine made, and if you fancy a snack to go with your beer or spirit, there is usually a plate of olives or cheese. These cafés define the Dutch word *gezelligiheid*, which means a state of cosiness or conviviality. This is where locals come for a few beers after work, to play cards, engage in political debates and tell tall tales.

The more elegant and stylish grand cafés serve lunch and desserts and tend to have high ceilings, more light, reading tables and a variety of music. There are also cafés where you can play chess, throw darts, or play pool or billiards. There are men's cafés, women's cafés and even night cafés, which close around 5am. Remember that the Dutch take pride in speaking English, so you should not be at a loss for conversation, if desired.

▷ **CAFÉ LIFE BEGINS HERE**
Warm weather offers the perfect excuse to sit on a bar or café terrace and sip a beer in the sunshine with friends.

WHAT'S THE ALTERNATIVE?

◁ **GREENHOUSE EFFECT**
There are cafés to suit one's every mood, including those offering "space cake". But don't overdo it on an empty or jet-lagged stomach.

△ **LIVING ROOM**
Local, or brown cafés, remain a strong tradition. Serving as a type of living room, for some they offer a home away from home.

Hash cafés attract their own mellow public, and most tourists who fancy a walk on the wild side place a visit to a hash coffee shop at the top of their itinerary. Although the police have clamped down in recent years, due to a rise in "hard" drug selling, you won't have to look too far to find one. Alternative cafés hang green and white placards in the window to distinguish themselves from regular establishments. These placards have replaced many of the marijuana leaf logos and Bob Marley imagery.

Other cafés which have opened in recent years include those known as "energy" or "smart drug" cafés, which sell psychedelic mushrooms and mood-enhancing drugs made of natural ingredients.

And for those hooked on the Internet, there are cyber cafés throughout Amsterdam where you can sip coffee while communicating with the world via the Internet.

◁ **HANGING OUT**
The hectic but lively Leidseplein remains a popular haunt for locals as well as tourists, particularly during the summer months.

△ **SOCIAL OR SOLITARY**
In a densely populated city like Amsterdam, the café is often regarded as a solitary retreat where one can read or sit in peace.

MODERN ART

Amsterdam's influence on art didn't end with the Golden Age; the 19th and
20th centuries saw the rise of Van Gogh, Mondrian and many others

When one thinks of Dutch art, the Great Masters of the 17th century come to mind: Rembrandt, Ruisdael, De Hooch, Steen, Cuyp, Hals, Vermeer, among others *(see page 31)*. The detailed work with its quiet power; the chiaroscuro portraits; naturalism of still lifes; intense raging seas; pastoral Dutch landscapes and interiors depicting daily life. The 18th century reflected earlier achievements in art with no new directions. Rather than the grand imagery of the past, a lighter attitude prevailed, with anecdotal portraits of Dutch life by painters such as Troost and De Lelie. In the 19th century Van Gogh's Expressionism was a contrast to Mesdag's Impressionist imagery of the Haagse School, the naturalism of Israëls and Breitner's visual realism.

Breitner chronicled Amsterdam until his death in 1927. His early work of ordinary moments in Dutch life has been described as "Amsterdam Impressionism", though it has none of the colour of the French Impressionists but more of the emotional impact of Expressionism. Breitner (who also was a pioneer in photography) would later be considered a Modernist, paving the way for Mondrian.

Vincent van Gogh

Although Vincent van Gogh "found" his style in France, his early work had a very Dutch character. The son of a parson, he almost followed in his father's footsteps but that came to an abrupt end in 1879 when his appointment as an evangelist was not extended. He decided, relatively late in life, to become an artist, convinced that it was his only chance to achieve any personal or social success. In a letter to his brother Theo, a successful art dealer, Vincent asked for prints of the peasant painter Jean-François Millet, which he wanted to copy.

His determination to draw and later to paint was most likely an extension of his thirst for self-knowledge. He would not paint his first

masterpiece until 1885, and he yearned for an artistic breakthrough that would bring him success. Relocating to Paris he had his first encounter with modern Impressionist and Post-Impressionist art. His work was considered old-fashioned, if not provincial, because of both the colours and the subject matter. In the next year

he would make an intense effort to work in other styles – from pointillist techniques to Japanese decorative painting – striving for his own medium.

Van Gogh was misunderstood throughout his life. More than 100 years later his legacy of masterpieces remains, and he continues to be misunderstood. Questions regarding why he cut off part of his ear after an argument with Gaugin and what drove him to admit himself to a mental asylum in France in the final year of his life have yet to be satisfactorily answered. One must keep the man behind the myth in mind. Only when one visits the Van Gogh Museum in Amsterdam is it possible to view his œuvre

LEFT: images of Vincent van Gogh.
RIGHT: *Dame in der Straßenbahn* by K. Malevich (1913)

in chronological order *(see page 193)*. In his Netherlands period, he sketched peasants and Dutch landscapes. Then he moved on to Paris where his palette grew brighter as he painted flowers, panoramas and portraits. Wanting to return to nature he relocated to Arles where he painted prolifically, often one canvas per day.

Van Gogh died by his own hand at the age of 37. He had painted his life's work in less than 10 years, and died having sold only one painting. But his legacy is the vivid colours and brushstrokes synonymous with his name. Today his works are famously valued in the millions at auctions.

The 20th century

The latter years of the 19th century were a tough act to follow, but there was no turning back. In 1917 the artists of the De Stijl movement emerged, intent on seeking a new and contemporary tradition. The problem being addressed by painters throughout Europe was what to paint and how to paint. This was the problem that De Stijl intended to address based on a theory that if the individual was the measure of all things, then anything could be art if the artist presented it as such *(see page 195)*.

Piet Mondrian was the movement's most prominent member and his work would mark

THE COBRA MOVEMENT

Constant, Corneille and Karel Appel joined forces with their Belgian and Danish counterparts Christian Dotremont, Joseph Noiret and Asger Jorn in 1948 to form COBRA, an international group whose new imagery, use of colour and playful elements moved away from the neutral postwar terrain. The works drew inspiration from folk art, naive painting, primitivism and the drawings of children and the mentally ill, and many incorporated text.

The COBRA Movement took its name from the first letters of three European capitals, Copenhagen, Brussels and Amsterdam, where its members were based. As Constant summarised the COBRA Movement: "A painting is no longer a construction of colours and lines, but an animal, a night, a cry, a man, or all of these together... after a period in which art represented nothing, art has now entered a period in which it represents everything."

Although the COBRA group existed for only three years, it became one of the 20th century's most influential artistic movements. In 1995 the COBRA Museum opened in Amstelveen, a suburb of Amsterdam. The collection features leading works from the COBRA Movement (Sandbergplein 1–3; tel: 547 5050; open Tues–Sun; entrance fee). The COBRA Café in Museumplein pays homage to this unique art movement in its decor and ambience.

him as one of the greatest of the 20th-century Modernist painters. Although his early work portrayed a romantic symbolism, his canvases would evolve radically over the next few years incorporating lines and rectangular shapes and eventually evolving to his easily identifiable "contra-compositions" in red, yellow and blue. In those classic paintings of the 1920s and '30s, space is evoked and structured with the use of black lines and small blocks of primary colour. His well-known *Victory Boogie Woogie* painting from 1943 can be seen in the Gemeentemuseum in The Hague, along with many other canvases *(see page 252)*.

Dutch either did not know about them or rejected them." Neither Dadaism nor Surrealism was significant in Holland. A group of original artists who painted in a cold, precise, realist style labelled Magic Realist were Carel Willink, Pyke Kock and Raoul Hynckes. Similar in style were Charley Toorop and Dick Ket.

After World War II there was more of a social involvement which seemed to be a requirement for the newly evolving art. Socialism brought together a group of freewheeling personalities which became the COBRA Movement. The COBRA Museum features their work, and work by the contemporary artists they inspired. ❑

Socialism in art

In his book *Dutch Painting* (1978), Rudi Fuchs, director of the Stedelijk Museum *(see page 196)* says that with the exception of Van Gogh, Expressionism never really caught on in the Netherlands. "Whether that is because the Dutch character is not given to the display of strong emotion is difficult to decide. In fact, Dutch art between the two wars, with the exception of De Stijl, found itself curiously apart from international developments. The

(see page 196)

FAR LEFT: *Suprematisme* by Malevich (1921).
LEFT: *Woman with Fish-hat* by Picasso (1942).
ABOVE: inside the Stedelijk Museum.

CONTEMPORARY ART

After a few quiet decades, Dutch art is having a renaissance. The works of Jan Dibbets, Pieter Struyckens, Ger van Elk and Marlene Dumas are often exhibited in art fairs and in museum collections. A new generation of Dutch painters includes Marijke van Warmerdam, Joope Koelewij, Krijn de Kooning, Gijs Stuyling, Arnold Mik, Gerald van der Kap, Marc Mulders, Ronald Ophuis and Rinneke Dijkstra. The following galleries are recommended for contemporary art: W139 Warmoesstraat 139; Metis 688 Keizersgracht; Stedelijk Museum Bureau 59 Rozenstraat; De Appel 10 Nieuwe Spiegelstraat; Galerie Fons Welters 140 Bloemstraat.

ARCHITECTURE

Architecture is Amsterdam's jewel in the crown, from its 17th-century gabled

canal homes to the stylish 20th-century additions of the Amsterdam School

On a wet dark night the locals are huddled in a café and the yellow light emitting through the Art Deco leaded glass spills out onto the pavement mixing with the soft light coming from 19th-century streetlamps. The reflections dance on the pavement and your eyes wander to the reflections of the houses in the canals; tall dark ships in the night each with its own special mast light at the top. From such a limited view as this, Amsterdam remains a beautiful city, and the great thing about being a visitor is that the architectural beauty the locals take for granted is everywhere to be found.

Taking pride in gables

Nearly all the houses that line the canals are graced with a gable at the top. Their basic shape defines them; these are the clock, step, spout, bell, neck (with side ornamentation), raised neck and frame gables *(see page 165)*. No two gables are alike and their ornamentation often reveals the profession of the original owner.

Much pride and effort was invested in the construction of the gables; after all, these decorated the homes of some of the wealthiest people in the world and this is particularly noticeable along the "Gouden Bocht" or "Golden Bend", a small stretch of the Herengracht. Faithful to its name, this area is now home to international banks and prestigious offices.

Bell gables were the forefathers of the popular neck gable; the neck gable offered more room for ornamentation and later evolved into the even more extravagant elevated neck gable. Fine examples of bell gables are to be seen on Brouwersgracht and two of special interest on Leliegracht, one at No. 60 in the French style with rococo ornamentation and the other at No. 36 surmounted by a Cypriot cat. Neck gables are by far the most common and can be seen everywhere, even though it became something

of a fashion in the 19th century to replace them with frame gables (common in the De Pijp area). During the Golden Age Italian and French influences made their mark and Tympana triangular gable tops started to appear on larger buildings. These classical forms can today be seen on the Dutch West Indies Com-

pany building in Haarlemmerstraat *(see page 157)* and Felix Meritis Theatre *(see page 168)*.

One of the most famous step gables to be seen looks out over the corner of the Brouwersgracht and the Prinsengracht. It is unique in that it is a twinned gable; one identical twin looks out over the Brouwersgracht, the other over the Prinsengracht. It's also a good place for a rest: the twins are perched above the oldest café in Amsterdam, Café Papeneiland.

Protruding from all the gables are hoisting beams, which would have been originally used to hoist up goods delivered from barges to the attic and, in warehouses, to different storage floors. The older warehouses are easily

---

PRECEDING PAGES: typical architecture in the Jordaan.
LEFT: gabled canal house.
RIGHT: hoisting beams were used to haul up goods delivered from canal barges.

distinguished from residences; they tend to have a central column of wider windows with hatches (to receive merchants' cargoes).

The hoisting beams are just as functional today. Since most houses still have their original extremely narrow and steep staircases it's impossible to move any furniture up or down. With the aid of a block and tackle the hoisting beam continues to be an indispensable architectural adornment.

For many centuries the houses and warehouses were not numbered, but had names instead. Many of the names have still survived and are to be seen in gable stones. Gable stones

are mini sculptural wonders that are embedded into the façades of the buildings. The house names are as diverse and humorous as the gable stones themselves. Often the names reflected an event in the owner's life, or an amusing anecdote. When the Netherlands was under Napoleonic rule people were forced to register their names; some, out of protest, registered pseudonyms such as Mr Born Naked. One wonders what Mr Born Naked's gable stone would have looked like.

By far the best way to see the gables is to take a round trip *(rondvaart)* on a canal boat with a guide *(see page 157)*. That way you avoid neck cramps and feeling like a whirling dervish since there are so many to see.

Almshouses

The wealthier residents of Amsterdam took their religion seriously, and nowhere is there better evidence of this than in the construction of the almshouses.

The most famous one in Amsterdam is to be found at the Begijnhof just off the Spui *(see page 133)*. It dates back to the Middle Ages and is today still home to widows and elderly women. The small courtyard contains the tiny former Catholic Church now used by the English Protestants. Next to the church entrance is a plaque dedicated to the Pilgrim Fathers. The courtyard is an oasis of quiet in the middle of the city and the residents' homes are adorned with gable stones dedicated to faith and devotion with the occasional Latin banner from the Catholic period – the gable stone of Abraham is quite striking. The centre of the courtyard has a small well-kept garden and judging from an

---

WAREHOUSES

For centuries warehouses played a very important role in Amsterdam. Originally merchants used to store their wares in their own homes, but later they started building warehouses next to their homes with substantial hoisting beams noticeably bigger than their domestic counterparts. To cope with the sheer weight of the goods a windlass was used from inside the building. Because of the bulky and heavy nature of the goods the beams inside these buildings are also enormous. It is not uncommon in some warehouses to see large holes in the beams – this was because the beams would have started their life as ship's keels, such was the need for strength to support the loads.

Indeed at one stage Amsterdam's grain reserve was large enough to supply the rest of Europe in the event of a bad harvest. Of course by this time trade had mushroomed and warehouses were being constructed on purpose-built islands on the IJ.

The warehouses, like the houses, were not numbered but given names (a tradition that survived well into the 20th century). As such the warehouses entered into a gable stone tradition of their own. The names often relate to the merchant or a motto such as "*D'Een-dragt*" ("Unity"). Today most warehouses have been converted into offices or highly fashionable apartments, popular among yuppies.

early painting little has changed over the centuries. Entry to the *hofje* or courtyard is free and it is well worth a visit, but remember that quietness is appreciated.

The Amsterdam School

At the turn of the 20th century, just as today, there was a housing shortage. However, there was still land available near the inner city to build on. With the introduction of a new housing act and a group of brilliant architects/artists, the Amsterdam School came into being.

They had set strict rules for themselves in terms of design and form, the results of which can be seen today. Every construction connected with this movement is a listed building. Characteristic of the Amsterdam School architecture are the expressive façades with projecting balconies, bay windows and sweeping curves. Lines, vertical and horizontal, were accentuated, thus making chimneys works of art, and for the first time people could enjoy the view from a wide window, hitherto impossible. Other window shapes, such as trapezoid and parabolic, are also a hallmark. Use of different coloured bricks as a sculptural medium integrating organic shapes and forms sometimes makes it hard to remember that you're looking at someone's home. The Amsterdam School was so thorough in design that they had even created their own typeface, which can be admired in the carvings and house numbers.

The architects did not confine themselves to housing, as the Beurs van Berlage (Berlage Stock Exchange) clearly demonstrates *(see page 135)*. Other public buildings that should be included in the list are the Scheepvaarthuis in Prins Hendrikkade by Van der Mey *(see page 219)*, a monumental building which boasts a series of figureheads; the Grand Hotel Centraal (Carlton) by Rutgers in Vijzelstraat; the former head office of the municipal transport company by Marnette in Stadhouderskade; and of course the old *Telegraaf* building in Nieuwezijds Voorburgwal by Staal.

In total there were 37 members of the Amsterdam School whose genius lay not only in architecture but a whole range of related disciplines from interior design and furniture to masonry. Maybe the greatest miracle of all is

that this radical early 20th-century omniscient approach has integrated so well with the rest of the city's buildings.

For a greater insight into this movement's achievements, a small but comprehensive pamphlet is available from the VVV tourist office *(see page 263)* outlining a walk that fully acquaints one with classic examples from The Amsterdam School.

Amsterdam Architectural Centre

Be your interest in architecture professional or that of a keen amateur, a visit to the Amsterdam Architectural Centre or ARCAM is a must.

It is located at Waterlooplein 213 (tel: 620 4878). Entry is free and there is always a small exhibition concerning contemporary architectural themes. There is also a wide range of relevant literature available in English and, for the dedicated enthusiast, €5 will buy you a detailed architectural map of Amsterdam to help you explore the city.

The centre focuses very much on current issues involving the role of architecture in Amsterdam. All the staff have an architectural background and view their role as a coordination point for anything architectural, thus they are an excellent reference point for students and professionals alike. ❏

LEFT AND RIGHT: creative examples of the Amsterdam School architecture.

PLACES

*A detailed guide to the entire city, with principal sites
clearly cross-referenced by number to the maps*

Go to a café on Keizersgracht on a wet Sunday afternoon in spring. A blonde woman, dressed in black, carefully tops two glasses of *warme chocolademelk* with generous dollops of whipped cream. This is Amsterdam. Go to Brouwersgracht and stand on the bridge facing the Westerkerk in the glow of an autumn sunset. With the trees stripped bare, the view of magnificent houses bordering Prinsengracht is like a painting of the city's Golden Age. This, too, is Amsterdam. Walk through the passage under the Rijksmuseum: there is a man sitting on the ground cross-legged, dressed in an embroidered Tibetan suit and singing. Return the next day and there may be someone else "in residence" playing the didgeridoo or exotic drums. These are other Amsterdam moments.

The city is composed of many memorable scenes, but there is also a list of "must sees". Museumplein with its impressive cultural triangle: the Rijksmuseum, Van Gogh Museum and the Stedelijk; the Royal Palace and the Nieuwe Kerk at the Dam; the Rembrandthuis and the Jewish Historical Museum near Waterlooplein – every visitor should find time to visit these. But after that, Amsterdam is what you want it to be, whether you sunbathe in Vondelpark, enjoy the outdoor pavilion of the NEMO museum or do a pub crawl from one brown café to the next.

Amsterdam has more than 1,000 bridges crossing more than 100 canals with a combined length in excess of 100 km (65 miles). Despite these statistics, the historic centre is very compact and lends itself to easy exploration. Take a canal boat to see the 17th- and 18th-century houses of the *grachtengordel*, the half-moon pattern of canals which stretches from the Amstel River to Brouwersgracht. Do plenty of walking: along the canals in the Jordaan; across the side streets between Leidsestraat and Raadhuisstraat; even to the warehouses of the east and the Maritime Quarter. Later, hire a bicycle and venture further afield. There are more than half a million bicycles in the city, which can be daunting. Start conservatively. Take your bike on the ferry behind Centraal Station and ride along the Noord-Holland Canal or go into the country heading towards Edam.

Above all, talk to the people. Language is rarely a barrier in a town where British entertainment is often preferred to the home-grown variety, and France, Belgium and Germany are regarded as neighbours. They will share, with frankness and generosity, their views on the city and the world in general. There are few places in Europe where human contact is so easy, and you will end up loving Amsterdam as much for its people as for its scenery. ❑

PRECEDING PAGES: city rooftops and the Oude Kerk; on the central canal circle at dusk; Damrak links the Dam with Centraal Station.
LEFT: a former warehouse converted into a chic apartment.

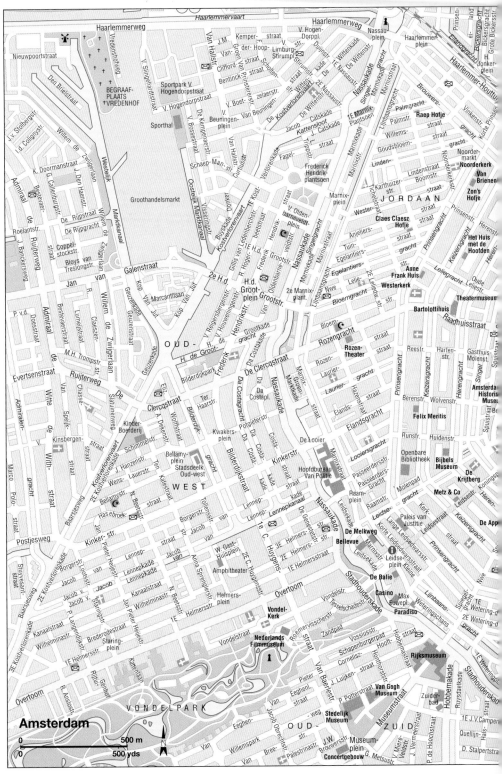

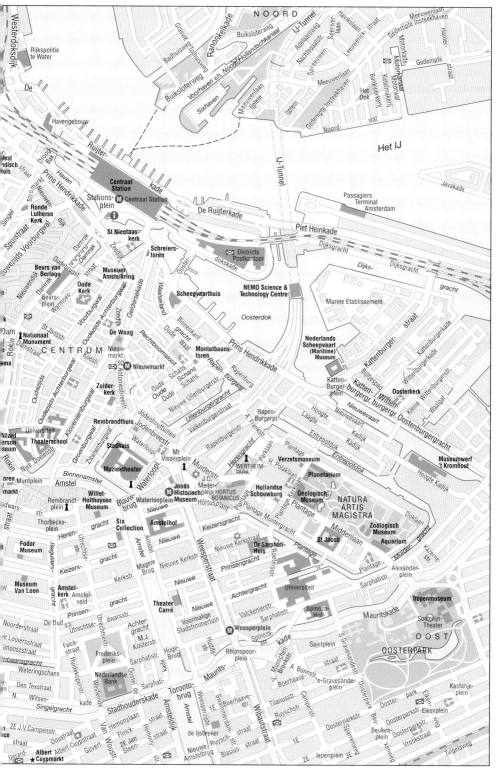

CENTRAL AMSTERDAM

*The heart of the city offers the best and the worst of Amsterdam,
but feasting your eyes on its historical treasures, it's easy
to imagine yourself back in the Golden Age*

Map
on page
128

S tanding in Dam Square today, it is tempting to try and block out the trams, cars and pedestrians for a moment and conjure up a romantic image of a medieval settlement built around a dam set back from the shoreline of the Zuiderzee. That ancient dam, of course, lives on in name only. But the very idea of it begs a few moments of mental reconstruction. Was it ever easier to imagine the way a modern European city looked in its earliest days?

The dam of old was built across the Amstel River sometime in the 13th century and proved to be the catalyst for rapid growth. By 1546 Amsterdam was a town of 14,000 people, an important transit point for Baltic grain and a place where tolls were paid on beer from Germany. One of the first clear pictures we have of Amsterdam is a town plan, dating from 1544 and drawn by the cartographer Cornelius Anthoniszoon. This "three-dimensional" view of the city shows the Amstel River flowing freely through the heart of Amsterdam, emerging beyond Dam Square as the Damrak. This final stretch of water extended all the way to the harbour, each bank crowded with small boats.

Much of that central waterway has since been built over and the Dam – Amsterdam's heart – is now landlocked. All that is left on the harbour side of the Dam today is a small cul-de-sac of water opposite Centraal Station. It still shares the same name as the street beside it, Damrak, but the cargo boats have been replaced by motorised canal boats which take tourists on nostalgic trips through the city's past. In the other direction, beyond the Dam to the south, the Amstel comes to a halt opposite the eastern end of Spui.

PRECEDING PAGES:
Prinsengracht
and Westerkerk
in winter.
LEFT: Dam Square.
BELOW: the Royal
Palace.

Historic centre

The **Dam ❶** has always been the heart of what was destined to become a mighty city and at different times much of Amsterdam's public life took place here. One of the original medieval buildings is the Nieuwe Kerk, first mentioned in 1400 and still dominating Dam Square today. Two other buildings – the old Town Hall and the Weigh House – have disappeared but are depicted in many surviving paintings and are familiar elements in the historic townscape.

The medieval Town Hall, with its squat tower, was a symbol of municipal independence and a busy administrative centre. This was where burgomasters made decisions affecting the city and the Republic. The meeting place of sheriffs and aldermen, it also housed the Exchange Bank, one of the most powerful financial organisations (at the time) in the world.

The Weigh House was constructed in 1565 and was the city's first large Renaissance-style building. Because navigation by small boats was possible from the seaward side as far as the Dam, this area was a

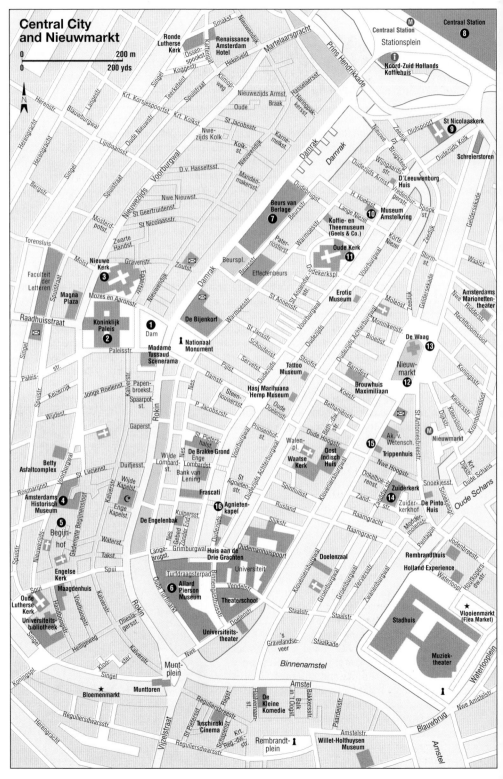

Central City and Nieuwmarkt

busy trading centre. During Amsterdam's heyday, all goods weighing more than 23 kg (50 lb) had to be recorded at the Weigh House. In the Amsterdam Historical Museum *(see page 131)* are some of the many contemporary pictures showing scenes of busy activity, with porters pushing wheelbarrows across Dam Square, wealthy merchants with their entourage and men in foreign dress making urgent business deals.

Another of Amsterdam's important early buildings was the 17th-century Exchange Building constructed across the river. The stretch of the Amstel River which stood behind it was named the Rokin. Barges departed with goods along the Amstel to the other major towns in Holland. Merchants came from all over the world to do business at the exchange. Depicted in many paintings of the time, the building was erected between 1608–11 but demolished in 1838.

The Dam continued to provide a busy focus for the city well into the 19th century and countless paintings and engravings show how it looked at various times. For a long while it was a fish market. A painting in the Amsterdam Historical Museum, for example, entitled *Dancing Round the Tree of Freedom at the Dam Square, 19 June 1795*, shows a long line of boats drawn right up to the edge of the 16th-century Weigh House.

The Weigh House itself, however, suffered an ignoble fate when in 1808 it was demolished at the order of King Louis Napoleon who, having made his headquarters in the new Town Hall, found that the building obstructed his view. Only the weather vane and a wooden statue have survived – they too are on display in the Amsterdam Historical Museum.

The Dam is still a hive of activity. Most days, especially at the weekend, it provides an impromptu stage for buskers, barrel-organs or street performers. Throughout the years, it has been the scene of parades, executions, political demonstrations, war remembrances, celebrations and noisy and colourful funfairs with larger-than-life Ferris wheels and other gravity-defying attractions. It is also the location of two of the city's major buildings, the former Town Hall, now the Royal Palace, and the Nieuwe Kerk. There are ambitious plans to make this historic intersection more pedestrian-friendly in the near future, but so far nothing decisive is in the works.

The Royal Palace

The scene at the Dam changed with the construction of the new Town Hall, the great building flanking the west side of the Dam today, which has since come to serve as the **Koninklijk Paleis ❷** (Royal Palace).

This new edifice was completed in 1655 and expressed the glory of what was by then one of the world's most powerful cities. Work began in 1648 with 13,659 piles driven into the ground to provide foundations. While it was under construction, the old Town Hall burnt down. Rembrandt provided a record of the scene when, curiously, he drew the old building in ruins, rather than the new one rising beside it.

The Dam was now an even more imposing hub. Executions were usually carried out on a scaffold in front of the new Town Hall. On such occasions the "staff of justice" was publicly displayed in one of the

Map on page 128

The National Monument is the focal point of Dam Square.

BELOW: Dam Square in the sunshine.

Town Hall windows. The corpses were taken from the gallows across the water of the IJ where they were hung as a warning to those entering Amsterdam by ship.

Although one might assume that the Royal Palace would be one of Amsterdam's top attractions, during parts of the year it is off limits to visitors due to the royal calendar. At such times, Queen Beatrix receives special guests at the palace, and it is quite obvious when she is "in residence" by witnessing the cordoned ropes, blue security vehicles and crowds of onlookers.

The large and imposing 17th-century classical-style building was designed by Jacob van Campen. When King Louis Napoleon came to Amsterdam in 1808, he transformed the building from a town hall into a royal palace, furnishing it with a rich collection of Empire furniture, clocks and chandeliers. Unlike its sombre exterior, the ornate interior reflects the power that Amsterdam enjoyed during its Golden Age, which makes a visit highly worthwhile (tel: 620 4060; open Jun–Aug daily 12.30–5pm; Sept–May: Tues–Thur 1–4pm; entrance fee).

The New Church

More rewarding, and more accessible, is the **Nieuwe Kerk** ❸ (New Church; tel: 638 6909; opening times subject to change throughout the year; entrance fee). With more than 500,000 visitors a year viewing such diverse and prestigious exhibitions as the Black Pharaohs, the Buddhas of Siam and the Art of Islam, to name but a few, the Nieuwe Kerk comes in after the Rijksmuseum *(see page 185)* and the Van Gogh Museum *(see page 193)* as the third most visited museum in the Netherlands.

Back in 1400 the construction of the Nieuwe Kerk had already begun; at that time the building was dedicated to the Virgin and St Catherine. Around 1500 the church was enlarged to its present size and decorated with paintings, sacred images and altars. After the Great Fire of 1645 the Nieuwe Kerk, by then in Protestant hands, was refurnished with elegant pews for the gentry, a copper gate in front of the choir and a highly decorative pulpit. Jacob van Campen, the architect of the Royal Palace, designed the housing for the enormous organ.

BELOW: the Nieuwe Kerk.

Through its many tombs and monuments to maritime heroes and poets, the church acquired national importance. Among the numerous famous Amsterdammers buried here are the naval hero Admiral Michiel Adriaensz de Ruyter (*d.* 1676) and the 17th-century poet Joost van den Vondel (*d.* 1679).

The investiture of Dutch monarchs has taken place here since 1841. Like kings Willem I, II and III, Regentess Emma and queens Wilhelmina and Juliana before her, Queen Beatrix took the constitutional oath in 1980 in a grand ceremony leading from the Royal Palace to the church. The church is also the venue for the national Remembrance Service held on 4 May.

In the late 1970s, the church re-opened its doors following a 20-year restoration. Since then, it has been operated by a foundation which has succeeded in transforming the grand building into an active and respected cultural centre. In addition to its exhibitions, there are also popular organ concerts held in the summer and on Christmas Day and New Year's Day.

History lesson

The city gives its best history lesson at the **Amsterdams Historisch Museum** ❹ (Amsterdam Historical Museum), a short walk south of the Dam (357 Nieuwezijds Voorburgwal or 92 Kalverstraat; tel: 523 1822; open daily; entrance fee). The museum's quiet courtyard location is reason enough to go – the museum occupies 17th-century buildings that were once home to the Civic Orphanage. In fact, upon leaving the museum and re-emerging into the neighbourhood with its 17th-century ambience, it feels like one is walking back in time.

In 1999, the exhibition space was expanded and updated with many hands-on exhibits focusing on life in Amsterdam, past and present. The renovation has created a much more visitor-friendly environment, with informative captions written in both Dutch and English and an efficient routing plan that gives one a clear and chronological insight into Amsterdam's rich history, making subsequent walks around town more informative and enjoyable. At the beginning of the route, one of the best displays is an illuminated flatplan of Amsterdam that shows clearly how the city grew. Starting in the year 1050, a light picks out particular periods down through the centuries and simultaneously illuminates the relevant phase of the city's growth.

The museum offers an excellent survey of the history of Amsterdam from the mid-13th century to the present, but given that the richest archives have come from the 17th and 18th centuries, the collection naturally concentrates on those periods. It is particularly strong on the era of Dutch maritime exploration. A selection of paintings depicts all of the city's landmarks as they appeared in their contemporary cityscapes. One gets a true picture of life in the Golden Age, at the turn of the 19th century and in the postwar years.

Map on page 128

Gable stones surviving from the Golden Age are a feature of the Historical Museum.

BELOW: Amsterdam Historical Museum.

As in London's Trafalgar Square, children enjoy the pigeons of Dam Square.

BELOW: 16th-century wooden house at the Begijnhof.
RIGHT: traditional costume.

The passageway from the Amsterdam Historical Museum to the Begijnhof is a modest history lesson in itself and a sudden unexpected art gallery as well. Hung along the walls are the oversized canvases of the Amsterdam civic guard, posing in attitudes of grandiose self-importance.

The civic guard originated at the end of the 14th century, when Amsterdam marksmen began joining together for civic defence and to help maintain public order. They founded three guilds: St George's for the crossbowmen; St Sebastian's for the archers; and the Guild of Harquebusiers, armed with early firearms. Each had its own meeting place, with rooms for social and business gatherings and a shooting range in the garden. Around 1530, the civic guard companies began to commission group portraits to hang in their guildhouses. The annual banquet was a favourite occasion for such paintings. The portraits grew larger and livelier over the years and culminated in the enormous canvases of the 17th century.

The guilds were merged in 1580 with other groups of militiamen drafted from Amsterdam's 11 municipal districts. In 1672, the old guilds were dissolved and the civic guard was reorganised. After 1650, no more group portraits were commissioned. Of all those painted in Amsterdam, some 50 have been preserved – the largest collection of paintings in this genre in existence.

The passageway serves as a link to the newest part of the museum, where the displays bring the history of Amsterdam up to date; paintings and photographs reveal the reasons why the city developed progressive welfare programmes from the mid-19th century and how it coped with the problems of unemployment during the Great Depression of the 1930s. There are numerous paintings tracing the development of the city, including two by Van Gogh, done during his

brief time in Amsterdam to visit fellow painter G.H. Breitner. Breitner's evocative paintings of his beloved Amsterdam are also on display, as well as his palette and easel with a half-completed painting of the Rokin.

The permanent exhibits are supplemented by temporary displays used to illustrate themes as diverse as personal collections of Amsterdam residents, the relationship between the Netherlands and Japan, fashion, Peter the Great's relationship with Amsterdam, and the diamond industry.

Map on page 128

Ancient glories and modern shops

Next door to the museum is the **Begijnhof** ❺, a magnificent diamond-shaped cobblestone courtyard of 17th-century buildings and easily the most picturesque place you can visit in Amsterdam's centre. The freshly painted houses with their bright windowboxes, the cast-iron lampposts and an unexpected air of solitude and tranquillity make it difficult to believe that the city's busiest shopping street, Kalverstraat, is just a minute away.

There are many *hofjes* (little courtyards) in Amsterdam, although the Begijnhof is the best known and the easiest to reach. It was founded in 1346 as a cloister-like home for Catholic lay sisters and today its quaint dwellings are occupied by unmarried retired ladies who appreciate having their peaceful garden treated respectfully by visitors. In 1578, with the Reformation sweeping over Holland, all the Catholic churches became Protestant, including the one standing within the Begijnhof and now known as the English Reformed Church. This is not the only church here, for the courtyard is also home to the concealed Begijnhof Catholic Church. Most of the houses date from the 17th century and are built of stone. One of the last two wooden houses remaining in Amsterdam,

The house at No. 34 in the Begijnhof dates from 1475 and is the oldest surviving house in Amsterdam.

BELOW: Centraal Station and the Koffiehuis.

Amsterdam's coat of arms adorns the wall of the Begijnhof.

BELOW: Dutch houses turned into fridge magnets.

dating from around 1550, has been moved to within the walls of the Begijnhof (the other can be found at Zeedijk 1).

You might have a little trouble finding the Begijnhof (you can also gain access from Spui) but you'll know soon enough when you are in **Kalverstraat**, one of Amsterdam's busiest shopping streets. On Saturdays in any month of the year this pedestrian-only boulevard is impossibly crowded. The fact that Kalverstraat was once home to Madame Tussaud's waxworks (now relocated to Dam Square) is proof of just how commercial this street is. Whether or not you take this opportunity to join "the millions of people who have visited Madame Tussaud in Amsterdam since it opened in 1970" is a matter of personal taste.

If you are in a serious frame of mind, you might head instead for the **Allard Pierson Museum ❻**, just a two-minute walk away (127 Oude Turfmarkt; tel: 525 2556; open Tues–Fri 10am–5pm, Sat–Sun 1–5pm; entrance fee). This museum contains the archaeological collection from the University of Amsterdam. Finds from Egypt, the Near East, Iran, Greece, Tuscany and the Roman Empire make for an academic but nevertheless captivating display of life in the Ancient World that occupies two floors. The changing exhibitions, which range from Myths and Music in Greek and Roman Antiquity to mummified monkeys in Egypt and Roman emperors on the Nile, are also of interest.

If you exit from Kalverstraat, in the direction of Centraal Station you will find yourself in **Nieuwendijk**, another pedestrianised shopping street but with a distinctly downmarket feel. The denim here is more faded than in Kalverstraat, but the fast food is faster and sex is creeping into the shopscape here as elsewhere in Amsterdam. On the plus side is the Hema store, a chainstore selling reasonably priced quality merchandise which locals swear by. This is a

good place to come to have if you need an umbrella, a pair of socks or tights, cosmetics, toiletries, film, writing materials and even postcards. They also have a small food hall which sells fine cheese, breads, chocolate and wine, and their coffee shop serves inexpensive hearty meals and snacks. There are two other Hema stores throughout the city, specifically in the Kalvertoren shopping complex by the Munt Tower and on Ferdinand Bolstraat near the Albert Cuypmarkt *(see page 230)*.

Nearby, parallel to Nieuwendijk, **Damrak** is similarly downmarket with souvenir stores, amusement arcades, exchange bureaux, cheap restaurants and fast food stands. Across the road, however, is a different story.

Monumental architecture

There are two monumental buildings which immediately catch the eye. The Bijenkorf department store and the former site of the Amsterdam Stock Exchange, the Beurs van Berlage.

The Bijenkorf is Amsterdam's oldest department store (with branches in other Dutch cities such as The Hague, Rotterdam and Utrecht) and boasts several floors featuring clothing, appliances, household furnishings and several restaurants and cafés. It is a good place to take a break in between tourist sights and busy Damrak.

But if you have to choose between the two, then it must be the **Beurs van Berlage** ❼ (Berlage Stock Exchange; 243 Damrak; tel: 624 0141; opening hours subject to change; entrance fee). This was one of the few large building projects undertaken in the last half of the 19th century and it replaced the Exchange Building, which dated from 1611. The Beurs van Berlage sprang up in 1896 from the designs of one of Holland's most famous architects, Hendrik Petrus Berlage. For many years the Beurs, also known as the Berlage Stock Exchange, was considered the most important Dutch architectural monument of the *fin de siècle* period. The stockbrokers have since moved away and these days the building is partly administered by the Stichting de Beurs van Berlage (Berlage Stock Exchange Foundation), which puts on a variety of exhibitions, cultural events, conferences and dinners.

Since 1988, the Beurs van Berlage has been the permanent home of the Netherlands Philharmonic Orchestra (the "NedPho") and the Dutch Chamber Orchestra, with one large hall and one small hall made of glass. This stately building is definitely worth a visit: within its cavernous and echoing interior is an impressive mix of pastel-coloured decorative brickwork, wooden flooring, stone pillars and steel roof girders from which hang long pendular globe-shaped lights. Around the periphery of the hall, small wooden cubicles, where deals were made, are a reminder of the building's original function as an exchange.

Around the station

Centraal Station ❽, north of the Beurs, dominates Damrak in a different way – it blocks off the view over the harbour (something which stirred up controversy during its construction at the end of the 19th

Map on page 128

TIP

At No. 62 Damrak is Allert de Lange, one of Amsterdam's finest bookshops. It was set up in the 1930s by a Jewish publisher to offer works of exiled German authors such as Bertholt Brecht.

BELOW: striking St Nicolaaskerk.

TIP

If you need a safe and sane refuge between trains, go to Platform 1 to the 1e Klas Grand-Café restaurant.

century). However, the elegant red brick neo-Renaissance building is hardly an eyesore. Designed in the so-called "national" style by P.J.H. Cuypers, who designed the similar-looking Rijksmuseum, one of its remarkable features is that it was built upon 26,000 wooden piles. Back-packing tourists and Amsterdam commuters crowd Stationsplein daily. Tram stops, bicycles and buskers set the scene here and, for anybody arriving by train, Stationsplein is unfortunately an untidy introduction to the historic heart of Amsterdam. Keep a tight grip on your luggage at all times.

Apart from the monumental sculptures that adorn the station building, the only other reason for anybody to come this way is for the VVV tourist office, situated in the **Noord-Zuid Hollands (or Smit) Koffiehuis** in Stationsplein just opposite the main entrance of the station (there's another VVV office inside the station, on platform 1). The ornate wooden coffee house, with its terrace overlooking the water, was built in 1911.

Near Stationsplein, are several places worth visiting. All of these lie in the direction of **St Nicolaaskerk ❾**, across the road to the east (left) as you emerge from the station. St Nicholas is the patron saint of sailors and the proximity of this church to the harbour easily explains the dedication. Built in 1887 in neo-baroque style, the interior is a striking mix of black marble pillars and wooden barrel vaulting. The church was extensively renovated in 1998.

Not far away is another example of a well-preserved historic building. **D'Leeuwenburg Huis**, in Oudezijds Voorburgwal, is a fine representation of early 17th-century architecture: a steep-gabled house dating from 1605 with a basement projecting out on to the street. The gable shows the arms of Riga, which points to trade relations with this Baltic port.

BELOW: Amstelkring Museum.

Hidden church

Another place in the centre of Amsterdam you should certainly visit is the **Museum Amstelkring** ⑩, or *Ons Lieve Heer Op Het Solder* (Our Lord in the Attic), just a few yards further along from D'Leeuwenburg Huis (40 Oudezijds Voorburgwal; tel: 624 6604; open Mon–Sat 10am–5pm; Sun and public holidays 1–5pm; entrance fee). Originally named "Het Hart" ("The Heart"), this is one of many clandestine churches that flourished in Amsterdam in the 17th century. Its discreet entrance right next door to the Red Light District means that, even today, it has managed to hide itself from view and it attracts nothing like the stream of visitors that justifiably flood to "sights" such as Anne Frank's House *(see page 162).*

Map on page 128

From the time of the Alteration in 1578 (the changeover from a Catholic to a Protestant city council in Amsterdam), Catholics were compelled to hold their religious gatherings secretly, in domestic rooms, an attic or a barn *(see page 28).* Around 1650 Catholic worshippers began to build clandestine churches, which in time were enlarged and heightened by the addition of galleries resting on pillars. There used to be scores of clandestine churches in Amsterdam. Wealthy merchants such as Jacob van Loon and Aernout van der Mye, who in 1662 were immortalised in Rembrandt's painting called *De Staalmeesters (The Syndics)*, were among the owners of these houses of worship hidden behind their simple domestic exteriors.

In 1661 a gentleman by the name of Jan Hartman started building a residence in Oudezijds Voorburgwal, together with two adjoining houses in Heintje Hoekssteeg. He furnished the combined attics of these three houses as a church. Although recent investigations have brought to light the remains of former attic

LEFT AND BELOW: details from *Ons Lieve Heer Op Het Solder* (Our Lord in the Attic) hidden church.

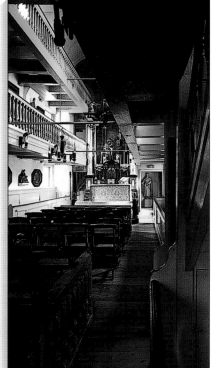

Map on page 128

Barrel organs are a common sight in the centre of the city.

BELOW: Oude Kerk.
RIGHT: imaginative decoration on the no. 13 tram.

churches in various Amsterdam houses, no other clandestine church throughout the Netherlands is as well preserved as the Amstelkring.

Over the years Hartman's buildings underwent various alterations but the **Sael** (living room) is still preserved in all its 17th-century sobriety and beauty: the combined coat of arms of Jan Hartman and his wife stands forth proudly above the imposing fireplace. The church was separate from the house proper, with its entrance in the side alley, and for more than two centuries this served as a parish church. In the beginning, when it was smaller, the officiating priest lived in a room in Hartman's family house. Around 1740 the church was enlarged and a new altar was built, while the priest moved into the house itself. This situation continued until St Nicolaaskerk, near Centraal Station, was completed.

It is difficult to imagine how anybody could have carried on clandestine services here. With 60 seats spreading back from the altar and additional seats in a further two storeys of galleries above, more than 150 people would have been easily accommodated. Neither does the church organ compromise on size. A full congregation singing the praises of the Lord would have been as discreet as a claustrophobic bull locked in a barn. The truth is that the existence of these churches was often an open secret, though they had to be unobtrusive enough for the city to be able to turn a blind eye.

Since 1888, the house has functioned as a museum. Fine statuary, ecclesiastical paintings, a Roman Catholic liturgical collection and 17th- and 18th-century furniture make this church all the more worth visiting. Do not let the sombre "museum" sign outside on the street deter you from investigating. The Museum Amstelkring is one of central Amsterdam's best-kept secrets.

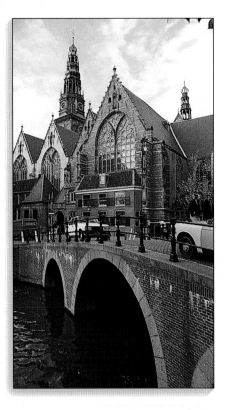

The Old Church

Just south by two blocks you will find the **Oude Kerk** ⓫ (Old Church; Oudekerksplein; tel: 625 8284; open Mon–Sat 11am–5pm, Sun 1–5pm; entrance fee). Do go in if it is open when you are passing. This is the city's oldest church, begun in 1200, though the present Gothic structure dates back to a rebuilding of the 14th century. Pilgrims flocked here at this time to witness the site of the Miracle of the Host *(see page 25)*.

Beautiful paintings survive on the wooden roof vaults, including pictures of ships, reminding us that the church is dedicated to St Nicholas, patron saint of sailors. The Great Organ, designed in 1724, is a mighty structure and is mounted on a square-columned marble base that spans the west door. Nearby is the gravestone of Saskia van Uylenburgh, the wife of Rembrandt.

The graceful spire was built in 1565 – in the summer it is possible to climb to the top (entrance fee) for spectacular views over the city. Guided tours of the church can also be arranged (tel: 689 2565 for information). On Saturdays, listen out for the beautiful 17th-century carillon of bells, which is played between 4–5pm. Since 1999, the Oude Kerk has been presenting exhibitions, and a series of organ concerts and events featuring soloists and ensembles. ❏

BIKER CITY: CYCLING IN AMSTERDAM

From the moment one arrives in Amsterdam, generally at the entrance of Centraal Station, the first impression is of bicycles everywhere

At any time of the day or evening, as one walks the city or crosses town on a tram, the bicycle ballet unfolds before one's eyes: mothers with children on front and back; passengers on handlebars or on the shoulders of the cyclist; others sitting gracefully perched behind the rider; septuagenarians on their *oma fiets* (granny bike) with high handle bars. Some bicycles have trailers attached for easy transport.

The bike of choice is basic, usually black, with no frills or gears – *de rigueur* for city life. Serious cyclists may invest in sleek, multiple-speed racing bikes, which are carefully locked inside their home or a bicycle garage in the neighbourhood.

TWO-WHEELED MAYHEM

For visitors, it often looks tempting to join the bicycle brigade, but in the city centre you do so at your own risk. Cycling in Amsterdam has become *levensgevaarlijk* (life-threatening) in recent years. The Dutch pride themselves on being "born on a bicycle", and weaving through traffic is second nature to them. But when that traffic also includes taxis who drive on tram tracks, aggressive drivers, skaters and pedestrians, then riding becomes a serious business. There seems to be a constant war between taxi drivers and cyclists and, in the anarchist style typical of Amsterdam, many cyclists run red lights. Still, many visitors do get around safely by bike in the city. If you are nervous, start out in a quiet area or at a quiet time, such as early in the morning, in the evening or on a Sunday, before mixing with the trams, traffic and crowds at Leidseplein. Or go out with Yellow Bike *(see page 266)*, who offer an orientation. One last warning: when crossing tram tracks go across them, *never* parallel, as the wheels get trapped and one is immediately aflight.

▽ HIRE A RIDE
There are numerous outfits throughout Amsterdam that will hire out bikes for the braver tourist, daily or for longer periods.

△ DESIGN STATEMENT
Not all bicycles are black: many are painted in fanciful patterns, stripes and bright colours to make them more recognisable.

◁ FAMILY RIDE
Child seats attached to the front or back of a bicycle are the most popular way for parents to take their little ones around the city.

◁ CITY OF WHEELS
With 600,000 bicycles in the city, these metal steeds serve as the primary form of transport to the Dutch populace.

△ LEISURELY PACE
The popularity of cycling gives Amsterdam's streets a peaceful atmosphere unusual in such a large city.

△ STREET ART
Bicycles are as much a part of the cityscape as the architecture and the canals, even when they are disused and discarded.

◁ VERSATILE CARRIER
People use bicycles to transport a variety of objects, from a ladder or chair to huge bouquets of flowers or a small tree.

UNDER LOCK AND KEY

Some say there are one million bikes sold in the Netherlands every year. Others say that one million are stolen. Which doesn't necessarily mean there are one million bikes, it just means there are often bikes that get stolen many times and, if you'll pardon the expression, recycled.

No matter how many sturdy, well-guaranteed locks one uses – generally two locks, one snap-on style for the back wheel and another chain style to link through the back tyre to whatever you are locking the bike to – the fact remains that there are clever thieves around who make an industry out of stealing bikes. One notorious fellow recently published a book about his exploits, which many booksellers refused to stock. There are also the local junkies needing cash for their next fix who roam the streets with their latest acquisition offering to sell it for around €20 to passers-by, which probably led to another infamous saying in Amsterdam: "You buy your first bike and steal the rest."

But that is not entirely true. Most locals prefer not to support the local junkie, and instead buy their second-hand bikes from specialist shops, along with a couple of good locks and some insurance.

NIEUWMARKT

From books to brewing, nuns to prostitutes, east to west,
Nieuwmarkt is like a microcosm of the entire city,
a living museum of all Amsterdam

Map
on page
128

Sex and drugs, noise and neon, antiques and old books, tastes of Thailand and China, one of Amsterdam's oldest medieval buildings and the once brave new face of 1970s redevelopment, photogenic Staalstraat and the seedy alleys off newly invigorated Zeedijk – Nieuwmarkt certainly presents an eclectic menu.

Nieuwmarkt proper is a small marketplace that sits between the two canals of Kloveniersburgwal and Geldersekade. But walk a few minutes in any direction and you'll see that Nieuwmarkt is much more than this. Head to the north-west for the Red Light District; make your way down Oudezijds Achterburgwal and you are in one of Amsterdam's centres of learning, full of books and bicycles. Go southeast and you are in St Antoniesbreestraat, a redeveloped street that leads into Amsterdam's old Jewish quarter. Walk northeast to the tree-lined canals of Kromboomsloot and Rechtboomsloot and you will find a tranquil neighbourhood that seems a long way from the busy city centre.

Protest and development

Start out at the wide square of **Nieuwmarkt** ⓬. This was at one time a fish market, supplied by boats that would tie up at the southern end of Geldersekade. To the west of the square a small group of stalls still ply their trade including a fishmonger, a cheese stall, a florist and a very good poultry and game stall. At the weekends there is an antiques, book and curios market.

The neighbourhood around Nieuwmarkt suffered severely with the construction of Amsterdam's metro system, which runs from Centraal Station out into the southeastern suburbs. In protest against the large number of houses around Nieuwmarkt that had to be demolished, squatters moved in. It took attacks by riot police to clear the way for the bulldozers. The city-wide protest was loudest around Nieuwmarkt; the station itself (on J.B. Siebbeleshof) recalls these events with depictions of the demolition work and the wider history of this area.

The bulky form of **De Waag** ⓭, Amsterdam's largest medieval building, has experienced its own share of redevelopment. The Waag started life as a turreted gateway, originally known as St Antonies-poort and built in 1488 as part of the city walls. By the end of the 16th century, the city was expanding rapidly and the gate was redundant so it was rebuilt around 1619 as a weigh house for checking the weight of ships' anchors and ordnance.

The octagonal tower at the centre wasn't added until around 1690; it served as the dissecting room (Theatrum Anatomicum) where the Surgeons' Guild gave lessons in anatomy. The guild commissioned Rembrandt's famous painting *The Anatomy Lesson*

PRECEDING PAGES: the infamous Red Light District. **LEFT:** Nieuwmarkt. **BELOW:** a local flea market.

of Dr Nicolaas Tulp (now in the Mauritshuis Gallery in The Hague, *see page 250*) and other pictures on similar subjects. In more modern times the Waag housed the Amsterdam Historical Museum, and then the Jewish Historical Museum. It is now home to a restaurant/café, **In de Waag**. Opened in 1996, the restaurant prides itself on its innovative reading table for old and new media – while more traditional daily newspapers and journals are available, clients can also surf the net and send e-mails. This modernisation hasn't tarnished the general feel of this remarkable building, which features two mezzanines and has converted one of the tower's ground floors into a private dining suite for up to eight people. Naturally it's very popular in the summer when the terrace offers a civilised introduction to Nieuwmarkt.

Many of the buildings on St Antoniesbreestraat, one of the few modern streets of central Amsterdam, were designed by architects Theo Bos and Aldo van Eyck. This area, too, has seen city planners do battle with conservationists. The Jewish quarter, which really begins with Jodenbreestraat *(see page 205)*, was dramatically changed by construction work in the 1970s. Plans to develop St Antoniesbreestraat controversially placed the much-prized 17th-century **De Pinto Huis** (at No. 69) under threat of demolition. Isaac de Pinto, a Portuguese Jew who fled first to Antwerp and then to Holland to escape the Inquisition, was one of Amsterdam's wealthiest bankers. He bought this building in 1651. Subsequent alterations nearly 30 years later gave it a number of painted panels and ceilings as well as an ornate exterior in the style of the Italian Renaissance.

Public opinion against the initial redevelopment won the day. The De Pinto House was saved and plans to make this road suitable for heavy traffic were shelved. This building is now a branch of the public library and visitors are

BELOW:
Geldersekade is at the heart of Amsterdam's Chinatown.

AMSTERDAM'S CHINATOWN

Standing in Nieuwmarkt and looking south you cannot miss the Chinese supermarket, which stretches across a whole building front. Upon entering you will discover an emporium of Oriental "goodies" ranging from exotic groceries to cooking implements and Chinese medicines. To the west and northwest of the square and leading up Geldersekade you'll notice Chinese apothecaries, acupuncturists, restaurants and bookshops. This is the heart of Chinatown. The local Chinese are proud of their roots and enjoy sharing their culture and hospitality with tourists and the Dutch alike. A Buddhist temple in Zeedijk was opened in 2000 by a member of the Dutch royal family, highlighting the beginning of the three-day "Chinatown Festival", an annual event which attracted 50,000 visitors in 1999. Nieuwmarkt and De Waag form the epicentre of this extravaganza. During the festival one may expect demonstrations of ancient crafts, music and dance, a Chinese market and culinary delights. The most spectacular event is the Lion Dance Championships; the colours and movements of the costumes are every bit as dazzling as the music. Little wonder that many locals refer to Nieuwmarkt as "*Het Chinese Plein*" or "China Square".

allowed inside (open Mon–Wed 2–8pm, Fri 2–5pm, Sat 11am–2pm; entrance free). Fittingly, the De Pinto House is home to a special section dealing with the protection of ancient monuments and city-centre restoration.

Map on page 128

Markets and mansions

Less than a minute's walk further south from the De Pinto House is **St Antoniessluis**, which provides a clear view all the way down to the Montelbaanstoren. St Antoniessluis was once a marketplace with a good share of street traders from the flourishing Jewish community east of Oude Schans and south of Jodenbreestraat. The presence of the market did not signify tolerance of Jewish neighbours, however. A petition by the non-Jewish inhabitants of St Antoniesbreestraat in 1750 asked that the city should find a separate living space for Jews, saying that "their shabbiness put the Christians who live in that district to the greatest inconvenience".

From St Antoniessluis, Zandstraat leads to the **Zuiderkerk ⓮**, the first Protestant church to be built in Amsterdam (open Mon–Fri; entrance free). It was completed in 1611 and its architect, Hendrick de Keyser, lies buried within. You can climb the tower (Jun–Sept Wed–Sat 2–4pm; entrance fee) for views over the surrounding area.

Along Kloveniersburgwal, the canal south of Nieuwmarkt, are five historic buildings that date from Amsterdam's Golden Age. At Nos 10–12 Koestraat is the Wijnkopersgildehuis (House of the Winebuyers' Guild) – actually three 17th-century buildings converted into one residence. Koestraat runs right through the middle of the grounds of a former convent. The Bethaniën Convent used to border Kloveniersburgwal, Oudezijds Achterburgwal, Barndesteeg and

Gables adorn the roofs of Nieuwmarkt's canalside houses.

BELOW: Oost Indisch Huis (East Indies House) on Oude Hoogstraat.

BELOW: searching
for second-hand
books.

Bethaniënstraat. Centuries ago the nuns would have water delivered to them by boat for washing and brewing, which would be hand-pumped from the boats into the convent. Beer, however weak it was, was a safer option than drinking water in those days. Today, at Nos 6–8 Kloveniersburgwal, within the grounds of the former convent, is Amsterdam's smallest brewery, **Brouwhuis Maximiliaan**. The brewery is well worth a visit – apart from the guided tours (upon request; closed Monday; entrance fee, includes one beer), the interior allows you the chance to consume their products in the brewing hall where you can admire a fresco outlining the brewing process and view the last surviving part of the Bethaniën Convent (tel: 624 2778 for information).

A more substantial landmark, on the eastern side of Kloveniersburgwal, at No. 29, is the grand façade of the **Trippenhuis ⓯**, designed in 1660 by Justus Vingboons for Louis and Hendrick Trip. The Trip family owned iron and copper mines and cannon foundries in Sweden. In acknowledgement of the owners' trade, the chimneys on the roof were made to resemble mortars. Even though the Trippenhuis has a single façade it once concealed two separate dwellings, one for each of the Trip brothers. The effect to the outside world was of a single household. Two main doorways at street level, however, provided separate access. The Trippenhuis was converted into one unit in 1815 to accommodate the forerunner to the Rijksmuseum.

On the other side of the canal, at No. 26, is the **Kleine Trippenhuis**, also known as the "House of Mr Trip's Coachman". The story that Mr Trip's coachman said he would be content with a home no wider than the front door of the Trippenhuis is probably apocryphal; another version says the house was built with stone left over from the Trippenhuis. In any event, at just over 1 metre (3 ft) across, the Kleine Trippenhuis is modesty itself.

Academic centre

If you go a little further south along Kloveniersburgwal and turn right into Oude Hoogstraat you can enter the courtyard of the **Oost Indisch Huis** (East Indies House). The house was built in the 16th century and rented to the Dutch East Indies Company in 1603. Today part of it is used by the University of Amsterdam. On the same street, Boekhandel Kok is a large antiquarian bookshop spread over two floors selling a wide selection of old prints and maps.

At the very southern end of Kloveniersburgwal you reach **Staalstraat**. A photogenic view of Zuiderkerk is to be had from the bridge that links the two sides of this street across Groenburgwal. Staalstraat itself is one of Amsterdam's many picturesque "film-set" streets, a stark contrast to the modern architecture that looms into view at the Zwanenburgwal end. A smart Thai restaurant, a cosy bookshop and a chic coffee shop make Staalstraat even more attractive. The linen trade once flourished here and at No. 7b Staalstraat sergeworkers met in the 17th-century *Saaihal* (Serge Hall). The stained-glass windows decorated with laboratory motifs originate from the 19th century when the *Saaihal* was occupied by the chemical laboratory of the Athenaeum Illustre, a forerunner to the University of Amsterdam.

Back in Kloveniersburgwal, a passageway leads off to the left on to Oudezijds Achterburgwal. This is Oudemanhuispoort (Old Men's Home Gate), a covered arcade of antiquarian bookstalls – you'll find some of these open every day except Sunday, but Saturday is busiest. Halfway along is a courtyard of late 18th-century buildings, originally used as almshouses for accommodating elderly men (almshouses had hitherto been exclusively for women.) The University of Amsterdam has occupied these buildings since 1877.

The surrounding streets form one of the centres of Amsterdam's university life. On weekdays in Grimburgwal, a narrow street which cuts across the southern end of Oudezijds Voorburgwal and Oudezijds Achterburgwal, there is always a tangle of bicycles attached to the canalside railings left by students attending lectures. Behind the former hospital, the Binnengasthuis (the building – converted into private houses – with the small white tower bearing the date 1875), and around Gasthuisstraat and Vendelstraat, are other university buildings.

Amsterdam is the only city in the Netherlands that has two universities: the University of Amsterdam and the Free University. The former has its roots in the Athenaeum Illustre, which was founded in 1632 in the **Agnietenkapel** ⑯ (Agnieten Chapel) at No. 231 Oudezijds Voorburgwal. Originally a chapel attached to the convent of St Agnes, dating back to 1470, today it houses the Historical Collection of the University of Amsterdam.

In streets such as Staalstraat, traditional bakeries sell mouthwatering pastries.

The Athenaeum originally existed to prepare students for higher schooling elsewhere but, ever since the French occupation of the Netherlands in the early 19th century, it has provided full tertiary education. The University of Amsterdam came into being in 1877 and today comprises a number of buildings throughout the city. The Free University is based in the southern suburbs.

BELOW: view of the university district in the 17th century.

Map on page 128

There's no limit to adult entertainment options in the Red Light District.

BELOW: advertising one of the city's biggest draws.

The names of the two main canals here, Voorburgwal and Achterburgwal ("before" and "behind" the city wall), refer to historic city boundaries. This southern tip of Oudezijds Voorburgwal was nicknamed the "velvet canal", in reference to the wealthy merchants who came to live in this neighbourhood.

Another building that serves the university today is the **Huis aan de Drie Grachten** (House on the Three Canals). Built in 1609, it takes its name from its location at the junction of Oudezijds Achterburgwal, Oudezijds Voorburgwal and Grimburgwal. Today it is a bookshop specialising in art and literature.

Red lights

At this end of Oudezijds Achterburgwal everybody is busy pursuing academic knowledge, but follow this canal north past Oude Doelenstraat and Oude Hoogstraat and the pursuit of carnal knowledge is the name of the game.

Amsterdam's celebrated Red Light District is concentrated in Oudezijds Achterburgwal but also occupies parts of Oudezijds Voorburgwal and the alleys connecting and branching off from them. There are sex shops, porn shops, live sex, video porn and video cabins everywhere. A sex museum, offering "erotic art and specialities", is another way of delivering the same product.

All of these are lit pink, purple, magenta, violet – and the canals themselves are occasionally hung with a canopy of red fairy lights reflected in the dark water below. Prostitutes in lacy underwear tempt from within their neon-lit glass-fronted cubicles. Some of the girls stand smiling and give a sharp beckoning tap on the window if you stop for just a second. Others look shell-shocked, expressionless, and stultified – often as a result of indiscreet groups of tourists ogling at them like some fairground attraction.

With so much to catch your eye on these streets you could be excused for missing a couple of incongruities. Above the main entrance to the **Erotic Museum**, at No. 54 Oudezijds Achterburgwal, is a historic stone decorated with maritime motifs; it proclaims boldly *God is myn burgh* (God is my stronghold). In Oudezijds Voorburgwal, on the other side of the canal to the Oude Kerk, is the Amsterdam Chinese Church, situated right next to a coffee shop with a brightly lit sex cinema below. A figure of Christ peers through the window on one side, a scantily clad prostitute touts for business on the other.

The **Hasj Marihuana Hemp Museum** (148 Oudezijds Achterburgwal; tel: 623 5961; open daily; entrance fee) is a showcase of this area's other preoccupation. Here, perhaps more than elsewhere in the city, the smell of marijuana is accompanied by the sure knowledge that harder drugs are there for the asking. This is the centre of street drug-dealing in Amsterdam.

The northern edge of Nieuwmarkt, around Zeedijk and Geldersekade, is the heart of Chinatown. **Zeedijk** itself traces the line of a sea-dyke which once protected Amsterdam from the sea. Zeedijk has long since "cleaned up its act" and this one-time haunt of pimps, pushers and addicts has undergone a transformation. Zeedijk now has a string of shops and restaurants representing not only China but other cultures too. A Buddhist temple opened here in 2000. ❑

Red Light District

A t 10pm, for €40 you could be sitting in the Bananen Bar in Oudezijds Achterburgwal, encountering various sexual displays by beautiful girls with bananas. The entrance fee includes free beer for an hour but there are many incentives to part with more cash.

The Red Light District is home to numerous such enterprises (varying in seediness), but it will always be most famous for the ladies in the windows. Worked on a shift basis, most windows are occupied all day. A girl can expect to pay up to €100 (depending on location) for a specified number of hours. There are some houses in the Red Light District where all the upper floors are empty – the owners make so much money from renting the ground floor for prostitution that they abandon the rest of the house. Other houses have two entrances; one leads upstairs where the owners live private lives, the other is controlled by the girl who rents the ground floor and plies her trade. Sex is big business in Amsterdam and the Red Light District is its showcase. When there is a conference at the Amsterdam RAI, there is a virtually guaranteed overspill at night into this neighbourhood. Tour groups, too, are often brought here to attend the sex shows at group discounts. But it is not just for tourists – customers include local men.

The neighbourhood has had its setbacks. In 1986, when Aids had become a recognised fact of life, the district went into a lower gear. Some of the girls gravitated to the city's clubs and stayed there. But new girls have taken their place and, so far as sex is concerned, the Red Light District has a rosy future again. Drugs are a different story. There is now a police presence in the area: locals protested that the drug scene was intrusive and asked for surveillance. There were also economic reasons for this. Many buildings have been renovated to improve the area. Prostitution has remained (it attracts tourists and so benefits the local economy) but drugs are being chased out.

RIGHT: waiting for passing trade under a strip of red light.

In addition, there is a strong support structure of government and religious agencies available to prostitutes who come to see their lifestyle as a problem. Many of the girls chose their career because of the money but, with help, some manage to break free.

In 1994 a crusading ex-prostitute, Mariska Majoor, set up the Prostitution Information Centre (PIC) at Enge Kerksteeg 3, in the heart of the Red Light District. Its key purpose is to remove the stigma attached to the "oldest profession" and generate acceptance. From the outside the PIC looks like a shop – it does indeed sell books and souvenirs – but of more interest is the reproduced prostitute's workplace, with its finer points explained. Entrance is free but donations are welcome.

Many prostitutes are members of their own union, *De Rode Draad* (Red Thread) which occupies itself with the welfare and working conditions of its members. Reassuringly, by law, the women in the windows are medically screened, eliminating STD dangers. The union and health authority ensure that safety always has the upper hand. ❏

CANAL CIRCLE NORTH

The concentric "canal girdle" of Amsterdam is the most distinctive feature of the city; along the banks of these four canals are some of the most important historical and architectural landmarks

Map on page 156

A msterdam's horseshoe-shaped network of canals is, in one sense, like a fingerprint. There is only one city in the world with a street plan like this and it is instantly recognisable. The long semi-circle of three parallel canals – called the Grachtengordel (literally: "canal girdle") – was part of the most ambitious piece of town planning the city has ever seen. Those three canals are probably among the first place names in Amsterdam that tourists learn. From inside moving outwards they are: Herengracht (Gentlemen's canal), Keizersgracht (Emperors' canal) and Prinsengracht (Princes' canal).

By 1600 Amsterdam was one of the most powerful trading nations in the world. For a long time the old city, with its walls and turrets, had been little more than a small horseshoe clinging to the Amstel River. Now, at the beginning of the 17th century, the medieval town that had grown up around Dam Square was spilling out beyond its boundary. Three canals on either side of the river had already been dug to drain land for expansion. But in 1609 city planners decided to build another three canals that would encircle the existing nucleus.

Hendrick de Keyser was appointed city architect and by 1613 the plan was underway. The first phase of digging took the new canals from near the port down to the bottom of the horseshoe as far as Leidsegracht. The second phase began in 1665 and the canals were extended to the Amstel. Parks were built on the opposite shore of the Amstel (the so-called Plantage) and the entire project was finally completed at the end of the 17th century.

It was a mark of distinction to build a house on the new canals. The elegant Herengracht was the most sought-after, followed in exclusiveness by the Keizersgracht. Prinsengracht and Singel had many of the warehouses and workshops. Today, in the summer, whichever part of the Grachtengordel you visit, the canals seem to form one long, leafy suburb.

PRECEDING PAGES: well-mannered architecture. **LEFT:** Zuiderkerk. **BELOW:** canal tour.

Starting point

It is appropriate to begin exploring these canals from the northwestern side, beyond Centraal Station *(see page 135)*, because construction actually started near here. This section of the canal circle is the least visited by tourists. Yet the area bounded by Haarlemmerstraat/Haarlemmerdijk to the north and Raadhuisstraat to the south is manageable and worthwhile.

In fact, the old Maritime Quarter, which begins at the corner of the Singel canal and Haarlemmerstraat and heads a mile or so west (when the street becomes Haarlemmerdijk), is a lively street full of interesting small shops, cafés and restaurants. It ends at Haarlemmerplein (a square which will undergo an ambitious renovation in the near future). Backtracking down Haarlemmerdijk to Korte Prinsen-

gracht, turn right and walk down the Prinsengracht canal where you will eventually find the Anne Frank Huis, one of the most visited places in Amsterdam *(see page 162)*. Just across the canal heading back towards the right is the Jordaan, a lively network of much narrower streets with second-hand shops, ethnic restaurants, boutiques and bookshops *(see page 158)*.

An easy landmark to start your exploration from is the great baroque dome of the **Ronde Lutherse Kerk ❶**, overlooking the Singel Canal. Built between 1668 and 1671, this church was extensively restored in the early 19th century after a fire. It has since been deconsecrated and now serves as an annexe to the **Renaissance Amsterdam Hotel**; it is not open to the general public but the exterior alone is very pleasing and forms a fine focal point to the views down the surrounding streets. After another fire in 1993, it was restored yet again in 1995.

Canal houses and views

Most of the canal-house façades which can be seen today date from the 17th and 18th centuries although the houses behind them are often older. Those buildings of significant historical and aesthetic value to Amsterdam *(Stadsmonumenten)* are the responsibility of a variety of institutions. Between them they spend many millions of euros annually on repair and restoration.

Near the Ronde Lutherse Kerk, at Nos 4–6 Kattengat, are two attractive but severely sloping 17th-century gabled houses. Dating from 1614, and therefore among the first to be built after the canals were dug, they carry the fetching names of **De Gouden Spiegel** (The Golden Mirror) and **De Silveren Spiegel** (The Silver Mirror). During World War II several Jewish families hid in the attics, and for the past few years there has been a restaurant here.

TIP

Located in Haarlemmerplein is a popular "art house" cinema called The Movies, with four screens offering a range of films, many in English (tel: 638 6016 for details).

BELOW: Ronde Lutherse Kerk.

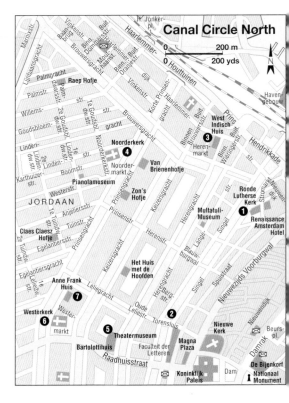

You will see grander houses than these, of course, but first take a look at one of Amsterdam's most curious dwellings. In the 17th century, taxes were levied on property owners according to the width of their house frontage. The original owner of **No. 7 Singel** (next to the Liberty Hotel) was perhaps determined to pay as little as possible and so he built the narrowest house in Amsterdam.

On the opposite side of the canal is another curious household, the "cat boat". The owner provides board and lodging for around 150 "orphaned" cats and these floating felines (best seen from a canal boat) have now become one of the sights of Amsterdam.

It is worth continuing a short distance southwards along the Singel to the first bridge past the "cat boat". In the stonework of the bridge itself is a 17th-century prison called the **Torensluis** ❷. The unfortunate souls who were incarcerated here would frequently have found themselves up to their waists in water as the level of the canal changed with the incoming tides.

If you go back up along the Singel to **Brouwersgracht** you will find yourself in one of the best places in Amsterdam to enjoy wide vistas down each of the three main canals. The picture is perhaps best in autumn and winter, preferably at dusk, when the trees bordering the waterways have been stripped of their leaves, allowing uninterrupted views to the point where the canals bend.

Traders, past and present

These canals were made possible by the wealth of the new Dutch empire. The East Indies (Indonesia) produced the greatest riches but the Netherlands had a foothold in the west as well. The **West Indisch Huis** ❸ (West Indies House) faces on to Haarlemmerstraat but backs on to Herenmarkt – a tidy little square

Map on page 156

West Indisch Huis (West Indies House), 17th-century HQ of the Dutch West Indies company.

BELOW: hanging loose in Westerstraat.

THE RONDVAART (ROUND TRIP)

Having arrived in the "Venice of Northern Europe" it would be bordering on the unforgivable not to go on a boat trip around the canals. There are several companies to choose from and the majority are located opposite Centraal Station, with a few opposite the old Heineken Brewery. After paying for your ticket you may buy a drink or snack to take on board and you will almost certainly be photographed as you step into the glass-roofed vessel which will glide you over the waters of the city.

Standing next to the skipper there will be a guide who will point out and explain the many features and buildings which seem more apparent from the water. Sitting in a *rondvaart* boat gives you a perspective rarely encountered – just above the water looking up at centuries of history unfolding before you. All the guides speak English and are happy to answer any questions. You can expect to see the narrowest house, the "skinny bridge" and the "seven sisters" bridges, among many other sights. The trip usually lasts about an hour. At the end you'll have the chance to buy a photo of your embarkation.

For wealthier tourists, there are water taxis, and for true romantics there are candlelit dinner cruises – relevant information is available at any of the ticket kiosks.

The Jordaan

The name Jordaan is said to be a corruption of the French *jardin* (garden). It is a feasible explanation: many of the streets – Palmgracht, Bloemgracht, Rozengracht and Laurierstraat – are named after trees and flowers.

The Jordaan grew up during the major phase of canal construction in the 17th century. It was the ambition of designer Hendrik Staets to create a self-contained community of artisans and the grid of streets and narrow canals was cut east–west along the course of existing polders (drainage ditches). However, at the beginning of the 20th century the Jordaan was a slum.

After World War II the area was refurbished and today it has a distinct charm. More than 800 buildings are listed as being of architectural or historical interest. The streets are narrower and the houses more compact here than in other areas of the city. There are also a number of concealed *hofjes* (courtyards) in the area. One of these, the small cobblestoned courtyard of Raep Hofje, is right at the "top" of the Jordaan at Nos 28–38 Palmgracht. Seven of the original 11 canals have been filled in but the area still retains its shops and artisans – there are more than 900 small businesses registered here: bookshops, second-hand stores, boutiques, bakeries, cafés and bars that give the neighbourhood a friendly feel. Above all, the Jordaan offers an escape from the crowds of tourists that are an inevitable part of Leidseplein or Museumplein. Things can be livelier in the evenings. In several cafés, such as Café Nol at Westerstraat 2 and De Twee Zwaantjes at Prinsengracht 14, locals join together in singing popular Dutch songs.

One famous resident was Jan van Riebeek, the founder of Cape Town, who lived in Egelantiersgracht from 1649 to 1651. Another was Rembrandt, who was forced by poverty to move to the Jordaan towards the end of his life. In 1656 the artist had been declared insolvent and in 1660, along with his mistress Hendrickje and son Titus, he went to live in Rozengracht. He died nine years later.

Rozengracht no longer has its canal; a tram line has taken its place. Bloemgracht, one of the most popular streets in the area, has fared better. With its numerous gabled houses, this street became known as the "Gentlemen's Canal". The step gables at Nos 87–91 are the most noticeable. This building (1642) belongs to the Vereniging Hendrick de Keyser, a foundation established to preserve the architect's works.

Egelantiersgracht has also retained its canal. At Nos 201–3 and 213–5 are four identical houses, bearing the same family coat of arms. Between Nos 107 and 114 is the entrance to the Sint Andrieshofje (1616). At the end of Egelantiersstraat is Café 't Smalle, the site of a distillery established in the late 18th century by Peter Hoppe. He produced a Dutch gin called Hoppe Jenever that became famous around the country.

At No. 109 Elandsgracht and No. 38 Looiersgracht there are two indoor antiques markets (open daily except Friday) which make for excellent browsing. ❑

LEFT: admiring the wares in one of the Jordaan's many boutiques.

Map on page 156

off Brouwersgracht – and is closely associated with those days of empire *(see page 41)*. Constructed in 1617, it owes its current name to the period when it was let to the Dutch West Indies Company, beginning in 1623. In 1625, one of the greatest western Dutch settlements, New York (then New Amsterdam), was born when an agreement was made to build Fort Amsterdam on the site of Manhattan Island. When the naval hero Admiral Piet Hein captured the Spanish "silver fleet" off Cuba in 1628, the booty (a prodigious prize of silver) was stored here. A statue of New Amsterdam's governor Peter Stuyvesant and a restaurant named after Hein are reminders of this past history.

On Monday morning and Saturday afternoon, the **Noordermarkt** (a short distance south along Prinsengracht) is just as its name suggests – a marketplace which hosts a flea market and farmers' market respectively, in addition to being one of the locations of the Jordaan Festival every summer. In the centre is the octagonal shape of the **Noorderkerk ❹**, the first landmark you see as you go down Prinsengracht. Construction of this church began in 1620. It is open for religious services and occasional concerts, and underwent an extensive renovation in 1999, with Queen Beatrix attending the opening ceremony.

Tranquil spots

On the other side of Prinsengracht are two *hofjes* (courtyards) that are well worth a closer look. **Van Brienenhofje**, at Nos 89–133 Prinsengracht, is an impressive square of almshouses overlooking a wide peaceful courtyard. The story goes that Jan van Brienen, who once locked himself inside his own safe and was rescued from suffocating just in time, showed his gratitude by founding these almshouses.

A little further along Prinsengracht, at Nos 159–71, is **Zon's Hofje**. The Frisian Mennonite community in Amsterdam bought a building here called "De Kleine Zon" ("The Little Sun") in 1720. It was used as a church and renamed "De Arke Noach" ("Noah's Ark"). This community merged with another and so in 1765 the church was converted into almshouses for widows. Be careful not to disturb the residents if you come here but sit quietly on the bench and enjoy what is surely the ultimate in secluded, tranquil living.

If you next turn left along Prinsenstraat you will come quickly to Keizersgracht. Turn right to follow the eastern bank of the canal until you reach No. 123, known as **"Het Huis met de Hoofden"** ("House with the Heads"). Built by Hendrick de Keyser for a wealthy merchant in 1624, the name of this building refers to the six classical busts on either side of the entrance depicting the deities Apollo, Ceres, Mars, Athena, Bacchus and Diana.

Preservation in the city

Also at No. 123 Keizersgracht are the offices of the main organisation involved with the conservation of Amsterdam's architectural heritage, the **Bureau Monumentenzorg** (Municipal Office for Historic Buildings' Preservation), established in 1953. Soon after its formation, the Bureau made an inventory of buildings in the city considered irreplaceable. In 1961, the

One of the six busts of Roman gods on the "House with the Heads".

BELOW: gables on Prinsengracht.

buildings on this list were given legal protection, so that Amsterdam now has 6,826 historic buildings in its old centre – more by far than in any other city in the Netherlands. These "monuments", as they are called, may not be modified or demolished without a permit from the Bureau. The Bureau has its own architectural office, a warehouse for storing valuable remnants of destroyed buildings and occasionally does some restoration work itself. It also assists private organisations and individuals involved in restoration work in the city.

In keeping with Amsterdam's entrepreneurial traditions, the private sector has also helped with the city's mammoth conservation task. One company active in this field is the Amsterdamse Maatschappij tot Stadsherstel NV (The Amsterdam Company for City Restoration). Formed in 1956, it aims to restore as many inner-city houses as possible while providing accommodation to help alleviate the city's critical housing shortage. **Herenstraat**, the side street that links Keizersgracht to Herengracht, owes much to the work of Stadsherstel and is just one example of what can be done. The company owns nine premises here and has helped revive a once run-down street in need of refurbishment.

Right at the north end of Herengracht, a short walk from Brouwersgracht, is **Het Huis met de Pilastergevel** (House with the Pilaster Gable) at Nos 70–72. This house dates from 1642 and, as its name indicates, has a gable ornamented with pilasters, the slightly protruding flat stone columns.

Dramatic heritage

Opportunities to see inside the grand buildings that border these canals are restricted to a handful of excellent museums that help preserve a sense of 17th-century opulence. A museum with a particularly attractive exterior is the

Delivering mail to houses along the canals must be one of the most picturesque postal jobs in the world.

BELOW: canalside contemplation.

Theatermuseum ❺ (Netherlands Theatre Museum) which is located in the stately **Bartolottihuis** at Nos 170–72 Herengracht just before you reach Raadhuisstraat (entrance at No. 168; tel: 551 3300; open Tues–Fri 11am–5pm, Sat–Sun 1–5pm; entrance fee). This bright and ornate four-storey building dates back to 1617 and was renovated as recently as 1971. The original house was designed by Hendrick de Keyser for Guillielmo Bartolotti, who made his fortune as a brewer and later in life became a rich and successful banker.

Map on page 156

The main building of the Theatermuseum, however, is a former residence designed by Philips Vingboons which dates back to 1638. This later bulding, at No. 168, called **Het Witte Huis** (the White House), has a grey, neoclassical sandstone façade. It was built for a certain Michiel Pauw, who in 1630 set up a trading settlement, which he called Pavonia after himself, close to the Dutch colony at Nieuw Amsterdam (New York). His house boasts the first-ever neck gable in the city, but subsequent owners excised some of the ornamental flourishes that emphasised Pauw's sense of his own importance, among them his coat of arms.

It is worth making a visit to this building to look at the two reception rooms on the ground floor. The grand murals and painted ceilings were part of an extensive redecoration scheme undertaken between 1728 and 1733 in the style of Louis XIV. Isaac de Moucheron and Jacob de Wit, two fashionable artists, were commissioned to paint the murals in oils on canvas. De Moucheron painted the landscape and de Wit was responsible for the figures and the ceiling. Other aspects of the dazzling interior ornamentation include a spiral staircase and complex stuccowork.

The museum's permanent exhibition is housed in a large glass cube which takes up the size of the room and includes a variety of props, shoes, hats, hand

BELOW: floating flowers.

Map on page 156

Just as London cockneys are born within earshot of Bow Bells, to be a true Amsterdam "cockney" one must be born within the sound of the Westerkerk's bells.

BELOW: the landmark Westerkerk.

puppets, masks and assorted paraphernalia from the museum's theatrical collection. An adjacent room features several period costumes made in a range of materials, from heavy damask to featherlight tulle.

The Theatermuseum also has a formal garden laid out in baroque and Renaissance styles. In the summer months, you can enjoy the "backstage" ambience of a canal house that benefits from a fine view of the Westerkerk tower.

Amsterdam landmarks

Heading west from here, along busy Raadhuisstraat, you reach Westermarkt, the best-known corner of this section of Amsterdam's Grachtengordel. The **Westerkerk ❻**, considered to be the masterpiece of Dutch Renaissance style by Hendrick de Keyser and his son Pieter, dates from 1630, was renovated in 1990, and is still considered the city's finest church. The soaring spire, the highest in the city at 85 metres (275 ft), is crowned by a glinting yellow and blue imperial crown, a reminder of former Habsburg rule. The view from the tower stretches to the Rijksmuseum in the south *(see page 185)* and to the harbour in the north. Anne Frank, who lived in a house bordering the Prinsengracht, described Westerkerk's carillon chimes in her diary. Today you can still hear them toll on the hour and there are occasional outbursts of a popular or classic refrain, depending on the occasion.

Compared with the Oude Kerk *(see page 138)*, the Westerkerk's interior is slightly disappointing. However, its popularity with tourists is secured by the fact that Rembrandt's grave was discovered here during excavations. It is also possible to attend classical music concerts and on certain days of the year (such as Monument Day), it is possible to climb to the top of the tower and see a remarkable view of Amsterdam. Look for the statue of Anne Frank on the square near the entrance to the church and if you want a snack, there are several good stands selling herring and Dutch chips, known as *patat*.

Visiting the nearby **Anne Frank Huis ❼** (Anne Frank's House) has become something of a tourist pilgrimage (263 Prinsengracht; tel: 556 7100; open Apr–Aug 9am–9pm, Sept–Mar 9am–7pm; closed Yom Kippur; entrance fee). As a symbol of Jewish suffering during World War II, this building certainly deserves a strong measure of respect. But the sheer volume of visitors has its down side. What should be a sobering and contemplative tour of rooms made world famous by a gifted Jewish adolescent diarist who spent two harsh years in hiding here with her family is, during the peak summer months at least, a crowded and sometimes frustrating procession through constricted passageways. After a renovation and expansion in 1999, however, visiting conditions have been vastly improved and now provide a better impression of the surroundings and circumstances which shaped Anne Frank's diary. With the addition of an adjacent building, there is now extra space for temporary exhibitions relating to racism and prejudice, as well as for the Educational Department, multi-media resource centre, bookshop and café. ❑

Anne Frank

On Monday 6 July 1942, Anne Frank accompanied her family into the *Achterhuis* (back annexe) of Prinsengracht 263; she was not escaping from Nazi persecution for the first time in her life. Born in Frankfurt in 1929, her family had already fled their native town in the summer of 1933: Amsterdam brought a respite that lasted just six years. After the Germans had invaded Holland in 1940, the country was subjected to the same anti-Jewish measures as other occupied nations. In February 1941, the Nazis began their first round-up of Jews in Amsterdam. Though Anne's father Otto had been forced by the Germans to leave his prosperous business, he was able to prepare several rooms on the top floors of his company's office as a secret hiding place. The safety of his family and four other Jews was to hinge on a swinging cupboard concealing the stairs to the back of the building. Another family, Mr and Mrs Van Daan and their son Peter, joined them. In November another refugee, Albert Dussel, became the eighth member of this clandestine household.

Anne's record of life in their secret refuge is remarkable not just as a diary of a Jewish family in hiding; the fascination of her book comes from witnessing the intellectual growth of a young girl blessed with literary talents as she passes through her adolescent years under fearful circumstances. The second entry of her diary is as a naïve 13-year-old: "I had my birthday on Sunday afternoon. We showed a film *The Lighthouse Keeper* with Rin-Tin-Tin, which my school friends thoroughly enjoyed. We had a lovely time." In July 1944, now 15, she wrote: "It is a great wonder that I have not given up all my expectations because they seem absurd and unfeasible. But I still cling to them, despite everything, because I still believe in the inner goodness of humanity. It's... impossible for me to base everything on death, suffering and confusion."

Just 20 days later, on 4 August, following a tip-off thought to have been provided by a Dutch informer, the Gestapo discovered the hiding place. All eight were sent to Westerbork, the Dutch staging post to concentration camps further east. On 3 September, the day the Allies captured Brussels, they were among the last shipment of around 1,000 Jews to leave the Netherlands. Of all the occupants of the "Secret Annexe", Anne's father alone returned. Anne Frank died in the concentration camp at Bergen-Belsen in March 1945 at the age of 15, only three weeks before the British liberated it.

Anne Frank's diary had been left behind among old books and newspapers lying on the floor. The most famous quotes come from the final paragraphs of her entry for 15 July. Three months previously she had written: "I want to live on after my death."

Anne Frank's House is more than the place in which a world-famous diary was penned or a voyeuristic opportunity to see the premises in which she and her co-refugees lived. It is a living monument to all victims of racism, fascism and anti-Semitism during World War II and since. ❏

RIGHT: bust of Anne Frank on display at the Anne Frank Huis.

CANAL CIRCLE CENTRAL

Map on page 166

Perhaps Amsterdam's greatest glory is its canals and the 17th- and 18th-century gabled houses lining the banks. But it is also a city of culture and has an exhaustive variety of nightlife

Amsterdam's greatest asset, the magnificent buildings lining Herengracht, Keizersgracht and Prinsengracht, often feel as if they are off limits. Your natural instinct is to want to stop and look inside, but the only houses you can visit as you walk along Amsterdam's three main canals are now museums. Some of these show you just how opulent these canalside buildings were in the 17th century when they belonged to the city's *nouveaux riches*. Today, due to absurdly escalating property prices, these houses are also off limits to most residents, commanding millions of euros often for only one storey.

Many of the buildings of the central stretch of the canal circle belong to banks and consulates; others serve as the Dutch headquarters of large multinational companies. One building on the Herengracht is the official residence of the city's mayor. Most of the time you can do little more than admire ornate façades, though you should take a walk along the canals at dusk to catch fleeting glimpses of the lit-up interiors through uncurtained windows. When the city expanded during the 17th century, Herengracht was undoubtedly the most sought-after of the three new canals.

Gables galore

Where Herengracht turns towards the southeast at Leidsegracht, and again towards the east just before Vijzelstraat, the richest and most splendid houses were built. This stretch was dubbed the "**Golden Bend**". From a visual point of view, the stretch of canals between Raadhuisstraat and Vijzelstraat is the most rewarding. If you don't want to walk too far or you have limited time, restrict yourself to this area.

Take a canal-boat tour and the first features that will be pointed out to you are the different styles of gable that the buildings possess. A typical "Dutch" gable is the ornate upper part of the façade used as an ornament to disguise the shape and appearance of the roof behind. This feature is not unique to Amsterdam. However, the fact that taxes based on the width of the frontage were once levied here means that many of the houses were deliberately built to be narrow but deep, "end-on" to the canals.

A range of ornamented gables developed throughout Amsterdam; the most common types are the step, spout, neck and bell gables. You don't have to be into architecture to spot these but a little guidance will make a walk along the canals more enjoyable. The step gable, a Gothic style, ascends geometrically like a small stairway up to the pinnacle; builders often used pale sandstone to offset the darker red brickwork. This type of gable is very much associated with Hendrick de Keyser, who died in 1621. Step gables

LEFT: canalside cycle lane.
BELOW: step gables.

are a good indication that the building dates from the late 16th or early 17th centuries (though there are later versions). Also a product of the same period, the spout gable, an inverted V-shape reflecting the slope of the roof, characterises many of Amsterdam's warehouses. The neck gable of the 17th century is often attributed to architect Philips Vingboons, who died in 1675. It takes the form of an elevated centrepiece culminating in a triangular pediment, often in association with heraldic statuary. The bell gable developed in the 18th century and is recognisable by its round top with concave sides like a church bell.

Gables do not account for all of the canalside façades. When the Golden Age had passed, Dutch architects imported much from France, especially the baroque style of Louis XIV. During the late 17th century and the 18th century, gable-fronted houses gave way to squarer façades and flat cornices.

Of the three main canals as they run between Raadhuisstraat and Vijzelstraat, concentrate first on Herengracht and Keizersgracht. First walk southwards along **Herengracht** from Raadhuisstraat down to Huidenstraat. Many of the finest houses were built to the east of Leidsegracht, and Herengracht was envisaged as a residential area from which many industries were banned; these included sugar refining because of the fire hazard, brewing because of the smell, and barrel-making because of the noise. On the way south to Huidenstraat there is a jumble of styles though there are several 18th-century gables on the west side of the canal. One good example is **De Witte Lelie** ("The White Lily") at No. 274, with a Louis XIV-style balustrade rising to a crested top.

Still going south, take the short stretch from Huidenstraat to Leidsestraat and walk along the east side. The ornate decoration at Nos 380–82 may not be to everybody's taste, but they were built in 1889 for a client who wanted to emulate

You can get an idea of how superior the buildings along the Golden Bend were by comparing property prices. In 1820, for example, a house on Herengracht would have sold for 30,000 guilders while a house in the nearby Jordaan would have fetched only 3,000.

BELOW: ice skating on the Keizersgracht.

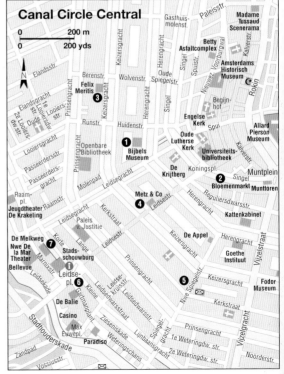

Canal Circle Central

Map on page 166

the chic mansions of New York's Fifth Avenue. Further along are good examples of twin houses, so called because they are double the width of most canalside plots. The gables of Nos 390–92 are adorned with a carving of a man and a woman stretching a rope between them; they date from the mid-17th century, as do Nos 396–98 and 409–11. No 386, with its classical pilastered façade, is one of many houses here that were designed by Philips Vingboons. Another highlight is No. 475, dating from the 1730s and built in an ornate Louis XIV style.

Another Vingboons building is the four-gabled Cromhouthuizen at Nos 364–70, dating from 1662. The name derives from the crooked piece of wood that was the trademark of a builder called Jacob Cromhout, who lived at No. 366. Today, his house is used as the **Bijbels (Biblical) Museum ❶** (tel: 624 2436; open Mon–Sat 10am–5pm, Sun and public holidays 1–5pm; entrance fee). Located in two adjacent canal houses, the museum's elegant interior features an elaborate painted ceiling and exudes the atmosphere of past centuries. The varied exhibits include a rare Bible collection, archaeological finds from Egypt and the Middle East, religious objects from the Jewish and Christian traditions, models of the Temple in Jerusalem, and a world-famous model of the Tabernacle dating from 1851. The tranquil garden is an oasis in the summer months.

Flowers and theatres

A short walk from the Golden Bend, **Muntplein** marks the junction of Kalverstraat with Rokin and Vijzelstraat. The **Munttoren** was built in 1490, though the steeple was added in 1620 by Hendrick de Keyser. For a short time in 1672 money was minted in the building adjoining the tower, hence the name. This area is always crowded – one of the attractions is the **Bloemenmarkt ❷**, the

Enjoy the canals the relaxing way, in one of the many pavement cafés.

BELOW: fine examples of bell gables.

"floating" flower market open from Monday to Saturday, which has been held here since at least the 18th century. Locals shop here as well as tourists.

On **Keizersgracht**, heading south from Raadhuisstraat, there are a number of stylish exteriors. At No. 209 is a statue of Hope holding a basket of fruit. A short way along, at No. 220, a Syrian Orthodox church breaks up the skyline.

Without doubt, the most notable building on this stretch of Keizersgracht is the **Felix Meritis Theatre** ❸ (formerly the Shaffy Theatre) at No. 324. It is instantly recognisable because of the four thick pillars that make up this classical façade. It was built in 1787 for the Felix Meritis (Latin for "deservedly happy") Society, whose aim was to broaden knowledge of the arts and sciences. At one time Haydn and Grieg conducted music in the building's concert hall. From 1946, the building was used as the headquarters of the Dutch Communist Party. Then, in the 1960s, the Shaffy Theatre Company took rooms here and it became one of Amsterdam's first experimental theatres. The communists later moved out and the Shaffy Theatre subsequently took over the whole building until 1989. Since then, the Felix Meritis has hosted many international theatre, dance and musical performances, as well as lectures and readings. The popular café is open daily. Look across to the other side of the canal to see another good example of a neck gable, at No. 319 Keizersgracht, designed by Vingboons in 1639.

Back on the western side of Keizersgracht, you'll see a gateway at No. 384. This was the entrance to the former Stadsschouwburg (City Theatre), destroyed by fire in 1722, after which it was re-built and functioned as an almshouse. It was renovated in 1999 when it was transformed into the exclusive Blakes Hotel. The Stadsschouwburg relocated to the Leidseplein in 1894 *(see page 170)*.

TIP

The Pulitzer Bar at No. 234 Keizersgracht, with its newly opened café/restaurant, offers lunch, high tea and dinner in a charming bistro atmosphere dominated by a modern and witty interpretation of a Frans Hals painting.

BELOW: majolica and Delftware in the Spiegelkwartier.

Look across the canal again to see the *Vergulde Ster* (Gilded Star) at No. 387, an excellent example of the elevated neck gable style, dating from 1668. The style of building changes here so rapidly that it is difficult to take in all the detail. Just look at Nos 440–54 Keizersgracht, near the junction with Leidsegracht. With its enormous windows and a decorative mixture of sandstone and red brick, No. 440 is a stark contrast to No. 446, a Louis XIV-style dwelling from the 1720s. The latter was at one time the home of a well-known art collector by the name of Adriaan van der Hoop. Both of these buildings back on to and form part of the **Openbare Bibliotheek** (Public Library). Another contrast is provided between the pillars and balconies of the bank occupying No. 452. And No. 454 is a stylish example of how Amsterdam's warehouses can be converted into comfortable apartments *(see page 79)*.

Map on page 166

Shopping for old and new

If all this street level façade-gazing is proving tiring, head for **Metz & Co ❹**, an up-market fashion, furnishings and furniture store on the corner of Keizersgracht and Leidsestraat. A large clocktower (designed by Gerrit Rietveld) makes it easy to spot; at night the roof of the building is illuminated. Go up to the top-floor café and enjoy rooftop views of Amsterdam. Unfortunately, the food is overpriced, unremarkable and served unenthusiastically. Settle for a cappuccino and some apple cake and hope to get a table by the window.

The Dutch love their tulips, whether real or woodcarved.

After refreshment, explore some of the cross-streets connecting Herengracht with Singel to the east and Keizersgracht with Prinsengracht to the west. The most interesting are Hartenstraat, Reestraat, Wolvenstraat, Berenstraat, Runstraat and Huidenstraat, beginning below Raadhuisstraat. They offer a wealth of exclusive shops specialising in candles, ceramics, leather, toothbrushes, chocolate, cook books – even buttons. But it is the wonderful old shops of the **Spiegelkwartier** that attract most visitors.

BELOW: antique dealer in the Spiegelkwartier.

Antiques dealers have been doing business here for more than a century, attracted by the proximity to the Rijksmuseum, which opened in 1885. The first dealers opened their shops in **Nieuwe Spiegelstraat ❺**. Later they were joined by art dealers who opened galleries along the canals, helping to create what has since become a centre for fine art and antiques. The area developed rapidly in the 1960s when antiques became more popular and some provincial antiques dealers, who saw their trade disappearing, moved to Amsterdam out of necessity, swelling the number of shops here.

Although the branch of Sotheby's auction house moved to larger premises in the southern suburbs of the city in 1999, other prestigious dealers have moved to the Spiegelkwartier. In a street only 300 metres (330 yds) long there are around 60 antique dealers and 15 galleries. Many shops have specialists who can advise buyers, though you should still ask for a signed certificate of authenticity when making a purchase.

At No. 34 Nieuwe Spiegelstraat a number of dealers have gathered together under one roof to create the **Amsterdam Antiques Gallery**, which offers icons, dolls and 19th-century paintings. At No. 58

Map on page 166

Buskers from all over the world, including Tibet, are a major feature of the city's entertainment scene.

BELOW: *maître d'* at the American Hotel.

Frans Liedelmeijer specialises in the decorative arts and Dutch design, Art Nouveau and Art Deco pieces. At No. 65, Inez Stodel is known for her period jewellery and at No. 3 Spiegelgracht, Jaap Polak specialises in Oriental art. Altogether the choice is wide and antiques available in the Spiegelkwartier include earthenware, furniture, porcelain, engraved glass, Asiatic art, sculpture, jewellery, clocks, medical and nautical instruments, drawings, books, pewter, tiles and engravings. Many of these "antiquairs" deal directly with the Rijksmuseum *(see page 185)* and have international reputations. Their shops are a bit like precious miniature museums – but don't be put off by the exclusive ambience; visitors are always welcome.

Buskers and nightlife

From here it is a short walk along Leidsestraat into one of the centres of Amsterdam nightlife: **Leidseplein ❻**. There are cinemas, bars, restaurants and clubs aplenty here. For jazz, drop by the Club Alto or Bourbon Street, while the Maxim piano bar attracts a loyal crowd of music lovers who like to sing along. For many locals and tourists, this remains a popular place to see and be seen. Street performers are invariably at the centre of attention; jugglers, mime artists, magicians and musicians take their turn at entertaining the crowds.

There are two unmistakable buildings on Leidseplein, each making its own contribution to an evening's entertainment. The red-brick building with its wide verandah and mini turrets is the new **Stadsschouwburg**. This venerable theatre has been entertaining Amsterdam with performances since 1894 and still offers many international dance and theatre performances. There is a different kind of ambience at the **American Hotel**. Its Café Américain overlooks most of Leidseplein and has long been a fashionable meeting place. Dessert and coffee are recommended rather than main meals, which tend to be over-priced.

Leidseplein caters to all tastes in entertainment – the conservative and the progressive. A shrine to the latter is the famous **De Melkweg ❼** (Milky Way) in Lijnbaansgracht. Rock, jazz, world, latin and reggae music, fringe theatre productions, art exhibitions and video performances all make for a lively "multimedia" arts centre that stays open into the small hours. De Melkweg first became the centre of alternative arts in Amsterdam when the former dairy building was converted in the 1960s and it is still going strong.

A kindred spirit to the Melkweg across Leidseplein and along Weteringschans, is the **Paradiso**, another nightspot which emerged in the 1960s and provides a lively venue for rock, hip hop and world music groups. Comedy clubs have become popular in the city in recent years and of the three in town, **Boom Chicago** is the best. Based on the US tradition of improvisational comedy, the troupe presents irreverent revues (in English) on current events and such topics as love and relationships. They are housed in the historic Leidseplein Theatre.

If at the end of a day tramping around the canals you are in need of refreshment and entertainment, spend at least one evening in Leidseplein. But don't expect to make an early start the next day. ❏

Grand Hotels

Amsterdam has many hotels at every price level and standard, but there are four in particular which you should visit, even if only for a cup of tea in one of their elegant cafés or bars.

The stately Amstel Hotel along the banks of the River Amstel has been the address for cosmopolitan society since 1897, when it opened as a spa. Back then, a Baedeker Guide listed it as one of Amsterdam's top hotels, with rooms priced at an astronomical three guilders a night. These days the prices are more amenable to captains of industry and the jet set. After an extensive facelift in the 1990s, the Amstel was returned to her former glory as the temporary address for guests such as the Queen of England, the King of Spain, Elizabeth Taylor and the Rolling Stones. It remains a popular spot to enjoy Sunday brunch or afternoon tea, and its La Rive restaurant has two Michelin stars.

The Grand Hotel Krasnapolsky is Amsterdam's oldest hotel, though no longer its grandest. The *grande dame* of Dam Square has seen many illustrious guests pass through her portals: composer Johannes Brahms, author Joseph Conrad, poet Paul Verlaine, numerous celebrities and countless political heads of state. It has certainly evolved from its early days as a modest yet colourful café, when it was said that "a traveller had not seen Amsterdam if he had not been to the Krasnapolsky". Opened in 1866 by Polish immigrant Adolph Wilhelm Krasnapolsky, the New Polish Coffee House quickly became popular – not only because of its selection of German beers, but for its good-value meals, high ceilings, reading table and billiards tables. Prior to the World Fair of 1883, Krasnapolsky added a new building with 80 guest rooms. Today, the hotel, with 469 rooms, still boasts the Winter Garden known for its breakfast and lunch buffet, but sadly lacks personality.

Just a few minutes away on a tranquil canal opposite the Red Light District is the Grand Westin Demeure Hotel, which opened in 1992 on the site of a former 16th-century convent. The convent became a hostelry for princes and lords, among them Prince William of Orange and the Earl of Leicester. In 1652 it became the temporary headquarters for the City Council after the Town Hall on the Dam burnt down. Today, the hotel has luxurious accommodation, and the Café Roux, run by renowned chef Albert Roux of London's Le Gavroche, is a popular meeting spot for the city's movers and shakers.

At the busy hub of Leidseplein is the American Hotel. It was built on the site of one of Amsterdam's city gates and dates from 1879. Its position opposite the Stadsschouwburg theatre made it almost immediately fashionable. As it grew in popularity, the old hotel was demolished to make room for a larger structure. The architect W. G. Kromhout recaptured the style of the previous building with his Jugendstil (Art Nouveau) design – sweeping arches, sumptuous decoration and elegant clocktower. The Café Américain remains a popular venue pre- and post-theatre as well as for afternoon tea. ❑

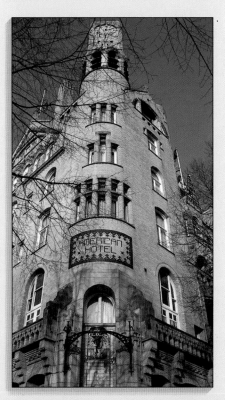

RIGHT: the glamorous American Hotel in Leidseplein, a fashionable meeting place.

CANAL CIRCLE EAST

*From viewing historic houses preserved in their original glory
to the modern pleasures of beer-drinking and shopping,
the eastern canal region is well worth a day's exploration*

Map
on page
176

The final stretch of the Grachtengordel, going east from Vijzelstraat, comes to a bold full stop at the Amstel. This stretch is part of the second stage of canal construction that took place after 1665. Commentaries on the canal-boat tours often dry up on this southeasternmost stretch of the canals and, if your stay in Amsterdam is governed by priorities, a thorough exploration of the canals between Vijzelstraat and the Amstel can be put low on your list.

But don't, for one moment, write this neighbourhood off altogether. Four of Amsterdam's best museums are tucked away here. A stone's throw north of Herengracht is Rembrandtplein, at night always bright and busy, and just to the south, overlooking Singelgracht, is the old Heineken Brewery, one of Amsterdam's most popular and convivial tourist attractions.

Rembrandtplein

If Leidseplein is Amsterdam's most popular haunt at night, then **Rembrandtplein ❶** comes a close second. The square was originally part of the 16th-century city ramparts; later it was the site of a butter market and a fairground. It took its name in 1876 from the statue of Rembrandt that stands at the centre of the square facing the Jewish quarter.

Topless bars, music bars, small bars, large bars – Rembrandtplein has them all. Unfailingly lively any night of the year, it has inevitably become very commercialised, reflected in the over-inflated prices of drinks and the relatively indifferent service one may encounter. In the summer it's the haunt of *nouveau* café society, massaging each other's egos and showing off their sunbed tans between endless gossip. At best, it's a place to meet someone en route to elsewhere. There is one oasis amid this world of posers, namely Café Schiller at No. 26. This café seems to have let time slip through its fingers: the pace is relaxed, the interior elegant and the service friendly.

The cobblestoned and shaded square of Thorbecke-plein, which leads on to Herengracht, is a tidy and deliberately quaint extension to Rembrandtplein that extends the nightlife repertoire. Ringed by cafés, hotels and restaurants, the pavement terraces are usually crammed full in summer and even in winter seldom lack custom. You can stagger from bar to bar here – and people do.

Standing in the middle of the square is a statue of J.R. Thorbecke, a significant figure in the history of the Netherlands. In 1814, after a brief interlude under the rule of Napoleon Bonaparte, the former Dutch Republic had become a monarchy. Belgium was then part of this new nation, but by 1830 Belgium had seceded and 18 years later the Netherlands had a new

PRECEDING PAGES:
Bloemenmarkt.
LEFT: cigar shop on
Reguliersbreestraat.
BELOW: Rembrandt
statue on
Rembrandtplein.

constitution, for which J.R. Thorbecke was responsible. It may seem ironic that the statue celebrating a man who played such an important role in the development of his country should stand amid all this carefree merriment, but Thorbecke was, above all, a liberal, part of a political tradition that ultimately accounts for much of this country's pragmatic outlook.

If you have already been on one of the canal-boat tours by the time you get to Thorbeckeplein *(see page 157)*, you'll probably recognise the six-arched bridges of Reguliersgracht just south of the square. The view down Reguliersgracht cuts across all three of the main canals almost as far as Singel; this particular perspective is a favourite with photographers.

Silver screen

Heading northwest out of Rembrandtplein, you enter crowded Reguliersbreestraat where, among the fast-food stalls, you will find the **Tuschinski Theatre Cinema ❷**. Go to see a film here just to enjoy the interior. The man behind this beautiful Art Deco building was a Polish Jew, Abraham Tuschinski. He first arrived in the Netherlands at Rotterdam, where he started a theatre company. When World War I ended, he came to Amsterdam with ambitions to build a unique theatre. Tuschinski purchased a piece of land in Reguliersbreestraat occupied by slum buildings known as Duivelshoek (Devil's Corner). He was closely involved in the design of the building, a lavish creation that is perfectly in tune with the era of cinema's heyday.

The cinema opened in 1921. Tuschinski himself died at Auschwitz in 1942, though the cinema – one of the most beautiful interiors in Amsterdam – ensures that his name lives on. The general public can enter the foyer for free, where a

BELOW: the wonderfully ornate Tuschinski Theatre Cinema.

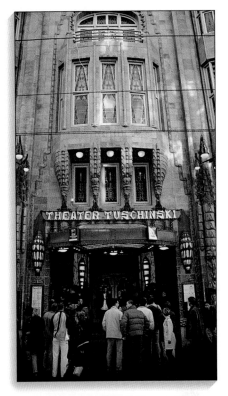

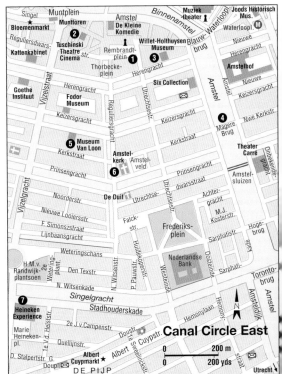

plaque behind the bar commemorates Tuschinski and his two co-founders. In summer there are guided tours (Jul–Aug Sun–Mon 10.30am). Fortunately, the current owners of this building have preserved all the fixtures and fittings intact so that the original style is just about unblemished. Amsterdam has a rich collection of Art Deco buildings and the Tuschinski is the proudest of them all.

Map on page 176

Lives of the gentry

You need walk only a short distance to the east of Rembrandtplein to enjoy a lavish interior from an earlier era. One of the most stunning insights into life in the grand canal houses of the 17th century is provided by the **Willet-Holthuysen Museum** ❸ (605 Herengracht; tel: 523 1822; open daily; entrance fee).

This three-storey building with a street-level basement was built in 1689 for Jacob Hop, a prominent burgher of Amsterdam, and his wife Isabella Hooft. The house changed hands many times and eventually, in 1855, came into the possession of Pieter Gerard Holthuysen. When he died three years later his daughter continued to live here. In 1861 she married Abraham Willet and together they built up a valuable collection of glass, ceramics, silver and paintings. Willet, who had a keen interest in art, was a friend of many of the artists of his time. The couple had no children and so, when Mrs Willet died in 1895, the house and its contents were left to the city of Amsterdam.

One condition of the legacy was that the premises were to be opened to the public as a museum. This was duly done on 1 May 1896. But the public showed no interest. A standing joke ridiculed this museum for being one of only two places in Amsterdam where a gentleman could meet his mistress unobserved (the other was Kalverstraat on a Sunday morning).

Extensive restoration in the 1990s has widened the scope of this museum so that it now contains a number of period rooms, including a fine 18th-century kitchen and a late 19th-century bedroom. Oriental cabinets, antique clocks, carpets, chandeliers, fireplaces, a grand stairway with gilded cast-iron banisters, painted ceilings, wall tapestries, silver, porcelain, pottery and glass are part of a valuable collection housed in an authentic and stately interior. During the restoration many new discoveries were made, notably the original wallpaper which has been faithfully reproduced. The attic houses temporary exhibitions.

Today the Willet-Holthuysen Museum is no longer ridiculed, nor does it lack visitors. Constructed three years after the final stage of the Grachtengordel was completed and almost the last building on this the most elegant of the three main canals, the Willet-Holthuysen Museum is a grandiose endpiece to the Herengracht.

River views

The Amstel was at one time the city's main artery. Amsterdam itself was named after this river, which during the 16th century flowed freely to the IJ. Once you have adjusted to the scale of the city's canals, the breadth of the Amstel seems strangely out of place in the heart of the old city, but it nevertheless makes for a popular Sunday afternoon walk.

BELOW: Willet-Holthuysen Museum.

The Amstel used to be an invisible border line that marked the beginnings of the Jewish quarter *(see page 205)*. Nieuwe Keizersgracht and Nieuwe Prinsengracht, because of their position on the east side of the Amstel, were not popular among Amsterdam's wealthier citizens and this allowed some of the richer members of the Jewish community to move in. The effect has survived and there is still a strong contrast between the streets on either side of the river.

One of the most prominent landmarks on this stretch of the river is the **Magere Brug ❹**, which means "skinny bridge". This restored wooden drawbridge, more than 300 years old, gets its name from an even narrower bridge that once stood here. Though there are many theories as to the actual origin of the bridge's name, experts tend to agree on the story of the two wealthy Magere sisters who lived on opposite sides of the Amstel; tired of making detours to visit each other, they built a bridge. Today, it is one of the last hand-operated drawbridges in existence. Featured on canal-boat tours, postcards and tourist brochures, the bridge has become one of the clichés of scenic Amsterdam.

A more remarkable landmark on the eastern bank is the **Amstelhof**, a nursing home dating from 1681. It is currently undergoing major alterations to accommodate part of the Hermitage collection. The collection will be on display from 2005 and the residents will be moved to Diemen, a modern suburb.

Art and religion

The museum theme continues back on Keizersgracht near Vijzelstraat, with two contrasting collections. The **Museum Van Loon ❺** (672 Keizersgracht; tel: 520 0400; open Mon–Sat; entrance fee) provides another glimpse into old Amsterdam, complemented by a modern gallery on the opposite bank.

BELOW: the
Magere Brug
("skinny bridge").

The centrepiece of the Museum Van Loon collection is a sequence of family portraits which provide a unique record of one of the most respectable families of the period. It is a giant family album that includes paintings from the 17th century all the way through to the 20th century, as well as photographs. The museum is run by the Van Loon Foundation.

Architect Adriaen Dortsman (1625–82) built this house in 1672 and the first tenant was the painter Ferdinand Bol, one of Rembrandt's pupils. Among subsequent owners were Abraham van Hagen and his wife Catharina Trip who lived here in the mid-18th century (they left a discreet note to posterity by initialling the staircase balustrade). The Van Loon family – who also helped create the East India Company – arrived on the scene when the building was purchased by Hendrick van Loon in 1884. The family lived in the beautiful house until after World War II.

Many years later, in 1964, the Van Loon Foundation started working on it, with the aim of restoring its late 18th- and early 19th-century appearance. The efforts the Foundation put into this venture have paid off handsomely. In contrast to the glitz of the Willet-Holthuysen Museum, the fixtures and furnishings here have been worn by time. It makes a morning or afternoon spent here all the more atmospheric. Uniquely among historic houses in Amsterdam, it also has a well-preserved formal garden, with lovely shrubs, flowers and statues.

The city is bursting with art and culture as home to almost 100 art galleries showing the work of established and new talent – there is always something to see and do. Some of the most popular exhibitions can be found in this area.

Tucked away between Keizersgracht and Prinsengracht, Kerkstraat is a thoroughfare with no canal. Go to the junction of Kerkstraat and Reguliersgracht and you will find the wooden **Amstelkerk ❻** sitting in the open space of the Amstelveld. Designed by Daniël Stalpaert, the church was built in 1670 as a temporary place of worship for Protestants but the plan to replace it with a more permanent brick structure was shelved. Nevertheless, the wooden church survived. It is best seen on Mondays, when a plant market is held in the adjacent square. The church has been subject to alteration, most notably during the 19th century. By the late 1980s it had fallen into a state of disrepair and was in danger of collapse. The City Restoration Company, with aid from the council, purchased it from the Dutch Reformed Church. Restoration began in 1988 and two years later it was officially opened by Prince Claus. Apart from now being the offices of the City Restoration Company, worshippers still attend services on Sunday mornings and concerts are given during the week.

Brewing traditions

A place to visit just for fun is the **Heineken Experience ❼** (Stadhouderskade 78; tel: 523 9666; open Tues–Sun; entrance fee; under 18s must be accompanied by a parent), on the site of the original brewery.

Mrs Anna Geertruida Cornelia Heineken, the mother of Heineken founder Gerard Adriaan Heineken, laid the first stone of the brewery here in 1867. When it closed in 1988, the site was used as a

Map on page 176

TIP

On the southeastern side of the church and facing the Prinsengracht is Café-Restaurant Moko, a somewhat chic place with a most agreeable terrace.

BELOW: the gardens of the Museum Van Loon.

Reception Centre for ten years, and the present museum opened in 2001. You can no longer take a full tour of the brewery proper, as the real brewing now takes place at two provincial plants at Zoeterwoude and Den Bosch.

Beer has been brewed on this site for around 400 years. The original brewery, called *De Hooiberg* (The Haystack), was established in 1592. Gerard Adriaan Heineken, founder of the present firm, acquired it in 1864. His company prospered; today it is an international operation with outlets in 150 countries. One ingredient in this success has been Heineken "A" yeast, developed by a pupil of Louis Pasteur. The formula has been closely guarded and passed down from generation to generation, thereby ensuring that the brew has remained a winner.

Its popularity, however, has been its undoing in that demand has forced Heineken out of Amsterdam. The small capacity of the Amsterdam plant was able to produce only 80,000 bottles of lager an hour – Amsterdam alone consumes beer at the same rate. The Heineken plant at Den Bosch has a capacity of 350,000 bottles an hour and the one at Zoeterwoude manages a hefty 700,000 (when demand requires, production can be boosted to a million bottles).

The former brewery building, with its striking façade, makes for an excellent museum preserving the company's history. Visitors are told about the invention of beer by the Sumerians, of how whole medieval villages in Europe were burnt down by careless brewing operations and of how the Teutons introduced public brewing houses where the product could be consumed at the point of origin. These stories are all part of a tour around vast, though now unused, copper vessels, antique brewing paraphernalia, malt silos and lager cellars where the beer was matured. The best part comes at the end when the separate groups reconvene in the Heineken beer hall. The ice is quickly broken by a couple of

Heineken is the city's most popular beer.

BELOW: inside the Heineken Experience.

glasses of beer, free snacks and a nostalgic film of the last horse-drawn cart laden with lager venturing out along Stadhouderskade.

Utrechtsestraat

South from Rembrandtplein a walk along Utrechtsestraat has much to offer. This street, once notorious for prostitution, has transformed itself into a rich row of shops and restaurants. A peek down the juxtaposing Utrechtsedwarsstraat will reveal the 19th-century **Theater Carré** on the opposite bank of the Amstel. Originally built to accommodate circus acts, its stage is circular. Today it is used by many international stars.

A lot of the locals are academics, so it comes as no surprise that there are four bookshops in the street, but there are many other shops of note: Concerto is a large CD shop spanning several buildings with every form of music; Loekie is a delicatessen of epicurean proportions; a shop towards the end of the street sells maps of everything (including the moon). Looking down Kerkstraat at night gives a view of the beautifully lit Magere Brug and if you're lucky the Russian Orthodox Church choir may be rehearsing. There's a wide selection of cafés, too. In **Café Krom**, apart from a lick of paint, nothing has changed in 50 years. **Oosterling**, at the end of the street, was originally a distillery – the large vats inside bear witness to the fact. This dark old bar is an archetypal "brown café" *(see page 102)*. Of particular interest are the prints displaying the People's Handicrafts Palace, a Crystal Palace-like structure that burnt down at the turn of the 19th century. The site where the palace once stood is now home to the National Bank of the Netherlands – Oosterling sits in the shadow of this modern glass and steel institution where the nation's gold is kept. ❑

Many theatregoers will be found after a performance dining in Restaurant Sluizer on Utrechtsestraat, a very traditional restaurant with a separate fish restaurant next door. It has a late supper licence (there are very few such licences) and is well worth a visit.

BELOW: the River Amstel.

THE MUSEUM QUARTER

*Amsterdam's museums rate among the finest in the world,
exhibiting priceless pieces from the Dutch Golden Age and
highlighting two Dutch masters: Rembrandt and Van Gogh*

Map
on page
186

Amsterdam has always been proud of its cultural heritage and in recent years the city has made major moves to make this more accessible to both its own citizens and the hordes of tourists who visit Amsterdam annually. This has not only involved the renovation and preservation of old buildings, but an expansion of and concentration on the city's museums. With the newly designed **Museumplein ❶**, Amsterdam's triple alliance of museums – the Rijksmuseum, Van Gogh Museum and Stedelijk Museum – have truly entered the 21st century. Their three separate visions of the presentation of their permanent collections enables them to tell their own story and maintain their own special presence. All three major art galleries are focused on Museumplein, south of the canal circle but only a short stroll from Leidseplein *(see page 170).*

The Rijksmuseum

The dominant building is the palatial **Rijksmuseum ❷** (42 Stadhouderskade; tel: 674 7047; open daily 10am–5pm; entrance fee), built by P.J.H. Cuypers in the late 19th century to house the national art collection. The façade, which looks more like that of a medieval French château than a Dutch national museum, reflects Cuypers' strong penchant for the Gothic style (he also designed Centraal Station and you can see the similarities in the towers and brick overlay).

The highlights of this great art collection are indisputably the paintings of the Golden Age, in particular *The Night Watch* and 20 or so other works by Rembrandt. This section alone merits several visits but constitutes only about a quarter of the museum exhibits. The rest is devoted to the decorative arts, Asiatic and foreign art and Dutch history and prints.

The proportions of the place are forbidding and it pays to be selective. Useful references are the floor plans at the entrance, but it is also advisable to buy the reasonably priced *Guide to the Rijksmuseum*, along with a new brochure which highlights a walk through the Dutch Golden Age (available at the information desk upstairs, next to the gift shop). There is also an audio tour which provides "instant information" on 200 paintings in the Rijksmuseum collection.

Upon entering the museum and turning left on the ground floor, you gain an instant insight into the Netherlands' rich heritage. Paintings, weapons, costumes, documents, models of ships and memorabilia relating to the seafaring history of the Netherlands are the legacy of this turbulent period *(see page 223)*. The earliest works in the Rijksmuseum date from the 15th century when art was still predominantly involved with religious life. The works of the 16th-century artists in Rooms 203–6 introduce large-

PRECEDING PAGES: the palatial Rijksmuseum. **LEFT:** the Rijksmuseum gardens. **BELOW:** *The Toilet* by Jan Steen.

scale narrative figure pieces or Biblical stories in real landscapes, with a gradual move away from religious themes. There is also the great 16th-century clock from the tower of St Nicholas's Church in Utrecht, but the main emphasis is on 17th- and 18th-century history: The Revolt of the Netherlands against Spain and The Seventeenth Century (Room 102), the latter a large open room covering colonial history, specifically the East Indies, the Eighty Years' War and sea battles, mainly against England. Rooms 105–9 cover the period of the *Stadholders* (1672–1702).

The dominant feature in the section on the French period (Rooms 110–12) is the monumental canvas of *The Battle of Waterloo* by Jan Willem Pieneman. The mounted Duke of Wellington is the focus of attention, while the Dutch Prince William lies on a stretcher. Nearby are some Pieneman studies of the details for his masterpiece, including the Duke of Wellington's horse.

The prosperity of the 17th century led to a prodigious output of painting. Art was no longer only judged on its aesthetic merits but was also seen as an investment and people of all walks of life were buying paintings to hang in their homes. Most artists restricted themselves to a specific type of art – landscape, genre, portraiture or history – often depending on the subjects they found most marketable. For the first time painters were independent of wealthy patrons.

Frans Hals and early Rembrandts

Frans Hals is now one of the most admired artists of the Golden Age and his paintings make a radical departure from the typical portraiture of the early 17th century. Compare the stiff, formal portraits of the regents and regentesses of the *Leper Asylum* by Werner van der Valckert (Room 208) with the more lively

Stained-glass portrait in the Rijksmuseum of the illustrious sculptor and architect Hendrick de Keyser.

BELOW: *Supplice de l'innocent* by Dieric Bouts (*circa* 1470).

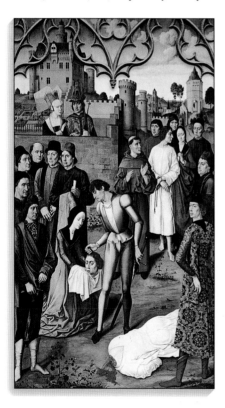

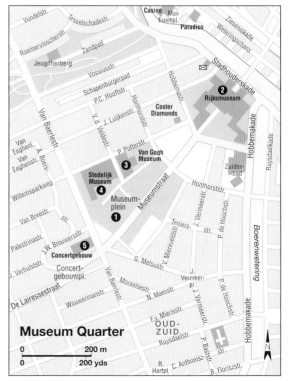

Museum Quarter

0 — 200 m
0 — 200 yds

and realistic portrayal of his subjects in the works by Frans Hals in Rooms 209–10. The *Marriage Portrait of Isaac Abrahamsz Massa and Beatrix van der Laen* (Room 209) is unusual in showing the married couple posing together. Husband and wife more commonly had their own portraits. Hals has set the newlywed pair in a fantasy garden with peacocks, which serve as a reference to the classical goddess Juno, the guardian of marriage. *The Merry Drinker* (Room 210), painted in swift Impressionistic brush strokes, shows Hals's remarkable capacity to depict a fleeting gesture. This portrait is typical of Hals's style at its most lively, and the sitter appeals to us through his smile and gestures.

Map on page 186

Room 211 contains some of the finest examples of Rembrandt's early period in Leiden, including an outstanding self-portrait of the artist at 22, one of more than 80 self-portraits he either drew, etched or painted, from young to old. It is a remarkable portrait since the face can hardly be seen. He probably made it as a study to experiment with light and dark. Rembrandt had many students who emulated his style. In Room 215, there is an impressive portrait which was the pride of the Rijksmuseum after it was acquired in 1880. It was thought to be a Rembrandt masterpiece, but in 1911, the director of the Rijksmuseum concluded that this portrait of Elisabeth Bas, a wealthy tavern owner was, in fact, painted by Rembrandt's pupil, Ferdinand Bol. The portrait became so famous that a brand of cigar was even named after her.

Landscapes and domestic scenes

The realistic country scenes in Room 214 show how landscapists had abandoned the Flemish Mannerist and schematised approach and instead had begun to paint what they actually saw. Pieter Saenredam's painting of the *Nave and Choir*

BELOW: Frans Hals' *The Marriage Portrait of Isaac Abrahamsz Massa and Beatrix van der Laen.*

Intricate wrought-iron railings in the Museum Quarter.

of the Mariakerk in Utrecht, 1641, is an excellent example of a church exterior of the Golden Age. The artist specialised in architecture and would first make extensive sketches of a building before painting it some years later.

The merry genre scenes in Rooms 216–9, typified by the bawdy tavern and chaotic household interiors of Jan Steen, are not just intended as realistic and witty portrayals of everyday life, although Steen took pride in being a storyteller by filling his paintings with cheery visual anecdotes. Like the still lives of the 17th century, these works are frequently filled with symbolism and allegorical allusions which were evident to most literate Dutchmen of the time. Steen's *Merry Family* (Room 216), in which children are following the example of their parents by smoking, drinking and disporting themselves with great abandon, warns against loose morals and bad upbringing. In his painting of *The Toilet* (Room 219) the allusions are erotic – red stockings symbolised a whore; a dog on the pillow, candlestick on the chair and chamberpot on the floor were all indications of lust.

There are only 30 known works by the Delft master Jan Vermeer *(see page 31)*, and four of the most famous are in Room 221A. They may well be familiar through reproductions but no copy can do justice to these superb works. His vivid interpretation of the street in Delft could have been painted in the present day. *Woman Reading a Letter* is a study of subdued emotion. Perhaps loveliest of all is *The Kitchen Maid*, a serene domestic scene of a woman pouring milk into a bowl. The beauty of the colour and the play of sunlight transforms an everyday chore into poetry. In the same room are some of the best works of Gerrit Dou, Gabriel Metsu and Pieter de Hooch, another master of domestic scenes who was also fascinated by and sensitive to the play of light.

RIGHT: *Merry Family* by Jan Steen.

The Night Watch and late Rembrandts

When you leave this gallery, walk on to Room 223 where "Facts about *The Night Watch*" are on display, including a miniature version of the painting by Gerrit Lundens, which offers a completely new perspective before you view the original. Armed with the facts, the large tableau will be even more impressive.

The most dazzling of Rembrandt's masterpieces occupies a whole wall at one end of the Gallery of Honour. The painting is a militia piece, an official portrait of the civic guard that defended the city. The subject matter is *The Company of Captain Frans Banning Cocq* and the captain is giving his company orders to march. Unlike the militia pieces that had gone before, in which the figures, seated or standing, looked stiff and lifeless, Rembrandt's painting portrays a group in action, each figure moving or about to move, and the overall activity is enhanced by the play of light. The layers of varnish and grime which had accumulated on *The Night Watch* led 19th-century experts to believe this was a night scene, hence the mistaken title.

The Night Watch is "guarded" on the right and the left by two other almost equally monumental paintings of militiamen by Bartholmeus van der Helst. The painting on the left shows the men celebrating the end of the Eighty Years' War, while the painting on the right shows a captain and his regiment in front of a brewery. There are 32 figures and one dog in the painting and wherever you stand in the room, most of the figures follow you eerily with their stares.

To the left of *The Night Watch* stairs lead up to Room 225 and the ARIA interactive centre. It was created in 1998 as a way for visitors to view and study the Rijksmuseum's superb collection. It offers 10 colour touch-sensitive monitors and 10 black-and-white printers. The accessed information can be printed out

Map on page 186

BELOW: sculpture of Rembrandt at the Rijksmuseum.

THE APPEAL OF REMBRANDT

Rembrandt Harmenszoon van Rijn is probably the most famous Dutchman in history. Although more has been written about him than perhaps any other prominent figure from Holland, the greatest painter of the Golden Age remains a mystery. There have been many scholarly works and in recent years efforts of the Rembrandt Research Project have helped to set the record straight on just how many paintings are credited to the master of *chiaroscuro*. Not long ago there were thought to be more than 650 Rembrandt paintings, but authenticity studies have reduced that figure to around 300. *The Night Watch* remains his most famous painting. Rembrandt completed it in 1642 at the age of 36, when he was one of the most sought-after painters in Amsterdam. According to the Rijksmuseum, which was specially constructed with the painting as the centrepiece, it remains priceless. And yet it was highly criticised at the time for being too dark and for breaking rules. Even the title is misleading because the figures in the painting are clearly not on watch duty. The painting has survived despite being cut down in the 18th century to fit into the old Town Hall on Dam Square and a lunatic slashing in 1975. Since then, it has been restored and the pilgrimage of visitors continues.

with a special card that can be purchased here. Floor plans are printed free of charge. If you prefer to view the collection the old-fashioned way, then the logical follow-on from *The Night Watch* is the Gallery of Art where the late Rembrandts are hung, along with the works of some of his eminent pupils.

Contrary to what people believed for many years, Rembrandt received some important commissions in his last years, among them *The Anatomy Lesson of Dr Deyman*, now in the Amsterdam Historical Museum *(see page 131)* and the *Sampling Officials of the Drapers Guild. The Jewish Bride*, now titled *Isaac and Rebecca*, is one of the great late works. The heavily impasted glowing golds and reds evoke a mood of warmth and tenderness. Van Gogh was so enamoured of the painting that he once said he would give 10 years of his life to be able to sit in front of it with a loaf of bread.

The Dutch School and Romantics

Paintings from the later schools of Dutch art are set out in Rooms 16–20 in the South Wing (soon these rooms will function as temporary exhibition space and the paintings held here will be on show in the main building). This was a time of prosperity and contentment and the theme "The Poetry of Reality" features paintings of the 19th century which made poetry of real situations, with an atmosphere still overshadowed by the achievements of the 17th century. Cornelis Troost's pretty conversation pieces and portraits show comfortable lifestyles and the influence of his French contemporaries, Watteau and Boucher.

Room 19 is devoted to Dutch Realism and features landscapes and beach scenes painted around The Hague by Anton Mauve and H.M. Mesdag. Room 20 features Amsterdam Impressionists, known as the "*tachtigers*" because their

BELOW: Rembrandt's *The Jewish Bride.*

movement began in the 1880s. Besides two early works by Van Gogh, there are several bold canvases by Georg Hendrik Breitner, considered Amsterdam's leading Impressionist, among them *Paleisstraat, Amsterdam* and *Horse Artillery*. Most of these paintings portray Amsterdam in winter with a typically grey and wet landscape, which was and still is considered romantic to many. In contrast to these very Dutch paintings are Orientalist canvases, two by the Romantic painter Sir Lawrence Alma-Tadema, *Egyptian Widow* and *The Death of Pharaoh's First-Born Son*, both evocative and rich in colour and detail.

Map on page 186

Sculpture, Delftware and dolls' houses

The huge and variable sculpture collection includes medieval sculpture and works from the Art Nouveau period. The medieval sculpture alone makes a visit worthwhile, particularly the lively oak carvings by Adriaen van Wesel in Rooms 238–42. Room 248 features bronze sculptures, majolica and furniture from the Italian Renaissance, the influence of which can be seen in the following rooms. Fine furnishings and sumptuous silver and glass portray the prosperity and comfortable lifestyles of the 17th century.

Delftware is one of the most well-known forms of Dutch craftsmanship and design.

There is a beautiful collection of Delftware, with delightful pieces such as a polychrome pair of pointed, high-heeled shoes and a violin, among the more familiar jugs and plates. The next highlight is in Room 164 (follow the signs and walk down the staircase from Room 261) where you will find exquisite and fantastically detailed dolls' houses modelled after real houses of the period and fully furnished, complete with tiny Delft plates, paintings, copper plates, as well as precious silver, glass and porcelain objects most of which were made in the 17th century by respected craftsmen. Comparable to the richly decorated

BELOW: detail from *The Jewish Bride.*

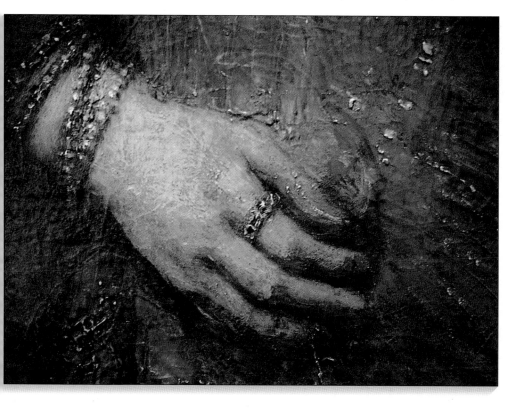

cabinets of collectors, these dolls' houses were clearly not playthings for children but for women of the regent and merchant classes. A series of rooms with French-influenced 17th- and 18th-century furnishings then leads you to the superb collection of Chinese-inspired Meissen porcelain. The remaining rooms on this floor contain mainly Dutch and French furniture of the 18th century.

Asiatic art

In 1997, the South Wing was reopened following an extensive renovation, allowing the collection of *objets d'art* from Asia to be showcased in a very striking exhibition with glass corridors and broad walkways. The Dutch empire's links with the east resulted in a fine array of Asian pieces that are now among the museum's most precious exhibits.

The reorganised wing allows more room to get a good perspective of the fascinating and somewhat forbidding stone sculptures from Indonesia, such as the pot-bellied, bearded Hindu god Agastya, complete with trident, rosary, water bottle and fly whisk. The Indonesian jewellery from the 12th century is priceless. Several rooms are also devoted to Japanese and Chinese fine and applied art. The 12th-century *Bodhisattva Akalokiteshivara* is an impressive example of late Sung wooden sculpture, skilfully rendering various textures such as metal, silk, skin and hair. From the same period, in an adjacent room, is the lively bronze south Indian statue of Shiva, dancing amid a halo of flames.

The last rooms show the development of Chinese pottery, from prehistoric pots through to Ming and later porcelain. The exhibition ends with Japanese textiles and earthenware from the 18th and 19th centuries. If you are interested in Asiatic art, this is one of the world's finest collections of its kind.

BELOW: wild elephant pen and ink sketch in the Asian art section.

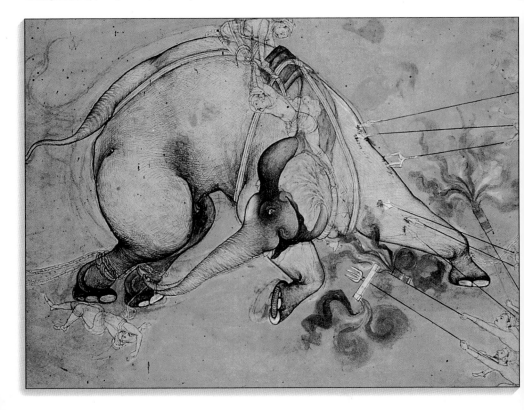

Vincent van Gogh and the Van Gogh Museum

A short stroll further down Paulus Potterstraat brings you to the **Van Gogh Museum ❸**, which has the world's largest collection of works by Vincent van Gogh (7 Paulus Potterstraat; tel: 570 5200; open daily; entrance fee). Designed by the De Stijl movement architect Gerrit Rietveld, it was built in 1973 as a permanent home for some 200 paintings and 500 drawings by Van Gogh, together with an extensive collection of works by other 19th-century painters and sculptors. There are also 700 letters, all bequeathed by Van Gogh's nephew, who was also called Vincent. The interior, which was given a complete facelift at the time of the construction of the new wing in 1999, is suitably light and spacious with whitewashed walls and open-plan floors.

The permanent collection features a selection of paintings by Van Gogh which are hung in chronological order on the first floor to give an overview of the main developments in his œuvre. The early works, typified by scenes from the daily lives of peasants, show Van Gogh's early preference for heavy forms and dark, sombre colours. The numerous studies of peasants in the province of Brabant culminates in *De Aardappeleters (Potato Eaters)*, a painting which Van Gogh regarded as one of his finest works but whose uncompromising ugliness did not impress friends or critics. Van Gogh's intent was not to idealise or sentimentalise, but to portray peasant life as he observed it.

Van Gogh's move to Paris in 1886 shows his vision transformed. Exposed to the rainbow colours and broad brush strokes of Impressionism and other new painting styles, he began to paint with a brighter palette. The intensity of his period in Brabant gradually disappears and gives way to lively scenes of Parisian streets, café interiors, windswept landscapes and vivid portraits of friends.

 Map on page 186

In response to criticism about the Potato Eaters, Van Gogh wrote: "I have tried to make it clear that those people, eating their potatoes in the lamplight, have dug the earth with those very hands they put in the dish, and so it speaks of manual labour, and how they have honestly earned their food."

BELOW: Van Gogh's boats.

Woman Sitting in the Café du Tambourin has the subject matter, the swift brush strokes of pure colour and the vivid effect of the Impressionists. It was a café he knew well; he took meals there, swapped canvases for food, was friendly with the Italian woman who owned it and used it as a venue to exhibit his collection of Japanese prints. Tiring of city life and passionate for "a full effect of colour", Van Gogh then moved to Arles. Enthused by the intense light and warm colours of the Mediterranean, he produced some of his most vivid landscapes and portraits, all created with great speed and intensity.

The famous *Sunflowers*, one of a series of five pictures of this subject, shows his love of warm colour, light and simplicity. The predominant colours of this period are blazing yellows, ochres and oranges, as in *The Yellow House* (where Van Gogh lived), *The Harvest at La Crau*, *Self-Portrait with Straw Hat* and *Van Gogh's Bedroom, Arles*. Of the latter picture, he wrote that the colour was "to be suggestive of rest or sleep in general. In a word, to look at the picture ought to rest the brain, or rather the imagination."

Following a quarrel with Gauguin, Van Gogh cut off a portion of his own ear and admitted himself to the asylum at St Rémy. He was physically and emotionally exhausted, had been drinking too much and was diagnosed with a form of epilepsy. The asylum provided him a refuge where he could be cared for and work in peace. His paintings of the landscapes around the asylum become bolder and more visionary, the canvases less colourful and heavily impasted. Of the *Olive Trees with Pink Sky* he writes: "What I have done is rather hard and coarse reality but it will give a sense of the country and will smell of the soil." In *Cypresses, St Rémy*, he shows the trees as swirling dark flames, reflecting his growing anguish and tormented sensibility. In the final period at Auvers, the

Sunflowers *is* Van Gogh's *most* famous work.

BELOW: face to face with Van Gogh.

landscapes are similar but fiercer, painted in a frenzy of creation between fits of insanity. *Wheatfields with Crows* is the most ominous and desolate of the last works. "They are vast fields of wheat under troubled skies and I do not need to go out of my way to try and express sadness and extreme loneliness." Only a few weeks later, Van Gogh shot himself. He was only 37 years old but in the last 10 years of his short life he had produced more than 800 paintings and 1,000 drawings, as well as sketches and watercolours. Unfortunately, the drawings and letters are no longer on permanent display as they are too sensitive to light.

Map on page 186

Other works

Works from the collection of 19th-century art are on show on the ground and third floors of the museum. These include works by Van Gogh's friends and contemporaries, as well as new acquisitions, which are displayed on a rotating basis. Among these are works by Toulouse Lautrec, Gauguin and Emile Bernard, all of whom had an influence on Van Gogh's own work. The second floor of the museum houses changing presentations of drawings and graphic art, as well as a study area with computers where visitors can view the reserve collection and the museum website and find out more about Van Gogh and the art of his time. The location of individual works may change from time to time – ask at the information desk for details on the current displays.

The new wing was created to house an ambitious programme of temporary exhibitions. Designed by the Japanese architect Kisho Kurokawa, the organic, highly modern structure stands slightly apart from Rietveld's original building on Museumplein, with almost two-thirds of it carved out below ground level, out of Kurokawa's deference to Rietveld.

BELOW: self-portrait by Piet Mondrian (1918).

MONDRIAN AND DE STIJL

With his distinctive paintings of grid lines and blocks of primary colours, Piet Mondrian (1872–1944) was the leading figure of the Dutch De Stijl ("The Style") Movement. But it was the dogmatic and polemical magazine called *De Stijl*, founded and edited by Theo van Doesburg, that would start the rumblings towards the subsequent development of modern art in the Netherlands.

Its purpose was "to state the logical principles of a style now ripening, based on a pure equivalence between the age and its means of expression… we wish to pave the way for a deeper artistic culture, based on a collective realisation of the new awareness." Moving on from Cubism, De Stijl captured the Dutch imagination, from art to architecture.

Mondrian's premise was that the bold colours and straight lines offered a "true vision of reality" by eliminating personal interpretation of the work. Another major artist in the De Stijl tradition was Bart van der Leck, whose work is distinctive for its use of triangles rather than squares. Mondrian himself abandoned the De Stijl Movement in 1925, producing even more abstract works before moving to New York and going against form with paintings that depicted the lively world of jazz music.

Ernst Ludwig Kirchener's Dancing Woman *(1911), at the Stedelijk Museum.*

BELOW: staircase at the Stedelijk.

Its striking forms are moulded in high-quality granite, aluminum and titanium, the latter taking on surprisingly varied reflections and colours in the changing conditions of light and weather. The museum café and gift shop have also been renovated and expanded.

The Van Gogh Museum remains dedicated to providing good service and educational facilities for its visitors, which include an improved audio tour, a permanently manned information desk, website, study area and auditorium. They have recently opened a shop annexe in co-operation with the Rijkmuseum on Museumplein, which sells a more extensive line of gift articles and souvenirs related to the particular museums.

Stedelijk Museum

The Neo-Renaissance Dutch façade of the **Stedelijk Museum ❹** (13 Paulus Potterstraat; tel: 573 2911; open daily 11am–5pm; entrance fee), embellished with gables and turrets, gives no hint of the strikingly modern interior where walls were ripped down to create large open spaces, ceilings partially glassed and rooms whitewashed to offset large, colourful canvases.

The collection consists of more than 100,000 works of art, including the collection of applied art and industrial design. Of these, a mere fraction have been on display over the years and the exhibition space of the museum is devoted to rotating the permanent collection every few months so that the Picasso one sees in January may be a different work in August. The museum's main challenge over the past two decades has been one of space: not for exhibition halls, but for art depots, work and office space for personnel. The Stedelijk is now in transition, with a new extension (two new buildings and an

annexe) and partial renovation being overseen by Portuguese architect Alvaro Siza Vieira, with plans for completion by the end of 2002.

Map on page 186

Identity crisis

The eccentric Dowager of Jonkheer Lopez Suasso, whose heterogeneous collection of antique furniture, coins, jewellery, watches and trinkets filled the rooms of the Stedelijk when it first opened in 1895, might be indignant if she could see the museum today. Her whole collection was cast out in 1975 in order to accommodate a large collection of paintings, sculpture, applied art and industrial design, for the most part uncompromisingly modern.

Over the past 50 years or so, the Stedelijk Museum has seemed to be experiencing an identity crisis. It has had several directors since 1945 when the dynamic Willem Sandberg began to steer the museum in a more modern direction. This visionary – the godfather of the COBRA movement *(see page 106)* which put the Stedelijk Museum on the world map – would prove to be a hard act to follow. Sandberg's aim was to concentrate on the evolution of art trends or of a specific movement, whether it was the Cubist works of Kasimir Malevitch which later evolved to his concept of Suprematism, the abstract compositions of Mondrian, the diverse periods of Picasso, the fanciful work of Chagall or the daring murals of Karel Appel. Sandberg's successor in 1963, Edy de Wilde, preferred to concentrate on the personalities of the newly emerging movement of the 1960s–70s: Pop Art, Fundamental Painting, Minimalism, Conceptual Art, and Environmental Art, to name a few. He felt it was "all about the individual artist, with his own language, his own syntax and his own imaginary world". In the mid-1980s, after a heated battle both politically and in the press, Wim Beeren (of the Boymans-van Beuningen Museum in Rotterdam) was selected to succeed Edy de Wilde as Director. With a philosophy similar to Sandberg's, Beeren wanted to restore the historical perspective to the museum. In 1989, he staged a Malevitch exhibition in co-operation with museums in Moscow and St Petersburg which attracted some 230,000 visitors. Three years later, Malevitch was shown in relation to the Russian avant garde, in an exhibition which drew 130,000 visitors. This was later followed up by popular exhibitions that featured the new and controversial work of Keith Haring and Jeff Koons, which attracted a younger public. During his tenure, Beeren purchased many acquisitions for the Stedelijk's collection, but there were to be still more changes ahead.

In 1992, Rudi Fuchs replaced Wim Beeren as Director. His series of exhibitions, "Couplets", which were a combination of works from the permanent collection and temporary exhibitions that changed every three months, had mixed reviews, but it was Fuchs's intent to serve as "an orchestra conductor" and arrange the works in a new tempo. Critics have accused him of favouring his "friends", citing German painters such as Baselitz, Rainer and Kiefer, and grow irate when high prices are paid for neon works by Bruce Nauman or Damien Hirst's *Waste*, which some consider "non-art". But Fuchs, as

BELOW: the neo-Renaissance façade of the Stedelijk Museum.

Map
on page
186

*The Museum Quarter
is one of the most
visited parts of the
city.*

BELOW: detail from
the façade of the
Concertgebouw.

museum director, art historian and author, has the privilege of moving from one century to the next, where he can continue to communicate his vision of contemporary art: to focus not only on "modern classics" of the past, but to consider the role of art in the 21st century and the relationship between the past and the present.

With some 500,000 visitors a year, it is clear that a museum devoted to contemporary art is essential, yet with no government support, museum conditions need to improve. Critics and many young artists feel that the museum should be concentrating more on the future social function of art, contemporary developments and the collections; to break from tradition and move ahead with the new century rather than going backwards. Based on the numbers who attended video artist Bill Viola's retrospective exhibition in 1998 it is interesting to observe that visionary (and former director) Willem Sandberg's maxim – "the museum of modern art looks from today's art to the past's" – is still valid.

Music on the square

Moving away from museums, at the southern end of Museumplein, the **Concertgebouw** ❺ has the reputation of being acoustically among the best concert halls in the world. Built in 1888, it houses two halls: the Grote Zaal, seating 2,250, and the Kleine Zaal, which accommodates 450. Famous European and US orchestras have performed here alongside the lesser-known Dutch orchestras, though the Concertgebouw's programme is not exclusively classical. Past performers have included Philip Glass, Wynton Marsalis and an Orchestra of 100 Gypsy Violins. It is also home to the Koninklijk Concertgebouworkest (Royal Concertgebouw Orchestra), which takes its place among the top international orchestras. Besides the regular concert schedule, there are also popular Sunday morning concerts held from 11am each week. Tickets can be purchased the morning of the concert. On Wednesday morning there is usually a free half-hour "surprise concert" where visitors can hear the resident orchestra or a guest orchestra in rehearsal.

The street to the side of the Concertgebouw is Van Baerlestraat which runs just a few blocks and leads up to the Vondelpark *(see page 232)*. It is a stylish street with a number of clothing, music and book shops and speciality stores selling perfume, cigars, coffee and language books. There are two cafés where you can stop, depending on your mood. The **Bodega Keyzer** at No. 96, directly opposite the Concertgebouw, is more than 100 years old and takes pride in its old-fashioned service and Old-World ambience. At the far end of the street is the **Small Talk Café**, at No 52, which is a popular spot for visitors between museum visits. Typical Dutch soups are served which hit the spot on a cold day; in summer one can sit outside. Just one block further up is the P.C. Hooftstraat, considered Amsterdam's smartest shopping street, with familiar designer names such as Armani, DKNY and Hugo Boss. While the shopping may be beyond some visitors' budgets, it is entertaining to watch Amsterdam's rich and famous double-parking their cars and taking a leisurely stroll with their dogs. ❑

The Van Gogh Phenomenom

In a letter to his brother Theo in 1883, Vincent van Gogh wrote: "One thing I know, within a few years I must bring a certain work to completion... I am concerned with the world only insofar as I have, as it were, a certain debt and duty... and also because I want, out of gratitude, to leave behind a sort of remembrance in the form of drawings and paintings... not made in order to promote this or that trend, but on account of them having in them something that expresses a sincere human sentiment. That is the goal of my work."

During his lifetime Vincent van Gogh sold only one painting. Today he is arguably the most popular and most reproduced modern artist and his paintings fetch world-record prices, with the last sold at auction for around $80 million (£55 million). After the reopening of the new wing at the Van Gogh Museum in 1999, there were almost 50 percent more visitors than in the previous year. With more than 700,000 visitors in the first five months, it is more popular than any other museum in the Netherlands.

Van Gogh's imagery continues to have an impact on people of all ages and backgrounds. The museum shop sells millions of postcards, as well as posters, calendars, diaries, pencils and paintboxes. In 1999 at the opening of the Museumplein, a new glass pavilion was built between the Rijksmuseum and the Van Gogh Museum which serves as a joint shop for the two institutions. Here there are even more collectibles which one can buy without having to pay an entrance fee. For Van Gogh fanatics, there are bath towels, coffee mugs, candles, mouse pads, refrigerator magnets and much more.

What an irony that a man who was considered a failure and a misfit and who died penniless and unrecognised should become such a commercial phenomenon. What is it about this sensitive painter that continues to be immortalised in songs, poetry, books and films? More than 100 years after his death, there are new generations from all over the world who continue to be inspired by his work: the homely ambience of the *Potato Eaters*, the pastoral landscapes of Holland and France, the sensual flowers, haunting self-portraits and turbulent skies of his final days at St Rémy. Perhaps it is the humanity which is seen and felt in these works. The spirituality which was such an important element of the troubled Van Gogh spirit.

Although his career spanned only 10 years, he produced close to 2,000 works. The paintings from Arles – amounting to a prolific 200 in 15 months – were produced in a frenzy of haste, as though he knew the end was near. Some of his most famous canvases were dashed off between fits of depression and insanity. Yet, in his letters to his brother Theo, he writes with great insight about his deteriorating health and state of mind and describes his paintings in detail. Although Van Gogh's art was rarely praised during his lifetime, he achieved his humble goal and his legacy remains. ❑

RIGHT: one of Van Gogh's many self-portraits in the Van Gogh Museum.

MUSEUMPLEIN: THE CULTURAL HEART

The Museumplein was reopened in 1999 after extensive improvements, creating a grand square linking the city's triumvirate of art museums

Before 1999, Museumplein was a somewhat bedraggled, wide-open space separating the Van Gogh Museum, the Stedelijk Museum, the Rijksmuseum and the Concertgebouw. It was a popular place for strolling, demonstrations, special events and skateboarding, but by that time it was clear that new challenges needed to be addressed: more tourist coaches were taking up space around the square, creating traffic problems as well as being an eyesore, and the city lacked a grand promenade like those found in other European cities. It was time for change.

GRAND DESIGN

Sven-Ingvar Andersson, a Swedish landscape architect, was selected to design the project which, at its centre, features a pedestrian promenade with a large green expanse for events such as the annual Uitmarkt festival. There is a separate area for sport and play, as well as a cycle path. Colourful benches and stylish lanterns have been placed throughout the area. Skateboarders still have their terrain on one side and boules and basketball players on the other. A grand café-restaurant paying homage to the COBRA art movement *(see page 106)* was constructed opposite the Rijksmuseum and its terrace can seat nearly 200 people. The Van Gogh Museum and Rijksmuseum have opened up a gift shop pavilion selling posters, cards and various souvenirs relating to their collections. The underground garage has space for 600 cars and 25 coaches and a grocery store. There are also plans for a Photography Museum. Traffic no longer flows through the square and the resulting tranquillity is a big improvement. Yet the overall effect of the changes, so far at any rate, is still a little cold and unfeeling.

△ **CENTREPOINT**
The heart of the Museumplein features a pedestrian promenade and the impressive structure of the Rijksmuseum looming over the square.

◁ **FLOOR SHOW**
Mime artists are a regular feature on the Museumplein, entertaining the regular flow of tourists.

▷ **WATER FEATURE**
A pond runs parallel to the promenade and has a stone border at seating level. In winter people can skate on the frozen water.

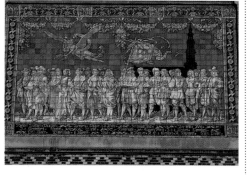

△ ARCHITECTURAL GEM

The exterior of the Neo-Gothic Rijksmuseum is as impressive as its interior, as seen by its decorative panels above the entrance door.

▽ REST SPOT

On the east side linden trees and a flower garden create a restful ambience for the Ravensbrück and Zigeuner (Gypsy) monuments.

A WORLD-CLASS ORCHESTRA

Considered to be one of the most beautiful concert halls in the world, the Concertgebouw opened its doors in 1888. Renowned for its fine acoustics, its historic environs have hosted such composers as Mahler, Ravel, Strauss, Debussy, Stravinsky, Schönberg and Hindemith, all of whom conducted the orchestra here more than once. In recent years many leading conductors have been in residence with the Royal Concertgebouw Orchestra, which – under the leadership of Riccardo Chailly – has earned a reputation for its versatility in the international world of music and is considered to be one of the leading orchestras in the world.

History continues to be made with the prestigious Robeco series of summer concerts held in the stately large hall with its elegant interior. The small hall on the upper level presents a number of concerts with solo artists and small chamber groups throughout the year, while the Sunday morning concerts continue to regularly attract sell-out crowds. Guided tours of the Concertgebouw are possible by appointment.

JODENBUURT AND PLANTAGE

*Although little remains of the pre-war atmosphere and bustle,
Amsterdam's Jewish quarter is today a sobering but fascinating
memorial to its once-thriving Jewish community*

Map
on page
207

The Jewish quarter of Amsterdam (Jodenbuurt) was once a lively, colourful and proud neighbourhood. Though poor, it was invariably hardworking. Those days have gone for ever. During World War II, the Jewish community in Amsterdam, which had numbered 80,000, was reduced to only 5,000. The Jodenbuurt became a virtual ghost town. Jewish street life disappeared.

Since then it has been a victim again, this time of property development and road-building. Stand at the broad junction of Mr Visserplein and look at the dull concrete embankments flanking Jodenbreestraat to the north, the gaping underpass which leads traffic from Weesperstraat north towards the IJ Tunnel, and the great square hulk of the Town Hall overlooking Waterlooplein, and you can't help feeling that Amsterdam is just another ugly modern city.

Yet the Jodenbuurt and neighbouring Plantage have a strong story to tell. There are enough places to visit to occupy a full day and, if you are interested in Amsterdam's Jewish past, more careful exploration is amply rewarded.

PRECEDING PAGES:
the Muziektheater
and Stadhuis
complex.
LEFT: the
Portuguese-Israelite
Synagogue.
BELOW: busker
on Waterlooplein.

Origins

Ironically, the thoroughly modern setting of **Waterlooplein ❶** is an appropriate place to start exploring the Jodenbuurt. At Nos 33–39 Waterlooplein, Amsterdam's first public synagogue was completed in 1639 (it was demolished in 1931). This area was known as the Vlooyenburg, a stretch of marshy ground regularly flooded by the Amstel, and was the site of the original Jewish quarter, accommodating the first Jews who came to Amsterdam.

The name Vlooyenburg comes from the old Dutch word for "flood". Two canals, Houtgracht and Leprozengracht, ringed Vlooyenburg to the north and east, creating an island. Here the Jews lived in poverty. In the 19th century, when Jews were allowed to practise trades for the first time, many small businesses were established in houses that were already too small and so conditions worsened. In 1882, the two canals were filled in to create Waterlooplein. Markets on Sint Antoniesbreestraat and Jodenbreestraat were transferred there and the marketplace became the focal point of Jewish life in the area.

Jodenbreestraat ("The Broad Street of the Jews") was once the business centre of the Jewish quarter. Today you can do little more than imagine all that colour and life. The concrete block that used to run down the northern side of Jodenbreestraat was until recently just one of the many modern buildings that have torn the heart out of the Jewish quarter.

The construction of the subway, which runs right under Waterlooplein, and extensive redevelopment at the southern end of Sint Antoniesbreestraat have

Unusual decorative pieces can be found at the flea market on Waterlooplein.

BELOW: flea-market trader.

further contributed to the changes that have completely destroyed the character of this area. In 1977 the flea market on Waterlooplein was moved to Rapenburgerstraat and did not return until the *Stopera* project (the combined Muziektheater and Town Hall) was completed. That market (open Mon–Sat) is worth visiting as the last vestige of the once-vital community life of the area.

The **Mozes en Aaron Kerk** ❷ (Moses and Aaron Church) is proof that Waterlooplein was not exclusively Jewish. It was completed in 1841, on the site of an earlier clandestine church.

Controversial culture

If you enjoy opera and ballet you would do better to make your visit here in the evening, having bought tickets for a performance at the **Muziektheater** ❸. The centrepiece of redevelopment on Waterlooplein, the Muziektheater and Town Hall complex was one of the most controversial pieces of property development that Amsterdam has ever seen. Opposition to the plan was widespread; many felt that the area should be residential and squatters rioted here in the late 1970s *(see page 81)*. Attempts to stop the building failed and the complex was completed in 1986. Ironically, the nickname *Stopera*, given by protesters to the complex, has stuck and passed into common parlance.

From a tour boat on the Amstel you will need little persuasion that the architecture of the complex is totally out of keeping with the scale and style of buildings nearby. But the Muziektheater (if not the Town Hall) has at least brought a measure of charisma to this area. Two resident companies perform here: the Netherlands Opera and the National Ballet, accompanied respectively by the Netherlands Philharmonic Orchestra and the Netherlands Ballet Orchestra.

Together they quickly earned the Muziektheater a place on the international opera and ballet circuit. Acclaimed guest performers have included Moscow's Bolshoi Ballet, London's Royal Ballet and New York's Martha Graham Dance Company.

Map on page 207

Rembrandt's home

The most-visited sight in the Jewish quarter is undoubtedly the **Rembrandthuis** ❹ (Rembrandt House; 4–6 Jodenbreestraat; tel: 624 5255; open Mon–Sat 10am–5pm, Sun and public holidays 1–5pm; entrance fee). A former home of Rembrandt, this has been a museum since 1911.

Rembrandt Harmensz van Rijn, to give the artist his full name, was born in Leiden and came to Amsterdam in 1631 when he was in his mid-twenties *(see page 32)*. Soon after arriving he took lodgings in what was then known simply as Breestraat, or Broad Street, later to be known as Jodenbreestraat. In Rembrandt's day this was on the edge of the town; he used to walk out into the country, eastwards to the village of Diemen, now an Amsterdam suburb.

Rembrandt purchased the house on Jodenbreestraat in 1639 by which time he was a celebrated artist. Even so, his comfortable new home (then just a two-storey building topped by a step gable) cost him dearly; he had incurred substantial debts to pay for it and the expense of furnishing and running it eventually contributed to his bankruptcy in 1656. Forced by his creditors to sell the house and many of his possessions, Rembrandt was nevertheless allowed to stay on until 1658, when he made a new home in the Jordaan *(see page 158)*.

On 7 May 1998 Prince Willem-Alexander opened the new wing adjacent to Rembrandthuis. This new wing has radically altered the role of the original house – intriguing as it was, it had become something of a receptacle for

The philosopher Spinoza is thought to have been born in 1632 in one of the houses demolished to make way for the building of the Moses and Aaron Church.

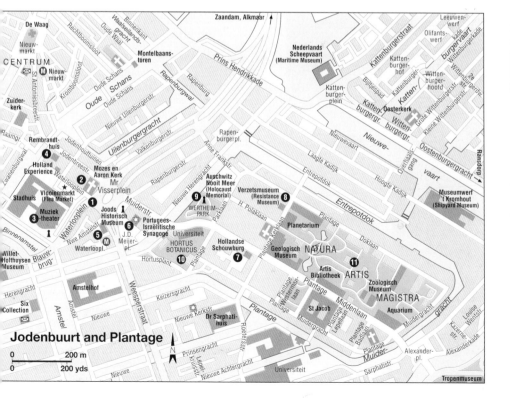

Jodenbuurt and Plantage

0   200 m
0   200 yds

Rembrandt's world-renowned prints and etchings. The new wing now houses these artefacts, thereby creating the opportunity to restore the residence to its pre-museum role. Rembrandt's house may now be seen as he lived and worked in it; the restoration has been carried out with scientific precision using, for example, floor and wall tiles of the same period and where possible using Rembrandt's own works as reference. The greatest point of reference however was the bailiff's inventory drawn up at Rembrandt's bankruptcy declaration. As a result the visitor gains a view of the artist's character hitherto inaccessible.

Entrance to the Rembrandthuis is now via the new wing. This spacious and well thought-out building houses temporary exhibitions in addition to the above-mentioned art treasures. There are also video and slide presentations in English.

Jewish life, past and present

On the opposite side of Jodenbreestraat from the Rembrandthuis is another important part of the Jewish quarter, bounded by Oude Schans and Valkenburgerstraat. In the 17th century there were two islands here – Uilenburg and Marken – thick with shipyards and wharves. When shipbuilding transferred to the newly developed islands of Kattenburg, Wittenburg and Oostenburg, large numbers of poorer Jews settled here.

A Jewish success story, in the shape of the former diamond factory of the Boas company, was founded here in 1878 and the building still stands overlooking the Uilenburgergracht. The processing of diamonds was very much a Jewish occupation and skilled cutters and polishers earned high wages. Today the area's principal attraction, particularly for jazz fans, is the **Bimhuis**. Housed in a former warehouse on the eastern side of Oude Schans (Nos 73–77), this is one of Amsterdam's best jazz venues.

While Waterlooplein was the embryo of Amsterdam's Jewish quarter, its heart today is a short walk away in the **Joods Historisch Museum ❺** (Jewish Historical Museum; Jonas Daniël Meijerplein 2/4; tel: 626 9945; open daily; entrance fee). The museum occupies the Ashkenazi Synagogue Complex, which comprises four synagogues built during the 17th and 18th centuries. The museum had previously been housed in the Weigh House (Waag) on Nieuwmarkt. When it moved here in 1987, Amsterdam's Jewish community achieved a long-standing ambition to have this major collection on Jewish life in a building where something of the Jewish spirit would reign.

The Jewish Historical Museum's stated aim is to provide a "place of reference for those whose links with past generations were broken by the war." Be warned that it is an enormous, sober and serious collection. If you want to absorb it fully, you should give yourself a full morning here.

The museum's detailed history of Zionism, collections of religious artefacts and insights into the lives of important Dutch Jewish personalities are part of a narrative that primarily appeals to practising Jews. This is counterbalanced, however, by exhibits of a more general interest: the story of Jewish settlement in the Netherlands, explanations of Jewish dietary laws and photographs that depict Jewish life today.

Map on page 207

The oldest synagogue in the museum complex, the Grote Schul, dates from 1671. Across the way, between Jonas Daniël Meijerplein and Muiderstraat, the **Portugees-Israëlitische Synagoge** ❻ (Portuguese-Israelite Synagogue) was completed just four years earlier. Both buildings are important in that they were the first synagogues of any size to be built in Western Europe.

The Portuguese-Israelite Synagogue is so large, in fact, that it dominates the junction of Mr Visserplein even today; in the 17th century the effect would have been more pronounced still. When wealthier Jews went to live in the extensions to the Grachtengordel – the new canals to the east – this locality became the new centre of the Jewish quarter. Paintings of the area soon after the synagogue was constructed depict tranquil scenes on the Muidergracht, a wide canal (now partly filled in; it re-emerges at the eastern end of Plantage Middenlaan) which passed through what is now Jonas Daniël Meijerplein. The synagogue was fully restored in the 1950s.

This triangular space flanking the Portuguese-Israelite Synagogue is named in honour of Jonas Daniël Meijer (1780–1834). He graduated as a Doctor of Law at the age of 16 and that same year, 1796, became the first Jew to be admitted to the Bar. It proved to be an auspicious year for the community as a whole, for Jews were also granted equal citizenship rights for the first time.

The huge copper candelabrum at the Portuguese-Israelite Synagogue.

Site of atrocities

Sadly, Jonas Daniël Meijerplein is today associated more with the annihilation of most of the city's Jews during World War II. Following the German invasion in May 1940, anti-Jewish measures had been introduced only gradually. The stakes were raised in early February 1941 when the Germans ordered the Jew-

BELOW: Jewish Historical Museum.

The statue of Anne Frank stands in memory of the city's Jewish victims of World War II.

BELOW: St Antoniesbreestraat and Zuiderkerk.

ish Council to be set up, supposedly to maintain order among the Jewish people. Following a disturbance on 19 February, the German chief of police decided to make an example and on 22 and 23 February, 425 young Jewish men were forcibly arrested, herded together and taken away in trucks.

What happened on this square sparked off the first organised Dutch resistance against the German Occupation. In the face of further round-ups by the Germans the following day, the communists called for a general protest strike. The dockworkers were among the first to respond and the strike spread through Amsterdam, only to be broken up violently the following day. The bulky bronze statue of *De Dokwerkers* (The Dockworkers) on Jonas Daniël Meijerplein, unveiled in 1952, is one of Amsterdam's most important war memorials and commemorates the February strike.

The strike merely delayed the inevitable. German policy against the Jews gathered pace in 1942. In January of that year, Jews from Zaandam were the first to be moved from their home town and Amsterdam was used as the collection point. The Nazis used the Jewish Council (whose headquarters were at No. 58 Nieuwe Keizersgracht) to coordinate the deportations. They evaded resistance by claiming that the deportees were being sent to work in German factories.

In Remembrance

A little further down Plantage Middenlaan is another sad reminder of World War II. The façade of the **Hollandse Schouwburg ❼** has been preserved not for architectural reasons but as a memorial. In September 1942, this theatre was appropriated by the Germans as an assembly point for Jews prior to deportation. Their length of stay varied but their route out was always the same: by train to

A VOICE IN THE DARK

The extent to which the Jewish Council contributed to the destruction of Dutch Jews is still intensely controversial. Did the Jewish Council know what would really happen to the Jews when they were taken east? Was it effectively collaborating? Could the Jewish Council have taken any other course of action under the circumstances?

One Dutch Jew, L.E. Visser, was of a clear mind on the matter. In 1939, Visser was President of the Supreme Court in the Netherlands but was dismissed the following year. He spent the final two years of his life in defiance of the Germans. He worked for the illegal underground newspaper *Het Parool*, protested against the implementation of separate Jewish education and refused to wear the yellow Star of David that the Nazis demanded all Jews sew on to their clothes. Visser also spoke out against the Jewish Council, saying: "I am quite overcome by the humiliation which you, who are well aware of the historical importance of these measures, have brought about." A few days later he died of natural causes.

Today, Visser's bravery and outspokenness have been commemorated in the former Jewish quarter for posterity – Mr Visserplein is the name of the junction next to the Jewish Historical Museum.

Map on page 207

Westerbork, the transit point for the death camps of Auschwitz and Sobibor. Through the doorway of this building is a quiet courtyard and a stark obelisk that stands as a monument to the 104,000 Dutch Jews killed by the Nazis. The building opposite is today a house for single mothers and their children; during the occupation, it housed a crèche which was used for the children and babies of those who were being kept in the Hollandse Schouwburg awaiting deportation. Almost next to this building used to be the Reformed Church Teacher Training College, which helped in the rescue of Jewish children. The building still exists and bears a plaque dedicated to all those who helped in the rescues.

The Jodenbuurt and Plantage, having been witness to so much suffering, now have a new museum that gives a well-balanced account of the struggles and achievements of the Dutch resistance movement during World War II. The **Verzetsmuseum ❽** (Resistance Museum), opened in May 1999 (Plantage Kerklaan 61; tel: 620 2535; open Tues–Fri 10am–5pm, Sat–Sun noon–5pm; entrance fee, except 5 May). It is difficult to imagine the circumstances in which the resistance came into being, especially when one considers that at the outbreak of war Dutch society was made up of four main persuasions: Catholics, Protestants, liberals and socialists – subcultures that were not necessarily trusting of each other. The permanent exhibition conveys chronologically the inevitable social changes and developments of a small country living under progressively worsening conditions imposed not only by an occupying enemy, but also by the horrors of an extreme winter which led to starvation in many areas. Of particular interest are the many interactive exhibits, such as a radio that one can tune in, desk drawers that one can open to read documents or the doorbell of a "safe house". Strolling through these corridors of time one gets not only an insight into

BELOW: the Hortus Botanicus.

Map on page 207

the dangerous underworld of the resistance but also an appreciation of the social pressures and why many people ended up collaborating with the Germans.

The museum's foyer also houses temporary exhibits reflecting present-day resistance to human injustice. Education is one of the museum's key objectives and its many facilities include a documentation and study room. All exhibits are in English and Dutch and a guided tour is available on request.

The 19th-century Wertheim Park, named after a leading Jewish banker, became the focus of much attention in 1993 when a **Holocaust Memorial** ❾ commemorating Jewish war victims and entitled *"Auschwitz Nooit Meer"* ("Auschwitz – Never Again") was unveiled. When the monument, designed by Dutch writer and sculptor Jan Wolkers, was vandalised, suspicion fell immediately upon neo-Nazis and there was public outrage. At the close of enquiries, however, it was found that one of the craftsmen involved, fearing failure within his trade, was the vandal and subsequently committed suicide. Nevertheless it is an impressive piece of work, with a reminder in Dutch and English listing the hideous atrocities the Jewish community suffered.

Parks and gardens

The **Hortus Botanicus** ❿ (Plantage Middenlaan 2a; tel: 625 9021; open daily; entrance fee) is one of the oldest botanical gardens in the world, founded in 1638 as a nursery for apothecaries' healing plants. It moved to its current location in 1682 and now houses more than 8,000 different plants, with more arriving daily. Most impressive of all is the three-climate greenhouse completed in 1993: under its immense glass roof one can stroll through a subtropical section, a desert section and a tropical section, with a gallery that can take you some 5 metres (16 ft) high through the "jungle". Of historical interest are the plants that were brought to the Netherlands by the Dutch East India Company in the 17th and 18th centuries. The Orangery, constructed in 1870, has been converted into an airy café where one can order simple meals and snacks – in the summer one may enjoy tea on the terrace under the pleasant scent of citrus trees.

BELOW: wolves at the Artis Zoological Gardens.

The **Natura, Artis Magistra (Artis Zoological Gardens)** ⓫ were founded in 1838 and contain the oldest zoo in the Netherlands (Plantage Kerklaan 38–40; tel: 523 3400; open daily; entrance fee). As well as the zoo, there is a planetarium, a geological museum, a zoological museum and tropical greenhouses. Its animals include lions, tigers, gorillas, polar bears and seals plus a reptile house, an aviary, magnificent aquariums and a nocturnal house.

In 1998 a multimillion-euro three-phase expansion programme was begun, in addition to refurbishment of several areas within the existing 10 hectares (25 acres) of the gardens. Phase one of this expansion, the African Savannah, was opened in June 1999. In keeping with the zoo's fanaticism for authenticity, this is a micro-plain, home to zebras, wildebeests, ostriches and other savannah birds – the only things to remind you that you're in Amsterdam are the surrounding 18th-century warehouses. There is also a self-service restaurant with a "kiddies corner". ❏

Jews in Amsterdam

Jews first settled in the Netherlands in large numbers in the early 17th century. The 1579 Treaty of Utrecht, under which the northern provinces of the Netherlands joined forces against the Spanish, stipulated that no one should be persecuted for their religious beliefs. The provinces were reacting to Spain's repression of Protestantism *(see page 26)* and did not necessarily have the Jews in mind, but nevertheless the new republic seemed to offer Jews a freedom that they did not enjoy elsewhere in Europe.

The first Jews to settle in Amsterdam were Marranos – Sephardic Jews from Spain and Portugal who had been forced to convert to Christianity. By the middle of the 17th century the pattern had changed. Most of the Jews coming to settle in Amsterdam were Ashkenazic – Jews of German or Polish origin.

Amsterdam's tolerance of its Jewish immigrants was not unbounded. In 1598 the city magistrates determined that the Portuguese merchants could purchase citizenship providing that they did not worship openly. A more serious restriction, dating from 1632, prohibited Jews from becoming members of the guilds. Since nearly all trades were run by guilds, the Jews were in effect excluded from most occupations. They were forced to pursue guild-free activities: retail trading; banking; diamond processing; sugar refining; silk manufacture; tobacco twisting and printing *(see page 28)*. Jews were also forbidden to own shops and another measure, passed in 1661, decreed that they should not attempt to convert Christians or have relations with Christian women.

It is hardly surprising, therefore, that Jews settled in the city's poorest neighbourhoods. In 1795, after two centuries of Jewish immigration, 74 percent of Sephardic Jews and 87 percent of Ashkenazic Jews received poor relief. A grain crisis in 1771 led to an increase in mortality in Amsterdam of 30 percent; for Jews the increase was 100 percent.

But 1796 was a year of emancipation for the Jews: with the disappearance of the guilds all occupations were open to them; they were free to settle anywhere; and they obtained the right to vote. As a result, the Jewish community grew substantially in the 19th century but the "boundaries" of the city's Jewish quarter had been established: St Antoniesbreestraat, Jodenbreestraat and east of the Oude Schans canal and Zwanenburgwal, especially the Uilenburgergracht and Waterlooplein. When the Grachtengordel was completed, wealthier Jews moved to the new canals – Herengracht, Keizersgracht and Prinsengracht. By the end of the century, Plantage Middenlaan was an affluent extension of the quarter. By the early 20th century, about 60,000 Jews were living here – more than half the total number of Jews in the country. At the outbreak of World War II that number had grown to 80,000.

By the end of the war there were only 5,000 survivors and Jodenbuurt was in ruins *(see page 53)*. It was one of the darkest eras in the city's history. ❏

RIGHT: *The Dockworker* memorial statue on Jonas Daniël Meijerplein.

AMSTERDAM HARBOUR

Amsterdam grew up around its maritime prowess and, although one of the least-visited areas of the city, the harbour gives a fascinating historical insight into this seafaring nation

Map on page 218

Amsterdam has always been a port and in the late 16th and early 17th centuries the city's phenomenal growth was built on its role as a mighty centre for shipping and world trade. Dutch maritime supremacy was founded on the fishing industry; a Dutchman discovered a recipe for curing fish and pickled herring which then became an important commodity. Dutch sailors subsequently opened up scores of new routes to the Far East and the Americas, and the port of Amsterdam became the biggest and busiest in the world. In 1824 the North Holland canal was opened, dug through the entire length of the province of North Holland to the naval base at Den Helder. In 1876 the North Sea canal followed. The latter, 270 metres (887 ft) wide, 14 metres (45 ft) deep and 16 km (10 miles) long, is connected to the sea via the locks of IJmuiden.

The port and its associated activities of shipbuilding and repair is still an important factor in the city's economy, not only providing jobs but making a significant contribution to the gross city product as well.

Docklands tour

The story of Amsterdam's role as a port can still be traced even if the surviving maritime sites – with the notable exception of the Maritime Museum – hardly count as scenic corners of Amsterdam; Prins Hendrikkade, the Eastern Docks and Oostenburgstraat can look rather forlorn. No matter. Amsterdam's wealth came in on boats and you cannot hope to understand what made this city tick without knowing a little more about its nautical past.

A maritime tour proper of Amsterdam should start with the **Schreierstoren ❶**, situated on Prins Hendrikkade and just a few minutes away from Centraal Station. This is the oldest tower surviving in Amsterdam and was built in 1482 as part of the city walls. The Schreierstoren ("weeper's tower") got its name from sailors' wives and lovers who would learn of the death of their partners when their ship returned.

The Schreierstoren, today a shop selling maps and books, gives three clues to Amsterdam's nautical past. A tablet from Greenwich Village Historic Society commemorates Henry Hudson's departure from here in 1609, the beginning of a long voyage to the harbour of New York and the eponymous Hudson River. Another tablet, dating from 1569, shows a weeping woman and departing ships. Yet another was placed in 1945 and reads: *Eerste schipvaart naar Oostindi' 1595* (First voyage to the East Indies, 1595).

While the Schreierstoren was once part of the city walls, an important area known as the Lastage, the site of the earliest shipbuilding yards, remained outside these fortifications. You can pinpoint this locality

PRECEDING PAGES:
ship in Amsterdam Harbour.
LEFT: Dutch Maritime Museum.
BELOW: Oude Schans canal and Montelbaanstoren.

Schreierstoren is the oldest tower in Amsterdam, dating from 1482.

BELOW: the NEMO Science and Technology Centre.

by finding the **Montelbaanstoren** on Oude Schans. This tower was constructed in 1512 as a fortification to protect the Lastage. The decorative spire was added in 1606 by Hendrick de Keyser, the architect responsible for many of Amsterdam's other pinnacles.

Science and history

Once a busy harbourside, Prins Hendrikkade is today a major road taking traffic in and out of Amsterdam via the IJ Tunnel. Unattractive as it may sound to the pedestrian, a stroll to the entrance of the IJ Tunnel is well worth the effort. Above the tunnel's entrance is a giant patina-sheathed building which, from the north, has the appearance of a large ship's bows. From Prins Hendrikkade one may ascend the roof of this building – having reached the top you will be standing on a terrace offering a panoramic view over the Oosterdok (Eastern Dock) and the IJ. From this point you can see most of the places mentioned in this chapter as well as shipping, Rhine barges and local harbour traffic.

The building is the **NEMO Science and Technology Centre ❷** (Oosterdok 2; tel: 0900 919 1100; open Tues–Sun; daily during school holidays; entrance fee), designed by the famous architect Renzo Piano and opened in June 1997. Amsterdam may be justifiably proud of this relatively recent project. This science museum, whose motto is "A world wherein you are the greatest miracle" certainly lives up to its promise. Nearly all the exhibits are interactive, from refilling radio-controlled model oil tankers to conducting light and sound experiments and carrying out your own investigation in a laboratory. The visitor creates his or her own voyage of discovery in six departments on four floors. There are guided tours and all exhibits are in English; very child-friendly.

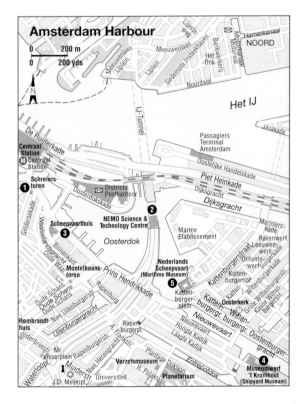

Walking between Prins Hendrikkade and the NEMO Centre, one can hardly miss the collection of vintage vessels along the quayside: they are all registered as floating monuments and all lovingly restored with plaques on the quay detailing the history and working life of each boat.

Scheepvaarthuis ❸ (literally "ship voyage house") is an appropriate name for the building that overlooks Amsterdam's Oosterdok even if it doesn't date from the city's seagoing heyday. It was constructed in 1915 and was designed by Van der Mey, one of the architects associated with the Amsterdam School of architecture that flourished in the early part of the 20th century *(see page 113)*. Internally and externally the building's motifs and decorations recount Amsterdam's maritime history in delightful detail, with ships, whales and mermaids ornamenting the façade and railings that ripple like the sea waves.

Admiral Michiel Adriaensz de Ruyter, the city's most famous nautical son and a man credited with making the Dutch fleet a strong enough force to withstand British and French attempts to destroy it, once lived at No. 131 Prins Hendrikkade. A frieze over the front door commemorates him.

New uses

There is no shortage of buildings surviving from the days when Amsterdam was a centre of world commerce. A walk along the Entrepotdok reveals a line of warehouses, recently converted into flats, built by the East Indies Company.

At the western end, the grand gateway emblazoned with the words "Entrepotdok" looks sadly out of place surrounded by the seedy bars and cafés of Kadijksplein. But go through the gate and walk along the waterside and you will be able to picture just how many shiploads of eastern promise at one time used these

Map on page 218

BELOW: the Nederlands Scheepvaart (Maritime) Museum.

waterways. Today these buildings have been turned into stylish offices and flats. Tucked between them are quiet bars that provide welcome ports of call as you retrace the footprints of Amsterdam's seafaring heritage.

Maritime museums

Just over halfway along Hoogte Kadijk, which runs parallel with the Entrepotdok, the Kromhout Shipyard, one of 30 shipyards that were established here by the end of the 17th century, still survives.

Gable stones in the harbour area graphically illustrate the maritime heritage.

The name Kromhout was first mentioned in 1757 in relation to a forge located on the site of the present shipyard. A shipwright, Doede Jansen Kromhout, developed the site. In the 19th century a new owner, Daniel Goedkoop, equipped the yard for building iron ships. His son turned it into one of the most modern shipyards of the area. One of his investments, an iron canopy over the slipway, stands today and is a protected monument.

Moves to preserve the shipyard for the future were first made in 1970 and later gained the support of the Netherlands Maritime Museum. The Kromhout shipyard was also subsequently placed on Amsterdam's list of protected monuments. Still an operating shipyard, it now restores and repairs historic vessels.

BELOW: boats moored on the city's canals.

There is also a modest museum, the **Museumwerf't Kromhout** ❹ (Kromhout Shipyard Museum; tel: 627 6777; open Tues 10am–3pm; entrance fee). The exhibits mostly consist of old ships' engines and pumps, along with models of old steamers, which really only appeal to people with a penchant for marine engineering; and some of the framed engravings on display, depicting the Nieuwe Vaart as a busy artery of floating repair platforms and tall ships at anchor, serve only to emphasise that the docks have long been dead.

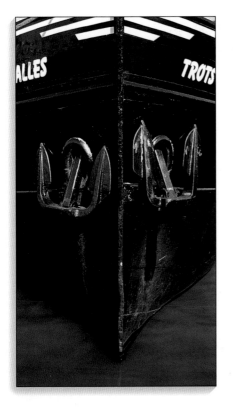

THE MARITIME QUARTER

From the Singel canal, cross a bridge sandwiched by lock gates, which used to separate the city from the sea. Partake in the delights of a herring sold on the prize-winning stall on the bridge. On the other side of the bridge, on a pedestal, is a ship's propeller; this marks the beginning of the "Scheepvaart Buurt" or Maritime Quarter. To the right a brick building forms the Amsterdam School of Architecture, formerly a school for barge skippers' children. Continuing along the Haarlemmerstraat you'll pass a ship's winch embedded in the pavement and, on the left, the Dutch West Indies House *(see page 157)*. Back on the Haarlemmerstraat at No. 105 is Café Prinsesse-Bar, an archetypal "brown café". The next bridge has a view of the Westerkerk *(see page 162)*. Crossing this bridge brings you to Haarlemmerdijk. If you peer down streets on the left you will notice a gradient reminding you that you're walking on top of an old dyke that used to face the sea. Take a right into Oranjestraat, cross a main road, pass under a railway arch and you're on Bickers-gracht, one of the city's gems. At the end of Bickersgracht is a children's farm where city kids get acquainted with nature. Halfway down, cross a bridge to Prinseneiland, a serene area of 17th-century warehouses and boatyards.

There are plans to create a new permanent exhibition here that will give a comprehensive picture of shipbuilding on the islands and of the people who lived here. The sad fact is that the Kromhout Shipyard currently lacks the money to do justice to the heritage of this sleepy corner of Amsterdam. At present the Kromhout Shipyard is really for aficionados only.

By contrast, the **Nederlands Scheepvaart (Maritime) Museum ⑤** (Kattenburgerplein 1; tel: 523 2222; open Tues–Sun, daily during school holidays; entrance fee) is one of Amsterdam's highlights. Even the hardiest of landlubbers will consider an hour or two here well spent. This rich collection occupies Amsterdam's old Zeemagazijn, the arsenal of the Amsterdam Admiralty. From this building, constructed in 1656, sails, ropes, cannons, cutlasses, food and fresh water were supplied to the newly built ships, launched at the adjacent yard, and to the fleet moored in the port.

In the 20th century the Dutch navy moved its facilities and installations to ports with direct access to the North Sea and the Zeemagazijn lost its original function. The building was renovated in the 1970s and a first-class museum was born. Its collection was assembled by the Society for the Netherlands Museum of Maritime History. The models and paintings are nearly all of the same period as the ships and events they represent.

The museum charts a detailed course through all of Amsterdam's and Holland's maritime achievements, starting with the V-shaped timber of a small medieval vessel found in the reclaimed land of the former Zuiderzee and finishing with glimpses into the lives of passengers cruising to South America, the United States, Asia and Australia in the luxurious liners of the early and mid-20th century. Between those two points, the collection provides colourful

Map on page 218

BELOW: decorative art on a canal boat.

Map on page 218

insights into the development of the three-masted ships of the 16th century which opened the way to the uncharted oceans, the many naval wars in which the Dutch fought, and how, in the 17th century, Amsterdam was the world centre of cartography, producing the first sea-atlas.

One of the highlights – particularly for children – is the full-size model of a Dutch East Indiaman, the *Amsterdam*. The ship has a crew of actors dressed in the costume of the day and lies moored along the landing-stage of the museum.

On the water

A walk to the rear of Centraal Station will bring you to the edge of the Het IJ. It has 18 piers with various "partyships", Rhine cruisers, a fine restaurant on Pier No. 10 with a grand view and a small booking office – probably the smallest building in the style of the Amsterdam School. It is also the site of numerous free ferries to **Amsterdam Noord** (North), where you may take a stroll along the Noordhollands Kanaal and take refreshment at the tollhouse.

For a longer trip you could take a ferry to the Java and KNSM islands. These two islands are separated only by a small canal and are crossable by bridges. The KNSM Island was once the domain of the Royal Dutch Steamship Company, but many of the old cargo warehouses were demolished to make way for residential projects and, like the NEMO Centre, there are many wondrous modern buildings to behold. It would be fair to say that the KNSM Island is like a modern architectural museum combining traditional and new elements: names such as Barcelonaplein or Venetië Hof reflect this. When disembarking this ferry it's best to walk along the quay where you get off, thus following the northern aspect; as you proceed you will notice some of the older buildings.

BELOW: an old salt.

When you get to the end there's a good viewpoint that takes in the entrance to the Amsterdam-Rhine canal and the Oranjesluizen, the locks that connect Amsterdam to the IJsselmeer (formerly the Zuiderzee). From here, follow round to the south where there are spacious terraces to enjoy a drink and look out over the barges and docks against the backdrop of residentially converted warehouses on the Zeeburgerkade. If not returning by ferry, a bus back to Centraal Station will take you past old warehouses in various states of repair and restoration, boasting their former trading glories in massive letters: "AFRIKA" or "INDIA".

A new terminal

With the growing size of luxury liners and passenger ships coupled with all the charms of Amsterdam, it has been necessary to build a new passenger terminal (Oostelijke Handelskade 9; tel: 418 6854). This addition to the harbour has room for 2,500 passengers in a building occupying 35,000 sq. metres (377,000 sq. ft). Facilities include a congress hall, boardrooms, restaurants, banks and shops. In addition, water transport to and from the city centre complements the existing bus connections. The terminal's official opening in August 2000 coincided with *Sail Amsterdam*, the city's week-long maritime festival held every five years. ❑

Supreme on the Seas

In 1597, a Dutch expedition reached the East Indies (Indonesia) for the first time, by way of the Cape of Good Hope and the Indian Ocean. Voyaging as far as Australia, they opened up the legendary spice routes to the Far East and began to displace the Spanish and Portuguese as rulers of the waves. The trade in tropical products became one of the largest sources of income for Amsterdam. In 1602, a number of small companies united to form the East Indies Company, based in the city. Shares in the company were traded in the Mercantile Exchange. A West Indies Company was also founded to maintain trade with New Amsterdam (New York) and Brazil. In 1609, when an exchange bank was established, Amsterdam was well on its way to becoming the biggest trade centre in Western Europe.

The main aim of the East Indies Company was to secure a monopoly on the spice trade, and for a long time it succeeded. The company's trading posts eventually became colonies. By 1669 the company owned 150 trading vessels and 40 warships, and employed 10,000 soldiers and 1,000 shipbuilders. The furthest outpost was the Japanese island of Deshima in the Bay of Nagasaki. By 1730 the East Indies Company was the world's largest trading enterprise, even creating its own coinage. Although it lost its leading position after 1750, its influence lasted much longer. The Dutch East Indies empire remained intact until Indonesia gained independence in 1949.

As carriers of trade, the Dutch were dominant in all parts of the world from the start of the 17th century and the Dutch fleet was the largest in existence. Dutch ship design was the envy of, first, Sir Walter Raleigh and later, Samuel Pepys. Czar Peter the Great came to live in Holland to acquire knowledge for a new Russian navy.

There are two sets of man-made islands dating back more than 300 years, off the east and west coasts of the city, projecting into the IJ. Each still bears its original name. The eastern islands – Kattenburg, Wittenburg and Oostenburg – were created to help Holland in the battle for maritime supremacy against Great Britain, which started around 1650. Constructed to provide building space for warships, these islands were lined with harbours and bisected with wide canals. Consecrated in 1670, the Oosterkerk (East Church) stands near the old island harbour.

The three western islands – Realeneiland, Bickerseiland and Prinseneiland – were also constructed for shipbuilding. The shipyards profited from the East Indies Company's policy of granting trading licences to companies that used Dutch ships. The islands were also used for storing inflammables away from the city centre.

Warehouses are today the most visible legacy of this maritime explosion. Many of these buildings have been converted into chic apartments. Unimproved warehouses, now scarce, are favoured by artists because of their space and character. ❑

RIGHT: sign at the front of the Kromhout Shipyard Museum.

GREEN CITY: THE PARKS OF AMSTERDAM

Every city has parks that its inhabitants and its visitors can enjoy, but few have the expanse and variety offered by Amsterdam's green spaces

Amsterdammers love their green spaces, and unlike many city dwellers around the world, make a great deal of effort to enjoy them at every opportunity afforded by time restraints and climate. From the wooded forests of Amsterdamse Bos, ideal for walking, to the duck ponds of Sarphatipark and the southern Amstelpark, a favourite with flower lovers, the city's natural areas offer something for everyone.

VONDELPARK

The most popular venue, however, is undoubtedly the Vondelpark *(see page 232)*. Named after the poet and dramatist Joost van den Vondel (1587–1679), it is the city's oldest municipal park. The park was designed in 1865–77 in the English style by two landscape architects who created water-ways, woody paths and bridges from one side of the park to the other. The bandstand has been the site of open-air summer concerts since 1974. The Film Museum presents old and new films throughout the year and its Café Vertigo attracts crowds to its terrace in warm weather.

Sunday remains the busiest day throughout the year, with joggers, skaters, cyclists, dog-walkers and vendors selling handicrafts and T-shirts.

▽ **WATER PARK**
The Bosbaan in the Amsterdamse Bos is the city's most popular place for boating and canoeing.

◁ **HIPPIE LEGACY**
Sometimes parks still feel like the 1960s with musicians playing and girls in long skirts. The smell in the air is not incense.

IN PRAISE OF NATURE

Amsterdammers love the outdoors and once there are signs of spring, they take to the streets, specifically to café terraces where they stretch out in their chairs, heads turned upward in praise of the sun. In May and June when it gets dark after 11pm, there is a special feeling of endless summer in the air.

Since Amsterdammers ride their bikes throughout the year, they seek other forms of recreation in the city. In-line skating has become extremely popular in recent years, with the Vondelpark now adding skaters to its active populace of runners, dog-walkers and sunbathers. Once a month on Friday evening, streets in the city are blocked off to car traffic for about two hours for a kind of skater's marathon. This is now attracting several thousand enthusiasts, some of whom dress in outrageous costumes for the event.

Amsterdam's canals continue to be a popular playground for locals. Many own small boats, which can often be docked in front of their houses. Friends invite friends, who bring a picnic and various liquid refreshments, and the Amsterdam canals become the site of festive boat excursions.

◁ **FLOWER POWER**
Outside the city, Keukenhof, near Leiden, is a popular place for strolls among the blooming tulips.

△ **SUMMER IN THE CITY**
In summer the city's parks are a haven for sunbathers, cyclists, skaters, joggers and families.

◁ **TROPICAL ENCLAVE**
The Hortus Botanicus gardens are 350 years old and have more than 6,000 plant species to admire.

△ **CROWD PULLERS**
No open space would be complete without the street entertainers showing off their skills.

AROUND THE CENTRE

Map
on page
230

*If you venture by foot, tram or bus just outside the city centre,
you will experience a very different Amsterdam, with characterful
neighbourhoods and peaceful green expanses*

Like many major cities around the world, the growth in population during the 19th century forced Amsterdam to expand its old boundaries and spread further south. As a result of these expansions, if you head just a short distance outside the city centre, there are numerous neighbourhoods worthy of discovery – as well as two wonderful parks which offer a welcome green refuge from the busy sightseeing trail of museums and shops that make up the majority of the central city.

Summer playground

Once you're outside the semicircle traced by Singelgracht you are already on your way into Amsterdam's suburbs. One of the best places to visit outside the city centre, however, is further afield. The **Amsterdamse Bos ❶**, on the city's southern fringes, is a great splash of green that would be the envy of many another modern European city.

The decision to turn a group of polders on the city's southern edge into a park was made by the Amsterdam City Council in November 1928. A year previously, the world had seen Black Monday and was adjusting to the idea of mass unemployment. When work on the Amsterdamse Bos began, it provided welcome jobs to many of the men who had become unemployed. It was all too literally a man-made landscape – the work was done not by machine but by men and horses. Yet the Amsterdamse Bos sprang to life quickly; the first tree was planted in 1936 and in 1937 the Bosbaan (rowing course) was officially declared open by Queen Wilhelmina.

To enable the trees to put down strong roots, the subsoil water level had to be lowered to 1.5 metres (5 ft) below the surface. This was achieved with thousands of porous pipes placed at intervals of between 15–25 metres (50–80 ft). Laid end to end, all these pipes would stretch a distance of nearly 300 km (200 miles). The result of this work was the creation of an 800-hectare (2,000-acre) park that draws people in their thousands all year round. With around 48 km (30 miles) of cycle paths and close to 160 km (100 miles) of footpaths, there is room for everybody.

There is also plenty to do and see. The rowing course, which exceeds the international competition length of 2,000 metres (6,560 ft), also provides a venue for canoe, speedboat and swimming races. There's a 1,500-seat open-air theatre, a farm, stables, playgrounds, a camp site, pancake house, wildlife preserve, a small ferry to take visitors across the lake, and even an artificial hill to provide a focus to the landscape. The **Bosmuseum** (Forest Park Museum) reels off the statistics of its flora and fauna with pride:

PRECEDING PAGES:
Amsterdam School
architecture at
Hembrugstraat.
LEFT: Albert
Cuypmarkt.
BELOW: peaceful
Amsterdamse Bos.

hundreds of species of birds, trees, herbs and fungi (56 Koenenkade; tel: 643 1414; open daily; free). The Amsterdamse Bos is also home to more than 700 different species of beetle.

In the summer, a novel way of getting to the Amsterdamse Bos is by catching an old-style tram from Haarlemmermeerstation, just north of the **Olympisch Stadion** (Olympic Stadium). The service is provided by the Electrische Museum Tramlijn (Electric Tramline Museum), which has collected and renovated antique trams from around Europe. Otherwise, it is a half-hour ride from Centraal Station with buses 170, 171, or 172 to the Bosbaan stop.

Shopping and tenements

Meanwhile, back in town, another place that pulls the crowds is **Albert Cuypmarkt ❷**, Amsterdam's busiest outdoor market, which attracts some 20,000 people on weekdays. One estimate puts the number of visitors on any Saturday at 50,000 – more than six per cent of Amsterdam's population. Albert Cuypstraat takes its name from an important 17th-century Dutch landscape painter (some of whose works can be seen in the Rijksmuseum). The market starts at Ferdinand Bolstraat and stretches east to Van Woustraat. If you walk through this market, ponder the fact that it is the centre of Amsterdam's first suburb, an area that sprang up in the late 19th century. And watch your handbag and wallet – it is a notorious haunt of petty thieves. Otherwise, do what the locals do and buy a herring to nibble on while you stroll.

Development beyond the Singelgracht had begun around 1870. The city council laid out the street plan but the construction of the houses themselves was in private hands and they were often of low quality. This new working-class neigh-

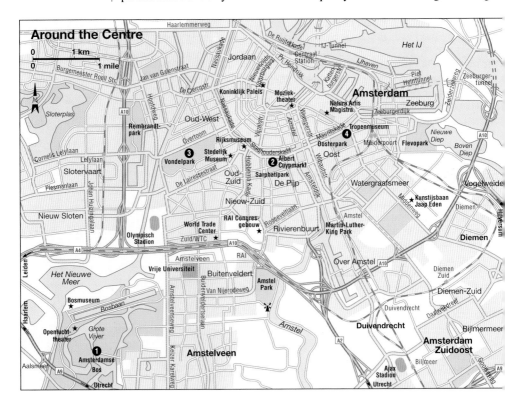

Around the Centre

bourhood, around Gerard Doustraat, Govert Flinckstraat and Albert Cuypstraat, was dubbed "De Pijp" ("The Pipe") after the long, narrow streets of three- and four-storey tenements. Albert Cuypmarkt originated soon after the first streets of "De Pijp" had been built. It gained momentum in 1905 when a local law allowed a greater range of goods, including livestock, to be sold.

The arrival of industry to Amsterdam in the 19th century brought with it thousands of immigrant workers, many of whom settled in "De Pijp". A second wave of foreign workers, after World War II, has widened the variety of ethnic groups represented here *(see page 84)*. Turkish and Surinamese restaurants point to the countries of origin of some of the inhabitants. The fortunes of Albert Cuypmarkt wavered in the early years but today it is a long, crowded, noisy and fascinating market. If you want to rub shoulders with a sizeable proportion of Amsterdam's population, this is the place to come.

These days the area is slowly becoming gentrified and locals are concerned about preserving its old-fashioned charm. Many new restaurants have opened in the past few years: the popular Ondeugd and the high-tech Zento Sushi Bar with its rotating, self-service counter, along the Albert Cuypstraat heading away from the market are among the several delicious ethnic "dives" featuring good food at low prices in no-frills settings. You can also choose from Kurdistan, Vietnamese, Chinese or Indian kitchens. Just across the road along Frans Halsstraat are two popular cafés, Carel's at No. 78 and Quinto at No. 42, which have a loyal crowd who come for their reasonably priced changing menu featuring many international dishes.

Cutting edge

Amsterdam can justifiably claim to be the "City of Diamonds" – diamonds have been processed here for more than four centuries. The "Cullinan" diamond, the world's largest, was cut in Amsterdam in 1908 by the Asscher company.

The Amsterdam diamond industry has always been dominated by Jewish families. When this business was new to Amsterdam, it was not governed by any of the guild regulations that would have disqualified Jews from becoming involved *(see page 28)*. It has been calculated that in 1748 around 600 of these prominent families earned their living from diamond processing. The great boom came during the Kaapse Tijd (Cape Age) when, around 1870, the first raw diamonds began to arrive from South Africa. The resulting surge in the supply of diamonds broke the monopoly of the Diamond Cutting and Polishing Society. Soon there were more than 3,000 people working with diamonds in Amsterdam.

Several prominent diamond workshops and stores have an open-door policy; they allow you to see diamonds in the raw and learn something of how the cutting industry took root here. One of these, **A. Van Moppes & Zoon**, is conveniently located at Nos 2–6 Albert Cuypstraat (tel: 676 1242). The Van Moppes firm was established on Plantage Middenlaan soon after the Kaapse Tijd, by David Levie van Moppes, the son of a diamond worker. Having taken refuge in

Map on page 230

Amsterdam's diamond industry has been an important part of the economy for centuries.

BELOW: relaxing in the Vondelpark.

Brazil during World War II, the Van Moppes family returned to Amsterdam and moved into their current premises at Albert Cuypstraat.

This building had previously been used by the Germans as part of their bid to get a slice of the lucrative world diamond industry. They assumed that the conquest of Britain would mean that the supply of South African diamonds would be theirs for the taking. In 1940 they founded a training school that would groom their own diamond cutters and polishers – Jewish skills were deemed unsuitable. Britain was not conquered, of course, and German entry into the industry failed. The Van Moppes' business meanwhile has flourished.

Park life

The Vondelpark has a carefree, family atmosphere.

If you have grown weary of museum exhibitions and overpriced boutiques, then it is time to take refuge in the green environs of the **Vondelpark ❸**, the oldest of Amsterdam's municipal parks. There is an entrance just a short walk up Van Baerlestraat. Opened in 1865, the park's namesake is the 17th-century playwright Joost van den Vondel; though German-born, he settled in the area and is sometimes referred to as the Shakespeare of the Netherlands.

Vondelpark's architects, J.D. and L.P. Zocher, made a deliberate move away from the symmetrical Dutch garden style when they drew up their plans in the 19th century and aimed instead for a romantic English garden. The park was built originally as a private park to accommodate the wealthy families who lived in the surrounding environs of Amsterdam Zuid (South Amsterdam). In the 1960s and '70s, it was the hippie happening place. These days it attracts an agreeable mix of locals and tourists who jog, stroll, picnic, make music or sunbathe. In winter, if the ponds freeze over, there is also the possibility of ice skating.

BELOW: summer in the city.

For such a relatively small city as Amsterdam, Vondelpark is a sizeable stretch of ponds, lawns, woods and even tennis courts, equivalent in length to the distance between Centraal Station and Leidseplein. A focal point is the striking form of Het Ronde Blauwe Theehuis (The Round Blue Tea House). The **Nederlands Filmmuseum**, on the northeast corner, is a resource centre that also shows a range of specialised films and documentaries (tel: 589 1400; box office open daily; entrance fee for screenings). It is also the site of a popular restaurant and summer terrace, Café Vertigo. During the summer, the Vondelpark hosts an open-air series of daily concerts, theatre, comedy, puppet shows and dance performances in a small amphitheatre in the middle of the park.

Map on page 230

Social architecture

If "De Pijp" shows Amsterdam pushing back its boundaries with little concern for visual style, elsewhere in the suburbs – especially in the Nieuw Zuid – there are strong examples of a much more inspirational kind of architecture. One of the best known of the city's architectural movements was the Amsterdam School, which emerged in the early part of the 20th century. The term was used for a group of socialist architects who developed a radically new style of building *(see page 113)*.

The work of the Amsterdam School has been described as "solid but rather playful housing... a kind of domestic sculpture in brick". Even though the style lasted for just a decade it has become a well-known ingredient in Amsterdam's street scene. An important piece of legislation in 1901, which introduced municipal subsidies into the construction of working-class housing, paved the way for more buildings in the distinctive style of the Amsterdam School.

BELOW: hippie traditions are still going strong in the Vondelpark.

Flowers and Dutch-style statuettes are just some of the finds at Albert Cuypmarkt.

BELOW: Albert Cuypmarkt.

If you want to pursue suburban examples, go to **P.L. Takstraat**, a few minutes' walk south of Sarphatipark, to see apartment blocks designed by architect P.L. Kramer. Nearby, on **Henriëtte Ronnerplein** to the east, and on **Thérèse Schwartzeplein** to the west, are good examples of the work of M. De Klerk, another accomplished Amsterdam School architect.

The very best examples of Amsterdam School architecture lie elsewhere in the city. The exuberant Scheepvaarthuis on Prins Hendrikkade was not only the building that launched the style, it is also one of its best expressions, decorated with lively, imaginative and humorous seafaring motifs *(see page 219)*. Further out, the northwestern suburb of **Spaarndammerbuurt** is entirely a creation of Amsterdam School architects, working here from 1914 to 1923. The colourful buildings are modernistic and yet hark back to the medieval *hofjes* with their intimate courtyards. The architects who worked here, De Klerk, Maard, Walenkamp and De Baozel, designed every last detail, even down to the letterboxes and the tiling. The neighbourhood post office is a good example.

Colonial heritage

You will notice throughout the city that certain neighbourhoods have streets with names which are related to one another. In the Jordaan, streets are named after flowers. Around Museumplein heading south there are streets named after painters and composers. However, moving back across town just southeast of the Plantage, there is another block of streets with evocative names. Madurasstraat, Javastraat, Celebesstraat and many others recall the former Dutch colonies. The Dutch Empire included most of modern Indonesia, and at times ruled territories in Africa, India, Australia and South America.

Just a few minutes' walk due east from the Plantage Middenlaan is the **Tropen-museum ❹** which started life in the early 20th century as the Dutch Colonial Institute (2 Linnaeusstraat; tel: 568 8200; open daily; entrance fee). At that time it was unashamedly a celebration of imperialism, but all that changed during the 1970s when the museum was carefully sanitised. Today it shows a more liberal face as a showcase for the lifestyles, as well as some of the problems, found today in many of the world's developing countries.

It is housed in a palatial 19th-century building, yet once inside you encounter a thoroughly modern and often provocative museum, one in which you can lose yourself for hours, After entering a magnificent hall with a high glazed dome, you will discover on the main floor and surrounding galleries some 10 separate exhibitions depicting daily life in towns and villages in West Asia, North Africa, Southeast Asia and Latin America. These exhibitions have recently undergone renovation and it is easy to become absorbed in the ambience of sights, sounds and scents, as if you have been transported to some exotic Third World location. Other rooms are devoted to themes such as clothing, music, dance and technology. Part of the museum is aimed at children aged from 6 to 12. The so-called Kindermuseum TM Junior attempts to bring the collection to life for kids who would be turned off by dry and dusty displays.

Frequent cultural performances are held in the museum's main hall, such as gamalan music from Indonesia, Japanese drums, fiery salsa or sensual tango sounds from Latin America, or evocative Andean panpipes. Exotic dining is offered in the Souterijn Restaurant on the lower level of the museum, which features a diverse menu of fish, meat or vegetarian dishes from at least 10 countries, and at Ekeko, a café on the main floor of the museum. ❑

Map on page 230

BELOW: rice-planting; a Tropenmuseum frieze.

BEYOND THE CITY

For a change of scenery from the busy city, a day trip offers a completely different ambience: historical towns such as Haarlem or Delft, Dutch cheese centres or traditional windmills

Map on page 240

L ike any major city, **Amsterdam** does not necessarily reflect the nation of which it is a part. The residents of this "cosmopolitan village" take pride in being more free, tolerant, outspoken, outrageous and independent than their Dutch counterparts in other cities, but enthusiasm can begin to wane when one's spirit starts to crave a bit of peace and a respite from dodging trams, taxis and bicycles. There is life beyond Amsterdam, and it is rewarding to discover on many levels: climbing inside a windmill; walking along a historic canal that once inspired the young Rembrandt; or eating pancakes in a pastoral village.

Some of these day trips are served by package coach tours, though you can find your own way, using various forms of transport – bus, train, bicycle or rented car. All the locations in this chapter can be reached by these methods; ask at a VVV office for details *(see page 263)*.

Just beyond Amsterdam, the tourist machine is allowed occasionally to get into top gear as coach-loads of visitors are herded daily to set-piece locations. The most popular places, and the nearest to Amsterdam, lie to the north: Marken, Volendam, Edam and Zaanse Schans. Souvenir gift shops loom large; demonstrations of cheese- and clog-making are *de rigueur*. These places are more soulful in winter when there are fewer tourists and the kitsch level is lower. If you must make one of these excursions, go to Zaanse Schans with its windmills and old houses.

PRECEDING PAGES: Zaanse Schans windmills. **LEFT:** Volendam harbour. **BELOW:** Zaanse Schans.

A step back in time

On the River Zaan, less than half an hour from the centre of Amsterdam, you can appear to travel back in time to the glory of Holland's Golden Age. **Zaanse Schans** ❷ is not an open-air museum but a typical "dyke-village", complete with working windmills, traditional wooden homes, merchants' stone mansions and warehouses.

Its picture-postcard appearance belies the fact that Zaanse Schans was one of the first industrial areas in the world, when windmills not smokestacks formed the skyline. After the invention of the first sawmill in 1592, more than 200 windmills were built on this site, engaged in the production of linseed oil, paint, snuff, paper and mustard. Eight still function today. Beside them stand buildings that were relocated in the 1950s with the aim of preserving a residential quarter typical of the district. Quaint shops are housed in well-preserved, authentic old monuments. You can buy hand-painted skates, timeless pewter objects, wooden toys, Delft pottery and clogs – all made in the traditional way. Each shop and windmill has its own ambience. At the cheese farm you can taste before you buy – and don't leave without a pot of the piquant Zaan mustard, produced in a mill by a family business that

dates back to 1786. There is also an historical museum, clock museum, bakery museum and antique costumier. Along the 8-hectare (20-acre) terrain with its tiny bridges and cobblestoned walkways is a pancake house, a bakery and a Michelin-star restaurant. There is also a *rondvaart* cruise along the waterways.

If you cross the bridge to the other side of the river, the small community of **Koog aan de Zaan** has another group of old-style green-painted houses. Here, the Molenmuseum (Windmill Museum) tells the story of the rise and fall of the Netherlands' windmills. For further information, contact the Zaanse Schans Visitors' Centre (tel: 075 616 8218).

No matter what form of transport one takes to **Ouderkerk-aan-de-Amstel ❸** – boat, bicycle or bus – the village is simply too beautiful to miss. Its scenic land- and waterscapes remain a popular destination for cyclists and boating enthusiasts alike, who travel along pleasant roads and waterways bordered on either side by farms and elegant country estates. Located at the spot where the Bullewijk, a picturesque tributary, joins the Amstel, this romantic village of

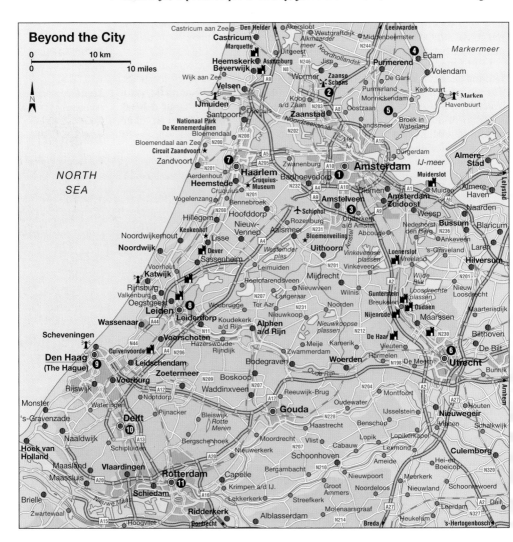

Beyond the City

Map
on page
240

windmills and wooden shoe factories dates back to the 12th century, making it the oldest village in the Amstelland region.

Its name derives from the reformed church which was founded in the area in AD 1000 and which now neighbours a row of houses from 1733. One of these is home to the Oudheidkamer which hosts exhibitions and provides historical information (open Tues–Fri 10am–noon; Sun 1–3pm). Just next door is the Out Bakery, a 100-year-old family-operated business offering a host of delectable confections made from recipes as old as the bakery itself. Across the bridge is the St Urbanus Catholic Church (1867), another stately masterpiece by P.J.H. Cuypers, architect of the Rijksmuseum *(see page 185)* and Centraal Station *(see page 135)*. The village's churches can be viewed by appointment only.

Established in 1616, the Portuguese Jewish Beth Haim cemetery is well worth a visit. It has served as a final resting place for some of Amsterdam's most prominent citizens, including the parents of philosopher Baruch Spinoza. It was renovated in 1997 and is renowned for its ornately carved gravestones and lush greenery (open Sun–Fri). Complete the day's outing by a visit to one of the popular restaurants and cafés in the area, such as the Paardenburg, De Oude Smidse, Het Kampje or De Voetangel.

The cheese market at Alkmaar.

Tourist favourites

Within easy reach of Amsterdam there are four villages on or near the IJsselmeer: Edam, Volendam, Monnickendam and the island village of Marken. The northernmost, **Edam ❹**, is less than 24 km (15 miles) from Amsterdam. The distinctive balls of cheese have spread the name of Edam to many parts of the world. With its picturesque canals, narrow bridges and 17th-century exteriors, the small village has done well not to give in to some of the worst excesses of tourism. Edam was at one time a port and shipyard. Although Dutch maritime power faded, the village of Edam lived on. Today the **Kaasmarkt** (cheese market) and the 16th-century Waag (Weigh House) ensure Edam's continuing prosperity.

BELOW: Zaanse Schans waterway.

If cheese alone isn't enough to attract you, a number of historic buildings provide another reason for coming here. The leaning **Speeltoren**, for example, is a remnant of Edam's 15th-century Kleine Kerk. The Grote Kerk (on Kerkstraat) also dates from the 15th century, though what you see today is the result of a reconstruction in 1602 following a fire. In addition you will find 16th-century almshouses belonging to the Beguine sisterhood, the same group associated with Amsterdam's Begijnhof *(see page 133)*. Overlooking the Dam is the Raadhuis (Town Hall), built in 1737 with an elaborate stucco interior. Inside you will find some good antique furniture. For a traditional Dutch treat, stop at the pancake house on the main street.

Volendam could learn much from its neighbour Edam. Once a quiet fishing port, today it is the most commercialised village on the IJsselmeer. A few fishing boats still use the small harbour, but it does not take much to see that Volendam has now put all its money into the tourist trade. No doubt this provides a

more reliable source of income than fishing ever did, but Volendam is still reputed for its fish and there are several good restaurants and herring stands along the harbour which you can choose from. Volendam's next greatest asset is its distinctive local style of costume, especially the winged lace caps of the women. On the seafront there are shops inviting you to dress up in traditional costume so that you can have your picture taken. Volendam is strictly for people who do not mind rubbing shoulders with coach parties.

The boat service from Volendam to **Marken** takes you swiftly away from the crowds. At one time this village did not sit on the edge of the IJsselmeer – it was an offshore island in the Zuiderzee. Before 1957, when a short causeway was built, the only way in and out of the village was by boat. Then there were just 70 families living in Marken, and they enjoyed being isolated from the mainland. Today the population is more than 2,000. Even so, Marken still hasn't lost its insularity and the inhabitants like to keep themselves to themselves. The narrow streets have no name and there are no doorbells or knockers to be seen. One of the concessions to tourism is the Marken Museum, and some of the female inhabitants still wear traditional costume *(klederdracht)* consisting of 10 pieces, including corset, bodice and skirt, with cap and clogs. Marken remains the quietest, prettiest and maybe the most eccentric of the IJsselmeer villages and you can't help feeling that the locals are going to keep it that way.

Monnickendam is equally unspoiled and, with Amsterdam just 13 km (8 miles) away, it makes for an easy day's excursion – a bus departs from opposite St Nicolaaskerk *(see page 136)*. A 15th-century church, a 16th-century bell-tower, a 17th-century weigh house (now a restaurant) and an 18th-century town hall account for just some of this village's charm.

Decorative clogs make popular souvenirs.

BELOW: world-famous Dutch cheese.

Although **Broek in Waterland** ❺ is not on the coach excursion itinerary, it is en route to Edam and makes a nice day trip by bus or bicycle if you take the path across from Centraal Station in Amsterdam Noord (North) via the ferry boat *(see page 222)*. This storybook village lies on a fertile stretch of land on the edge of the IJsselmeer and has brightly coloured gabled houses amid a pastoral landscape of meadows and windmills. There is a cosy pancake house in the village for a cheap, filling and traditionally Dutch meal, as well as a more elegant restaurant.

Map
on page
240

Castles and poets

There are two towns within easy reach of Amsterdam by car or bus (and in summer by boat excursion) to the east. At **Muiden**, you can take a guided tour of the red-brick Muiderslot, a moated castle built by Count Floris V of Holland. Floris was murdered here in 1296 by noblemen who were unimpressed by his efforts to help the common people. The castle as it stands today dates mainly from the 14th century. The interior, however, is a recreation of the castle as it appeared when it was occupied by the poet and historian P.C. Hooft in the first half of the 17th century.

In summer, it is possible to take the boat excursion from Amsterdam which includes admission to the castle as well as a stop at Pampus Island to visit the Stelling van Amsterdam, a fortification which was placed on the UNESCO World Heritage List in 1996 for its exceptional construction, historical importance and authenticity of design. This once-mighty fortification with 45 separate forts was considered the most modern ring of defence works in Europe and protected the Dutch capital against advancing enemies in times gone by.

BELOW: the island village of Marken.

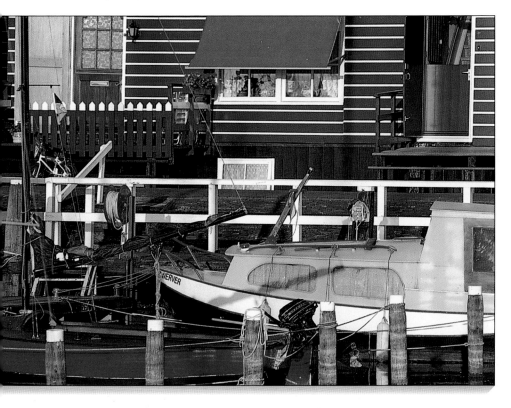

Watching the world go by on the IJsselmeer.

BELOW: Dom cathedral in Utrecht.

The fortification theme continues at **Naarden**, a little further east. This town's impressive double line of ramparts was built at the end of the 17th century. Naarden had already suffered its worst attack a century earlier, when, in 1572, Spanish invaders massacred the town's inhabitants. One bastion of Naarden's fortifications houses the Vestingmuseum (Fortress Museum), complete with underground passages and cannon. Climb the tower of the Grote Kerk and you will be treated to a bird's-eye view of the whole town.

Utrecht

Utrecht ❻ is known for its medieval city centre with its pedestrian wharves alongside the canals, lined with inviting cafés and restaurants. It is also the hub of the Dutch railway network. When arriving by train (just a half-hour ride from Amsterdam), you must first quickly navigate the Hoog Catherijne shopping centre (the Netherlands' largest covered mall) – a maze of shops, cinemas and fast food places, as well as the Vredenburg concert hall, before at last reaching the outdoors. Once you escape this modern monstrosity, then the delights of the city await you. As there are no trams (apart from a service to the suburbs), only buses, walking is the best form of transport in this easily accessible city.

The first canal you reach is a landing where you can take a pleasant hour-long *rondvaart* cruise through the old city. Almost wherever you go, an impressive backdrop is the tower of the **Dom** cathedral, which was founded in 1274. The nave collapsed during a storm in 1674, which has now divided the complex into two buildings. The Dom has the tallest tower in the Netherlands – 112 metres (370 ft) – and a climb to the top gives a good impression of the city.

Utrecht has an historic past. It all began in AD 47 when the Romans built a fortress as part of their reinforcements along the Rhine River. At the end of the 7th century, the Northumbrian missionary Willibrord settled in Utrecht and over the next centuries, under the influence of various bishops, Utrecht gained great ecclesiastical power. The Dom church and tower stand at the centre of a crucifix of four churches: the Pieterskerk, Pauluskerk, Janskerk and Mariakerk, which are all usually open to the public in summer.

The **Dutch Railway Museum** just outside the city centre (Maliebaanstation; open Tues–Sun; entrance fee) displays antique steam locomotives as well as scale models of the latest trains. The **Centraal Museum** (1 Agnietenstraat; open Tues–Sun; entrance fee) in the city centre offers a varied collection of art from the Middle Ages to the present, as well as interesting temporary exhibitions. Heading out of the city centre, for those fascinated by modern architecture is the **Rietveld-Schröderhuis**, which was designed in 1924 by furniture designer and architect Gerrit Rietveld, who also designed the Van Gogh Museum *(see page 193)*. It is the epitome of Jugendstil architecture (50 Prins Hendriklaan; tel: 030 236 2310; open Wed–Sun by appointment only). On Saturday there is a popular market along the Oudegracht (Old Canal), a street lined with shops, pubs and restaurants. Drop in at the Stadskasteel Oudaen at No. 99, a brewery-pub housed in a 13th-century building.

Haarlem

Just 12 minutes west of Amsterdam by train, **Haarlem** is one of the Netherlands' true gems. It is small and manageable, and once you are in the old city at the Grote Markt, a square with elegant Renaissance and Gothic architecture, there are many side streets to discover filled with galleries, antiques shops and cafés.

Walk from the station towards the tower of the imposing **Grote Kerk**. The Grote Kerk, dedicated to St Bavo, is the city's biggest landmark and was constructed during the 15th and 16th centuries. Inside, a magnificent vaulted cedar ceiling is supported by 28 columns. Equally grand is the famous Müller organ, one of the world's largest, with 5,068 pipes, said to have been played by both Joseph Haydn and the 10-year-old prodigy Wolfgang Amadeus Mozart. Frans Hals is buried here, as is Laurens Coster; Haarlemmers claim that Coster was the co-inventor, with Gutenberg, of printing in 1423. At the eastern end of the church, a statue of Coster pays another tribute to the man.

If you turn left on to the Damstraat and walk down to Spaarne along the canal you will come to the **Teylers Museum**, the Netherlands' oldest museum and one of its most eccentric (Spaarne 16; open Tues–Sun; entrance fee). Housed in a number of interconnecting buildings, the museum is based on the collections of Pieter Teyler van der Hulst, a wealthy Haarlem merchant who died in 1778. It boasts a priceless collection of drawings, including works by Michelangelo, Raphael and Rembrandt which are displayed in traditional style in a new wing of the museum. There are also collections of fossils and bones, crystals, coins and a marvellous array of scientific instruments and ingenious gadgets.

Nearby, in a quiet 17th-century *hofje*, is the **Frans Hals Museum** (Groot Heiligland 62; tel: 023 511 5775; open Mon–Sat 11am–5pm, Sun 1–5pm;

Map on page 240

BELOW: Haarlem's Art Deco railway station.

Detail from De Verri-
jzenis *by G. David
(1460–1523) at the
Frans Hals Museum.*

entrance fee). Frans Hals, one of the great Dutch portrait artists, lived most of his life in Haarlem and died here in 1666 *(see page 31)*. He became a special-ist in the group portraits commissioned by bodies such as the civic guards and the militia companies, arranging the subjects so that they each played an equally important role in the finished work. He also painted individual portraits. Many of his works, including *The Laughing Cavalier* in London's Wallace Collection and *The Merry Drinker* in Amsterdam's Rijksmuseum, are world-famous. The museum has the best collection of Hals's work, but other artists are represented here too. In particular, there are a number of important works that reflect the role played by Haarlem in the development of Dutch landscape painting. Refugee Flemish landscape artists came here in the late 16th century when conflict with Spain was at its peak. Before long, Dutch painters came to the city to join them. Haarlem landscape painters include Salomon van Ruysdael and his nephew Jacob van Ruisdael, both of whom are represented in the museum.

If you do visit Haarlem during the summer, bear in mind that you are only a short bus or train ride from **Zandvoort**. After Scheveningen, near The Hague, this is the most popular of the Netherlands' coastal resorts. In the summer months Amsterdammers flock here, but there is space enough for everybody. Behind the 8-km (5-mile) long beach is an extensive area of sand dunes called the Waterleidingduinen. More dunes, known as the Kennemerduinen, are to be found to the north of Zandvoort. This is a great place to hike as well as swim.

Spring garden of Europe

Below: sunbathing at Zandvoort.

The next stop to visit after Haarlem (between March and May) is **Keukenhof** in the village of Lisse (en route to Leiden). Keukenhof (open Mar–May daily;

Map
on page
240

entrance fee) has been a tradition since 1949 when a group of prominent Dutch bulb-growers from the region created an annual exhibition showcasing the variety of the Dutch bulb-flower industry. The spectrum of flowers consists not only of tulips, in all their Technicolor glory, but daffodils, narcissi, hyacinths and other small varieties.

In the Middle Ages, the grounds were part of an estate belonging to Countess Jacoba van Beieren (1401–36), whose three husbands included a Duke of Gloucester and a Dauphin of France. The annual "open house" which now attracts some 900,000 visitors, is located on the site of her former kitchen gardens, thus the name: *keuken* for kitchen and *hof* for garden. There are more than 28 hectares (70 acres) of land, with 16 km (10 miles) of paved paths. The main paths are surrounded by stately beech and oak trees that were planted in 1830. Fountains, canals and streams make a watery chorus, and there are benches everywhere to encourage visitors to sit down and smell the flowers while listening to birdsong. At the season's height, this expanse explodes into a rainbow of colour.

The two-month exhibition enables visitors to enjoy the beauty of the plants during their entire flowering period. Don't be put off by the crowds. Once you get past the car park with the blur of coaches and the multicultural food pavilions at the entrance and proceed past the windmill, you will appreciate the Keukenhof phenomenon, preferably in the later moments of the afternoon. There are special combined tickets, including rail/bus fare and admission, which can be purchased at Amsterdam's Centraal Station If you really love flowers, then put a trip to the flower auction at Aalsmeer on your itinerary *(see page 255)*.

(see page 255)

BELOW:
Haarlem's canals.

Keukenhof is ablaze with colour in the summer months – a must for any flower lover.

BELOW: brilliant colours at Keukenhof's flower show.

Leiden

The rich history and university atmosphere of **Leiden** ❽ make for an interesting visit. Just a half-hour by train from Amsterdam, this medieval city, famous for its cloth-making and brewing industries, joined the Dutch revolt against Spain and was besieged. It eventually rallied after the dykes were broken and the land was flooded, enabling a rescue fleet to sail directly across the countryside and save the city. Rembrandt was born in Leiden as well as other Dutch Masters such as Gerrit Dou, Jan Steen, Gabriel Metsu and Jan van Goyen. This is also where the Pilgrim Fathers formed a community in 1608 seeking refuge from Spain. Leiden University is probably the most prestigious in the Netherlands, with alumni including René Descartes and the 17th-century international lawyer, Hugo Grotius.

When you first walk into town from the station, along the Stationsweg and the Steenstraat, it is hard to imagine that there is so much to see. Visit the **De Valk** windmill on Binnenvestgracht, which today functions as a museum, and the **Museum De Lakenhal** on the Oude Singel, with its fascinating rooms illuminating Leiden's history. The inner city is ringed by two concentric canals, so a stretch of water is never far away and there are many bridges to cross. Make your way to the marketplace where the old and new Rhine meet and where open markets are held on Wednesday and Saturday. Then cross the bridge to the Old Rhine and turn right where you will find the Burcht, Leiden's 12th-century castle, which continually takes visitors by surprise. Have a drink at the Koetshuis in the courtyard. The Botanical Gardens along the Wittesingel are also worth a visit after an afternoon of sightseeing. The Leiden tourist office offers special guided walking tours with recorded commentary.

Map on page 240

The Hague

The combination of culture and history, monumental as well as modern architecture, museums, stately hotels, antiques shops, gastronomic delights and natural beauty give **Den Haag** ❾ (The Hague) an air of sophistication and elegance. The city centre is manageable by foot and public transport – both trams and buses make travelling from the town to the sea quick and comfortable. The Hague is also easily accessible from Leiden and Delft – less than 15 minutes by train and not much longer from Rotterdam and Amsterdam, making day trips a pleasant possibility. The Hague also has the distinction of being the only Dutch city to border two seaside resorts, Scheveningen and Kijkduin, giving it a second reputation as a "seaside city" with miles and miles of sand dunes and woods to explore.

The Hague was originally a hamlet close to the count's castle built in the 13th century. It grew up around a hunting lodge of the Counts of Holland, which gave The Hague its curious Old Dutch name of 's Gravenhage ("Count's hedge"). The village first became important in 1586 when the States Generals of the new Dutch Republic met here, and The Hague gradually assumed the role of political capital, even though officially it was not even a town, since it had no city walls or medieval privileges. Although The Hague was never granted a charter, which it still does not have today, it does boast its own Town Arms which were officially laid down in 1861 and depict a stork with an eel in its beak. This was seen as a sign of fortune, as the local storks would finish off all the remains after the fish market closed for the day; otherwise a rotten stench and infectious diseases could set in. Thus, the image of the stork is depicted on all municipal institutions to this day.

BELOW: The Hague at night.

The main attraction of this "village", which is still referred to as "the largest village in Europe", was that it offered a neutral meeting ground for representatives of the seven northern provinces, who each guarded their independence. Attractive streets and squares were laid out around the old castle in the 17th century, including the Plein and Korte Vijverberg which were designed by the diplomat and poet Constantijn Huygens. Further improvements were made in the 18th century along Lange Vijverberg and Lange Voorhout. By the 19th century The Hague had become a fashionable literary and artistic centre, while the nearby village of Scheveningen was one of the most elegant resorts on the North Sea. During the postwar years, The Hague lost much of its allure, due to the disappearance of many of its canals and the unchecked development of roads and office blocks. Fortunately, the extensive woods where the Counts of Holland hunted have been preserved, and the windswept dunes where the Impressionists of The Hague School painted are as wild as ever.

The Hague celebrated its 750th anniversary in 1998. In the 1990s it began an extensive plan to create a modern city centre. It started with projects such as the Anton Philipszaal concert hall on Spuiplein which is the residence of The Hague Philharmonic Orchestra and hosts many other cultural events. The AT&T Danstheater, designed by acclaimed architect Rem Koolhaas, is the residence of the equally acclaimed Nederlands Dans Theater. The new Town Hall is an impressive white complex which also houses the public library, and has become a meeting place for locals and visitors alike.

The most attractive area of the city lies around the old castle of the Counts of Holland. A gateway on Buitenhof leads into the Binnenhof, the former courtyard of the Count's castle. The building that looks like a chapel in the middle of the courtyard is the **Ridderzaal**, a 13th-century hall built by Count Floris V. Heavily restored in the 19th century, the building has come to symbolise the Dutch Parliament, though it is now only used on ceremonial occasions. A new building has been designed for the Second Chamber with a glass façade on Hofsingel to provide the public with a glimpse of the government in action.

A gateway behind the Ridderzaal leads to the **Mauritshuis**, rising out of the water like a Venetian palace (Korte Vijverberg 8; open Tues–Sun; entrance fee). This was the former home of Count Johan Maurits, an enlightened governor who ruled over Brazil on behalf of the Dutch West Indies Company. Built in 1633–44 by Pieter Post from plans by Jacob van Campen, the classical building embodies the Dutch principles of reason and balance. Maurits' house was famed for its "cabinets of curiosities", rooms filled with exotica brought back by Dutch trading ships. In the 19th century the Koninklijk Kabinet van Schilderijen (Royal Picture Cabinet) was moved here to create one of the most beautiful small picture galleries in the world. More like a private house than a museum, the Mauritshuis has a collection of Flemish, Dutch and German Old Masters. The works are hung in a series of period rooms, ranging from gilded salons to woodpanelled chambers. The permanent collection on the ground floor is mainly devoted to Flemish paintings,

BELOW: the Mauritshuis in The Hague

including the *Descent from the Cross* by Rogier van der Weyden and the *Portrait of a Man* by Hans Memling. The rooms on the first floor contain some of the finest works of the Dutch Golden Age, including Rembrandt's first major commission, *The Anatomy Lesson of Dr Tulp*, executed in 1632. There are also several self-portraits from different periods of Rembrandt's life. In the earliest, dated 1629, he looks almost arrogant, but by the time of the 1669 portrait (the year he died), the artist's face has weathered to an expression of infinite sorrow.

A pleasant walk around the lakeside brings you to the **Schilderijengalerie Willem V**, the oldest picture gallery in the Netherlands (Buitenhof 35; open Tues–Sun; entrance fee). Founded in 1774 by Prince William V, this small stately gallery has been restored to its original appearance, and paintings are crammed on the walls in several tiers. The collection of Dutch Old Masters does not compare with that in the Mauritshuis, but this eccentric gallery is nevertheless well worth a visit.

Buitenhof divides the government quarter from the old town, now an area of pedestrianised shopping streets. The Passage, off Buitenhof, is an elegant shopping arcade dating from 1885. Groenmarkt, not far from here, is the centre of the old town. Here stands the Oude Kerk, a 15th-century Gothic church with an early 16th-century choir. The Oude Stadhuis (Old Town Hall) opposite was built in 1564–65 in Renaissance style. A wing was added in the 18th century.

Noordeinde is the most elegant shopping street in The Hague, and has several well-preserved Art Nouveau shop fronts. Here you will find the Paleis Noordeinde, the royal residence, also known as the **Binnenhof**. The palace has a history dating from 1559 when Emperor Charles V assigned Prince William of Nassau to the post of *stadholder* of the provinces of Holland, Zeeland and

Map on page 240

Ornate decoration reflects the importance of The Hague's Binnenhof.

BELOW: Mauritshuis interior.

Utrecht. In 1689 when William III, married to Mary Stuart, was crowned King of England, they alternately resided in England and the Netherlands. Some of the pomp and circumstance can be witnessed on the third Tuesday in September on Prinsesdag, when Queen Beatrix travels in the Golden Coach from the palace to the Ridderzaal to read the Queen's Speech to Members of Parliament and presents a summary of the plans of the Cabinet for the next year.

Continuing down Noordeinde and across a canal, you reach the **Panorama Mesdag** (Zeestraag 65; open daily; entrance fee). Inside, you enter a darkened tunnel and ascend a spiral staircase to a mock pavilion, from which you obtain a life-like panoramic view of the coast and dunes at Scheveningen. The panorama was painted in 1881 by the Hague Impressionist Hendrik Willem Mesdag on a canvas 120 metres (400 ft) long by 14 metres (46 ft) high. The realistic effect is obtained by the indirect daylight falling from above and the artificial foreground strewn with real objects. Not far from here is the **Rijksmuseum H.W. Mesdag**. The museum is under the same management as the Van Gogh Museum in Amsterdam *(see page 193)*. It contains paintings by Mesdag and other members of The Hague School, plus a collection of melancholy works by members of the Barbizon School, including Corot and Millet. A short distance to the northwest is the **Gemeentemuseum**, with a fine collection of Mondrians, including his last work, *Victory Boogie Woogie*.

Delft

BELOW: Delft's Town Hall.

Delft ❿ is one of the Netherlands' best-preserved villages with its maze of canals, cobbled alleyways, classic homes and medieval buildings in the old city centre. In the Golden Age, Delft was a wealthy merchant city, housing the Dutch

East India Company (VOC), as well as the home of prominent scientists and painters such as Jan Vermeer *(see page 31)*. Relive its glorious past as you cross arched bridges and stroll past massive churches, stately courtyards, and the beautiful market square, which also hosts a flower and flea market. You can also take a boat tour or ride in a horse-driven tram.

Delft has special ties with the Dutch monarchy – Prince William of Orange was murdered here in 1584 and the bullet holes are still visible in the Municipal Museum Het Prinsenhof, his former residence. His marble mausoleum can be seen in the Nieuwe Kerk (New Church) over the vault of the royal family.

However Delft is best known around the world as the city of Delft blue earthenware. This goes back to the 17th century when dozens of small potteries were set up in former breweries. Delft was one of the home ports of the VOC and when the potters became acquainted with imported Chinese porcelain they began making their own earthenware inspired by these patterns, which are still made by hand today. Do beware of machine-made products when purchasing such earthenware.

Rotterdam

Rotterdam ⑪ is hard to recognise these days. In the 1990s the city was reborn, with a dynamic modern skyline and the largest and busiest port in the world. This is a city on the move.

In 1898, Rotterdam rapidly transformed itself into a modern port and the first skyscraper in the Netherlands, the 10-storey Witte Huis, was erected beside the old harbour. After suffering heavy bombing in 1940 (the Witte Huis was one of the only buildings that didn't crumble), the port was rebuilt, with massive invest-

Map on page 240

BELOW: traditional blue and white Delftware.

Map on page 240

The Euromast is Rotterdam's most prominent landmark.

BELOW: Rotterdam's busy harbour.

ment, to meet modern requirements. The spacious, pedestrianised streets of the Lijnbaan quarter, completed in 1953, inspired similar developments elsewhere. Rotterdam is now realising its ambitions of being one of the country's major cities. It has a prestigious orchestra, an internationally respected film festival and its city centre reflects cultural and culinary diversity. In summer take the **Circle Bus Tour** through the city, stopping at a number of museums, shopping areas and other points of interest.

Just a 10-minute walk from the station, the Museum Park was created in 1993 around the **Museum Boymans-van Beuningen**, which was founded in 1847 and has one of the best art collections in the Netherlands, including a number of early Flemish paintings by Hieronymus Bosch, and Pieter Brueghel the Elder. The modern collection has canvases by Monet, Van Gogh and Kandinsky as well as surrealist works by Magritte and Dali. The **Kunsthal** exhibition gallery focuses on contemporary art which is shown in a series of changing exhibitions in a building designed by the well-known architect Rem Koolhaas,

The **Oude Haven**, the former harbour, now contains a collection of redundant Rhine barges owned by the Maritime Museum. This area was devastated in 1940 and the only medieval building still standing is the Grote Kerk, gutted during World War II but restored with great skill. For many years the devastated area around the old harbour remained a wasteland, but it was transformed in the late 1980s by the construction of a huge public library in glass and steel, with fantastic views over the port and the city as well as its own hanging gardens. The **Blaakse Bos** nearby is a bizarre cluster of tilted cube houses (Kijk Kubus) on concrete columns, designed by Piet Blom. A raised pedestrian street lined with shops runs beneath the houses to create a modern version of the Ponte Vecchio in Florence. You can visit the Kijk Kubus for an impression of life in these strange futuristic houses, where every item of furniture has to be adapted to the sloping walls.

At the end of Leuvehaven, behind a redundant red lighthouse, is the **Maritime Museum Prins Hendrik**, devoted to Rotterdam's maritime history. The interior is somewhat like a ship, with gangplanks leading to the upper floors. The museum also displays exhibits on the quayside, including a reconstructed rope walk. The restored 19th-century warship *De Buffel* is moored here and is worth visiting to see the opulent officers' quarters furnished in the style of a Victorian club. Hemmed in by modern office blocks, the **Historisch Museum Schielandshuis** occupies a 17th-century classical building. This small museum has a collection of paintings, furnished period rooms and dolls' houses providing a visual history of art and culture in Rotterdam.

A good way to see the old harbour is by taking a boat tour from the quay at the southern end of Leuvehaven, heading downstream to the modern port. The **Euromast** rises above the trees on the west side of the park to a height of 185 metres (607 ft). The observation platform, at 100 metres (330 ft), offers a panoramic view of the city and port. Those with a head for heights can continue to the top by means of a slowly revolving cabin. ❑

Aalsmeer

At the Aalsmeer Flower Auction, held five days a week, millions of plants and flowers start their journey across the globe. Around 4 billion flowers and 400 million plants are sold each year. Annual turnover is €1 billion.

Flowers have been sold at the Aalsmeer site since 1912. In 1968 two separate auction houses based here merged to form the Verenigde Bloemenveilingen Aalsmeer (VBA). It is now the world's largest flower auction, occupying 600,000 sq. metres (150 acres), equivalent to 90 football pitches – the largest commercial building in the world.

Aalsmeer is just a 45-minute bus ride from Centraal Station. The annual total of around 200,000 spectators are free to walk around a long walkway that gives a clear view over the whole complex and the lightning-speed transactions. Information points are used to deliver pre-recorded commentaries explaining how the VBA works.

The VBA is a co-operative organisation made up of more than 5,000 growers, all of whom must sell their products here. The growers pay a commission of about five percent and this money is used to finance the running of the building and staff costs.

The VBA auction is nocturnal; flowers arrive at night pre-packed into boxes or containers and are examined by inspectors early in the morning for quality before the auction begins at 6.30am. Arrive at this time if you can – most of the action is over by 9am.

There are five auction rooms in all, each accommodating around 300 buyers, and a total of 13 clocks which control transactions. Each clock is used for the same sort of produce each day so that buyers know where to go. On registering, a buyer receives a computer card which has to be inserted into the desk at which he sits to unlock the "buy" button and link the customer into the computer.

Appropriately, Aalsmeer uses the "Dutch auction" system: the pointer of a large clock face marks decreasing prices as it turns back from 100 to 1. The clock gives the unit of currency in which the transaction is being offered, the number of flowers in each lot, the minimum purchase quantity and the price per flower. By pressing the "buy" button each buyer can stop the pointer at a price he is prepared to pay. The buyer informs the auctioneer whether he wants the entire lot or just part. If a part-lot is sold the clock goes back to 100 and the process is repeated until the entire contents have been sold.

The system processes an average of 50,000 transactions a day. After each batch has been sold, it is driven to an area where VBA staff divide up the flowers or plants according to each sale. Some 350 buyers rent spaces in the packing area. Only 15 minutes elapse between the auctioning and the delivery of consignments to the buyer.

More than 80 percent of everything sold at Aalsmeer is exported and, on average, 2,000 trucks leave the building daily. The proximity of Schiphol Airport means that these flowers and plants are on sale in florists around the world the same evening or the following day. ❑

RIGHT: Dutch tulips on sale in Aalsmeer.
OVERLEAF: Vondelpark sculpture.

INSIGHT GUIDES

Travel Tips

CONTENTS

Getting Acquainted

The Place

The Place

Amsterdam lies below sea level, so if the North Sea dykes collapse while you are in town you're going to get wet. The heart of the city is the Dam. North of the Dam is Centraal Station, which is also the main tram, bus and metro terminus. A ring of concentric canals – Singel, Herengracht, Keizersgracht and Prinsengracht – forms a wide semicircle around the Dam, ending at the River Amstel in the east.

Area: 219 sq. km (85 sq. miles).
Population: 725,000.
Language: Dutch, although almost everyone speaks English. However, it is always more diplomatic to enquire first if someone speaks English and not make assumptions.
Religion: Dutch Reformed Church (Calvinist), but with a large Roman Catholic community and a substantial Muslim minority.
Time Zone: GMT + 1 hour Oct–Mar; + 2 hours Apr–Sept (Daylight Saving Time).
Currency: Euro (€), divided into 100 cents.
Weights & Measures: Metric.
Electricity: 220 volts AC. Plugs have two round pins, so British and US plugs need adaptors.
International Dialling Code: 31 (Netherlands) followed by 20 for Amsterdam.

The People

Amsterdam is a genuine melting-pot, with immigrants from many countries. The city has a history of receiving political or religious refugees with open arms over the centuries. Indeed a browse through the Amsterdam telephone directory will quickly reveal many surnames of foreign origin. The fact that you may choose from at least 40 different nations with regard to cuisine is a good indication of the city's cosmopolitan lifestyle.

Postwar industrial development, economic growth and a housing shortage contributed to a substantial deficit in skilled and non-skilled workforces. To overcome this shortage people were drafted in from other countries as "guest workers". Many of these "guests" enjoyed living conditions previously unknown to them and instead of returning home opted to bring their families to the Netherlands *(see page 84)*. This phenomenon was not always well received by the indigenous popu-lation; however the more liberal are quick to point out that the guest workers often undertook work that the Dutch were too proud to do. Certain ethnic groups are to this day still associated with particular trades which never seem to be that appealing. For example in the steel foundries west of Amsterdam there are now second- and third-generation Spanish and Italian workers. The postwar return to independence for certain Dutch colonies (especially the East Indies) also led to an influx of immigrants who had inherited Dutch citizenship and rights from bygone colonial days.

It is far from surprising that the population of Amsterdam is so mixed, and even now refugees from war-torn corners of the world (such as Afghanistan) seek out the Netherlands and particularly Amsterdam as a new home.

Government

The Netherlands is a constitutional monarchy with a parliamentary system of government. Government operates from a constitution set up in 1814. The head of state is the hereditary monarch (currently Queen Beatrix). The political head of state is the prime minister, who is appointed by the queen. The prime minister presides over a cabinet that is responsible to parliament.

Due to the mixed political climate the cabinet is always a coalition of several parties. The parliament is referred to as the States General and consists of two chambers. The upper chamber has 75 members who serve a period of four years and are elected from the provincial legislature. The lower chamber has 150 members who also serve a term of four years but are elected from a system of proportional representation. The lower chamber is responsible for passing new laws and acts. The upper chamber has a limited power of veto that is rarely

Climate

The Netherlands has a temperate climate, typical of northwestern Europe. Extremes of heat and cold are rare, and the relatively long coastline and flat landscape results in frequent strong, chilly winds from the North Sea. Temperatures in the east of the country are slightly lower in winter and higher in summer.

Amsterdam itself has a mild, maritime climate similar to that of southern England, but it is generally wetter, and colder in winter. Average winter daytime temperatures are around 5°C (41°F), falling to 1°C (34°F) at night. When there is a cold spell, however, temperatures can plummet to minus 10°C (14°F) and canals freeze over. Summers are quite warm; the July daytime average is 21°C (70°F), falling to around 13°C (55°F) at night. Occasional heatwaves see temperatures up to 30°C (86°F).

You can expect rain at any time of year. Spring is the driest time and a favourite time for tulip enthusiasts. The advantages of a visit in winter are the cut-price package deals and the fact that museums and galleries are pleasantly uncrowded.

used and acts more in an advisory capacity. The monarch has the right to dissolve either or both chambers on condition that new elections take place within 40 days.

Amsterdam city council is headed by a powerful mayor who invariably sets his stamp on the city's social and economic affairs.

Economy

Don't get carried away by Amsterdam's reputation for free-living. Nowadays, that anything-goes lifestyle is more a product of wealth than of hippie values and hashish. Thanks to assiduous promotion and heavy investment, the Amsterdam-Schiphol Airport region is a booming enterprise zone, as can be seen in the city's extensive suburban business developments. It is also a favoured place for multinational corporations to locate their European headquarters and distribution operations.

The Netherlands has always held a unique role in European trade and economy. From the 16th century onwards, shipping, fishing, banking and trade have been the staple economic activities.

The Chamber of Commerce and Industry represents businesses ranging from the individual freelancer to heavy industry and trade unions. As a whole the organisation is a powerful decision-maker and on occasion it influences new legislation.

Culture and Customs

Amsterdam has a reputation for being supremely tolerant. Foreigners, including minorities, are always welcome and as a tourist to Amsterdam you are likely to find the locals pleasant, polite and civilised. They may not be very demonstrative or vivacious but they are rarely inhospitable or unfriendly. The Dutch love to show off their talent for languages and enjoy speaking English with visitors.

First-comers are frequently surprised at the leniency towards both drugs and prostitution.

Although there has been a crackdown on hard drugs, you can still buy marijuana in many cafés, which by law must be called "coffee shops" and are distinguished by a green and white licence displayed in the window *(see page 102)*. Many locals argue that the drugs problem is no worse than in any other major city – just more open. Make it a rule *never* to buy anything from drug dealers who approach you on the street. If you want to smoke marijuana or hashish, go to one of the better-known shops such as the Bull Dog with locations throughout the city. Most tourists get in trouble over-indulging in the notorious "Space Cake", which when consumed on an empty stomach will give the false impression of offering nourishment along with the high which can cause unpredictable side effects. Moderation is the key. In recent years a number of "smart drug" shops have opened around town, offering psychedelic drugs and so-called brain stimulants made of "natural" ingredients.

It is hard to offend Amsterdammers, whose approach to life is that whatever works for you is OK by them. But live-and-let-live has its limits. They don't like boorish, loud and aggressive behaviour any more than most people, nor do they take to being treated like servants or serfs. Like all Dutch people they are proud of their country, though not in a shallow, flag-waving way, and don't like too much criticism of its ways.

You certainly shouldn't trust the junkie in the Red Light District who asks to take a picture of you with your own camera, nor most of the hard-luck stories you might hear at Centraal Station from people whose money has mysteriously vanished and who need someone to pay their ticket home (their story *might* be true). Watch out for pickpockets in all busy places, especially at Centraal Station and on crowded buses and trams.

Although there are enough weird folks in Amsterdam to go around, one of its delights is its people. Strike up a conversation in any bar

or restaurant, at a tram stop, or in the Metro. The Dutch speak excellent English: they will probably place your accent, follow your colloquialisms, and laugh at your jokes.

Holland is a mostly Calvinist country, with the Dutch Reformed Church in the spiritual driving seat, but has a substantial Catholic minority (in the south, the reverse applies). Take a look inside any church in Amsterdam at service time on Sunday, though, and you will find that religion appears to be honoured more often in the breach than in the observance.

Tips are included in taxi fares and prices in restaurants and bars, so all that is required is some small change if you think the service warrants it. In most up-market restaurants, a tip of 10 percent is advised. In theatres and in many grand cafés, the washroom attendant generally asks for 50 cents.

Planning the Trip

Entry Regulations

Visitors from the European Union, the US, Canada, Australia, New Zealand and most other European and Commonwealth countries require only a valid passport. Citizens of most other countries must obtain a visa in advance from Dutch embassies or consulates in their home countries.

Customs Regulations

Personal possessions are not liable to duty and tax provided you are staying for less than six months and you intend to take them out of the country again. There is no restriction on the amount of currency that you can bring into the Netherlands. Among prohibited or restricted goods are plants, flowers, weapons and recreational drugs.

Duty-free shopping is no longer available to travellers within the European Union. Despite the change in regulations, travellers departing from Schiphol Airport to destinations in and out of the EU may still take advantage of reduced prices on all goods except for alcoholic beverages and tobacco. In a unique action, the airport and the shop owners decided to band together to pay the sales tax themselves; in this way the prices for perfume, electronic equipment, cameras and other items remain at duty-free levels. Alcohol and tobacco are still available for sale, but at prices comparable to normal shops in the city. Travellers to the Canary Islands (Spain) and the Channel Islands (UK) are not affected by the ruling.

Health

No health certificates or vaccinations are required for European Union citizens. EU citizens who have obtained an E111 form from their local post office before departure are entitled to free treatment by a doctor and free prescribed medicines. This insurance is not comprehensive and won't cover you, for example, for holiday cancellation or the cost of repatriation. For full cover, take out separate medical insurance.

Money Matters

Since January 2002 the unit of currency in the Netherlands (and in most other countries of the European Union) has been the euro (€), which replaced the old Dutch guilder. A euro is divided into 100 cents. Euro notes come in denominations of 5, 10, 20, 50, 100, 200 and 500; coins are 1 cent, 2 cents, 5 cents, 10 cents, 20 cents, €1 and €2.

Changing Money

The best rates of exchange are at national banks; beware high commission rates at hotels. Major credit cards and Eurocheques are accepted in all main hotels, restaurants and shops.

The GWK (Grenswisselkantoren NV) is a national financial institution where you can exchange any currency and also use credit cards or travellers' cheques. Although the Centraal Station GWK exchange office is open 24 hours a day, the station itself is closed for security reasons from 1am to 5am! Change is also available at post offices (at good rates) and banks.

There can be a considerable difference in commission charged between the various institutions and at the different times of night or day.

There are automatic cash-dispensers all over the city. Most can be accessed by foreign credit card holders, some also by the major charge card holders or cash cards with the Cirrus symbol. GWK

and other currency exchange outlets also accept major credit cards.

Credit Cards

Credit cards are accepted at hotels, restaurants, shops, car hire companies and airlines. Master-Card, American Express, Diners Club, Eurocard, Visa and JCB card are all recognised, plus many more.

Airlines

British Airways:
Tel: 020 346 0066 (Netherlands)
Tel: 08705 222 999 (UK)
www.britishairways.com
BMI:
Tel: 020 601 5459 (Netherlands)
Tel: 0345 554 554 (UK)
www.britishmidland.co.uk
EasyJet:
Tel: 023 568 4880 (Netherlands)
Tel: 08706 000 000 (UK)
www.easyjet.com
KLM Royal Dutch Airlines:
Tel: 020 474 7747 (Netherlands)
Tel: 08705 074 074 (UK)
www.klmuk.com

Getting There

By Air

Schiphol Airport, 14 km (9 miles) southwest of Amsterdam, has connections to 250 cities in 100 countries. With its enlarged terminals with shops, casino, business centre, two hotels and a children's play area, along with its reputation for efficiency and easy access to all parts of the Netherlands, Schiphol remains one of Europe's most popular international airports. There is a 24-hour rail service from Schiphol to Amsterdam Centraal Station, with up to six trains an hour at peak times. Trains also depart frequently to Amsterdam RAI Station and Amsterdam Zuid/WTC (South/World Trade Centre) Station. The journey time to Centraal Station is about 20 minutes. Taxis to the city centre leave from in front of Schiphol Plaza and cost around €30. KLM operates a hotel shuttle bus from the airport, serving 16 city-centre hotels every 20–30 minutes from 7am–9.30pm.

Taken together, British Airways, KLM Royal Dutch Airlines and British Midland operate an almost hourly service during the day between Amsterdam and the UK from London Heathrow and East Midlands airport. The best value for British visitors, however, is the Amsterdam Air Express from Gatwick, departing on Friday afternoons only and returning on Monday evenings. Services from regional airports are covered by various British and Dutch airlines.

Several airlines offer cut-price fares which work out as little more than the cost of a standard rail ticket. These cheaper flights usually mean that you have to spend a Saturday night in the Netherlands. Very regular flights link Schiphol with all major European airports, and there are several flights a week from North America, Canada and Australia. The Amsterdam Travel Service and Tours, with offices in the UK and in Amsterdam, offers specially priced excursion packages to Amsterdam and many other cities throughout the Netherlands *(see page 264)*.

By Train

There are good rail connections to all parts of the Netherlands from Brussels, Paris, Antwerp, Cologne, Berlin and the North Sea ports. The **Eurostar** Channel Tunnel train goes direct from London's Waterloo station to Brussels, from where trains run to Amsterdam. The total journey time from London is about six hours. The **Thalys** high-speed train (for which reservation is mandatory) connects the city with Brussels, Paris and Cologne).

Eurostar:
Tel: 0990 186 186 (in UK);
Tel: 1233 617 575 (from overseas).
Rail Europe (in UK):
Tel: 0870 584 8848
Thalys:
Tel: 0900 9296

By Sea

From the UK, **Stena Line** operates two ferries a day (for passengers

Rules of the Road

To drive in the Netherlands, you must carry a current driving licence (an international licence is not necessary), vehicle registration document, Green Card insurance policy and a warning triangle for use in the event of an accident or breakdown. The Netherlands has an excellent network of roads and signposting is good. But once you're in the cities, a car is often more of a hindrance than a help. And do be aware that in most large cities you are required to buy parking tickets at specially posted vending machines on the streets, marked with a "P". Amsterdam is notorious for high fines, parking clamps and an enthusiastic parking enforcement team.

with vehicles) from Harwich to Hoek van Holland: crossing time is around 8½ hours. **P&O North Sea Ferries** has a daily sailing from Hull to Rotterdam, taking 13 hours. **DFDS Seaways** has a daily overnight car-ferry service from Newcastle to IJmuiden: crossing time is 14 hours.

Stena Line:
Tel: 08705 707 070
www.stenaline.com
P&O North Sea Ferries:
Tel: 01482 377 177
www.ponsf.com
DFDS Seaways:
Tel: 08705 000 333
www.dfdsseaways.co.uk

By Coach

This is generally the cheapest way of getting to the Netherlands. From the UK **Eurolines** (tel: 0990 808 080; www.eurolines.com) operate frequent coach services to Amsterdam.

By Car

Four Euro-designated motorways converge on the city from Belgium and Germany: the E19, E22, E35 and E231. From the UK, the Channel Tunnel's Le Shuttle

provides a 35-minute drive-on service between Folkestone and Calais, from where there is a straightforward motorway connection to Amsterdam up through Belgium.

From Hoek van Holland to Amsterdam, driving time is roughly 2½ hours. If you don't mind a longer drive on the Continent you can, of course, take the shorter cross-Channel ferry routes: Ramsgate–Dunkirk (2 hours 30 minutes); Dover–Calais (1 hour 30 minutes).

Children

Tram trips, canal cruises, water pedaloes, bicycle excursions outside the busy city environs, barrel organs and mime shows are all likely to amuse the young. The Vondelpark has a playground, duck ponds and free entertainment in summer. The Amstelpark provides pony rides and the Amsterdamse Bos, reached in summer by vintage trams, provides a huge expanse of parkland with lakes, swimming, riding, fishing, biking and canoes *(see page 229)*.

Favourite childrens' attractions in the city are Madame Tussaud's, the Children's Museum at the Tropenmuseum *(see page 235)*, the Artis Zoo, Aquarium and Planetarium *(see page 212)*, the Maritime Museum *(see page 219)* and the delightful dolls' house section of the Rijksmuseum *(see page 185)*. Also exciting is NEMO *(see page 218)*, where games and hands-on exhibitions allow children to explore the world of science and technology.

As an excursion for children, you can't beat Madurodam – a Dutch town in miniature complete with churches, castles, farms, ships and planes, followed, perhaps, by an afternoon on Scheveningen beach; just 45 minutes by train to The Hague and then a 10-minute tram ride *(see page 249)*. Closer by is Zaanse Schans which offers authentic houses and windmills from the 1700s *(see page 239)*.

Gay Travellers

Amsterdam, has plenty to offer gay travellers. There are special hotels, restaurants, bars, bookshops, shops, nightclubs, cinemas and plenty more.

The best point of reference and information for gays and lesbians is undoubtedly the COC. Regardless of one's tastes, the COC provides something for everyone, is a key source for Amsterdam gay information and a non-profit organisation there to help gay people, be their needs social, legal or medical. The COC's big social night is Friday which attracts up to 600 gays and lesbians. The evening starts at 8pm for the youth section (16 years upwards), the café opens its doors at 10pm, and the disco starts at 11pm, with festivities continuing until 4am. It really is a big night out. Saturday night is exclusively for women but follows pretty much the same pattern. Sunday is multicultural night, open to all, and closes at the much earlier time of 12.30am. The COC is a large complex housing numerous halls including a small theatre where some English productions are played. In addition to these activities there are six leather and S&M parties a year, which have become something of an international event. Of interest to English speakers is the Wednesday English-speaking group from 8–10pm where one can discuss all aspects of gay life in Amsterdam.

The *Man to Man Gay Guide*, available at **Vrolijk Gay and Lesbian Bookshop**, is full of useful information. A list of books for lesbian readers is available on request at the bookshop.

Finally, a very user-friendly street map of Amsterdam entitled *Amsterdam Columbia Fun Map* gives details of all gay and lesbian bars, restaurants, hotels, beauty salons, shops, cinemas and anything of gay/lesbian relevance. Available from the COC or other gay bookshops *(see page 280)*.

COC:
Rozenstraat 14, 1016 NX.
Tel: 623 4596.
Vrolijk Gay and Lesbian Bookshop:
Paleisstraat 135. Tel: 623 5142

Disabled Travellers

The **Royal Association for Disability and Rehabilitation** (RADAR) has information on planning holidays, transport and equipment for rent, and accommodation.

Information is also available from the VVV-Amsterdam *(see page 263)* which gives advice on the accessibility of hotels, restaurants, museums and other places of interest with disabled facilities. The Uitbureau on Leidseplein has a brochure on the accessibility of theatres, concert halls etc, but it's written in Dutch.

Most of the major museums and galleries have access for wheelchairs, although the city in general, with its cobbled streets and wealth of steep narrow staircases, is not ideal, and you should check before booking into a hotel whether it has a lift, as some staircases can be almost as steep as ladders.

RADAR:
Unit 12, City Forum, 250 City Rd, London EC1V 8AF; tel: 020 7250 3222.

Student Travellers

Young people under 24 can get reduced-rate admissions to most museums, though you may need to produce a passport as proof of your age. The magazine *What's On in Amsterdam*, available at local book shops and VVV offices is crammed with information on current exhibitions and all cultural events.

The local student campus restaurants are called Mensas and anyone can eat there. Food is filling and cheap but served only Monday to Friday lunch and dinner. Two popular ones are: Mensa Agora Universitair Restaurant 11 Roeterstraat (near the Artis Zoo) and Mensa Atrium Universitair Restaurant in the city centre at 237 Oudezijds Achterburgwal.

Practical Tips

Media

Newspapers and Magazines

The main national newspapers are *NRC Handelsblad*, the most respected paper, the more left-wing *De Volkskrant*, and *De Telegraaf*, on the political right. English newspapers arrive on the same day they are published and are widely available. The monthly English-language *Day by Day/What's On in Amsterdam* gives listings and reviews of events, available from VVV offices. Brown café noticeboards are another source of information on events.

The *Uitkrant*, available at the Uitburo on the Leidseplein is a free monthly publication which, although in Dutch, is easily readable for concert venues and dates of performances. Pick up their English brochure, *Culture in Amsterdam*, at their offices at Kleine Gartmanplantsoen 21, tel: 0900-0191, for reservations to events. There are also brochures available from the VVV – *Amsterdam Winter* and *Summer Arts Adventures* – costing €2.50. These are part of the "language is no problem" performances and exhibitions.

Television and Radio

On cable TV you can watch Britain's BBC channels, plus Sky, CNN, NBC and various other international networks. English-language films are frequently shown on Dutch TV channels, undubbed. On the radio, you can tune into BBC World Service, BBC Radio 4 and Sky Radio.

Postal Services

Most post offices are open Monday to Friday, 9am–5pm; the main branch, behind the Palace at Singel

Public Holidays

- **1 January** New Year's Day
- **March/April** Good Friday, Easter Sunday and Monday
- **30 April** Queen's Day
- **May** Ascension Day (sixth Thursday after Easter)
- **May/June** Whit Monday (eighth Monday after Easter)
- **25/26 December** Christmas Day, Boxing Day

Banks and most shops are closed on these days.

250–6, is open until 8pm on Thursday evenings and 9am–1pm on Saturdays. Stamps are available from post offices, tobacconists, and some newsstands and stationary shops.

Poste restante facilities are available at main post offices – you need a passport to collect your mail. You can also send a fax and make long-distance calls at post offices (buying a telephone card), make photocopies and bank via the Post Bank.

Telephones

Most telephone boxes take phone-cards (€5, €12.50, €25 and €50), which you can buy in post offices, large stores and cafés. Some take coins (5, 10, 20, 50 cents or €1).

To dial a number outside the Netherlands, first dial 00 (international access number), then the country code, the area code and the subscriber's number. For information about phone numbers within the Netherlands, tel: 0900 8008; for information about phone numbers abroad, tel: 0900 8418.

To use US phonecards dial the following access numbers:
AT&T: 0900 022 9111.
MCI: 0800 022 9122
Sprint: 0800 022 9119

If you bring your **mobile phone** with you, remember that if you are calling a local number it is necessary to dial the international access code (eg "00" from the UK) followed by the code for the

Netherlands (31) and Amsterdam (20), and therefore calls are expensive. This is because you are still operating through your service provider at home; they may be able to arrange a temporary transfer so that your calls can be routed through the Dutch system.

Internet

Each internet café has its own ambience, so choose accordingly. Most have several types of PCs to work on and some have scanners, colour printers and other extras. The **easyEverything** chain has two Internet cafes: at 33 Damrak (tel: 020 320 8082), open daily 7.30am–11pm; and at 22 Reguliersbreestraat (tel: 020 320 6291), open 24 hours a day. **The Internet Café**, 11 Martelaarsgracht (tel: 020 627 1052), is open Sunday–Thursday 9am–1am, Friday–Saturday 9am–3am.

Tourist Information

The main tourist office (**VVV**) is opposite Centraal Station at Stationsplein 10, tel: 0900 400

4040 (www.visitamsterdam.nl), and there is another office in the station. There is also a VVV bureau at Leidsestraat 104.

There is a tourist information office at the airport, which is useful if you have not already booked your accommodation. The booklet *What's On in Amsterdam* lists events in the city. Other guides can also be bought at the VVV.

The **GVB Office**, also at Stationsplein, alongside the metro entrance, tel: 0900 9292 (50 cents per minute), provides information and ticket sales for local and city public transport. Open Monday–Friday 7am–9pm, Saturday and Sunday 8am–9pm.

Useful Addresses

The website for visitors wanting information specifically on Amsterdam can be found at: www.visitamsterdam.nl
The Dutch tourist office website can be found at: www.goholland.com

Netherlands Board of Tourism USA
355 Lexington Avenue
New York, NY 10017

Embassies and Consulates

Australia
Carnegielaan 19, 2517 KH
Den Haag. Tel: 070-310 8200
Belgium
Lange Vijverberg 12
2513 AC Den Haag
Tel: 070-312 3456
British Consulate
Koningslaan 44, Amsterdam
Tel: 676 4343
British Embassy
Lange Voorhout 10
2514 ED Den Haag
Tel: 070-364 5800
Canada
Sophialaan 7, 2514 JP Den Haag
Tel: 070-311 1600
German Consulate
De Lairessestraat 172
Amsterdam. Tel: 673 6245
German Embassy
Gr. Hertoginnelln 18-20
2517 EG Den Haag
Tel: 070-342 0600

Ireland
Dr. Kuyperstraat 9
2585 JD Den Haag
Tel: 070-363 0993
New Zealand
25 Mauritskade
2517 KH Den Haag
070-346 9324
South Africa
40 Wassenaarseweg
Den Haag
070-392 4501
US Consulate
Museumplein 19
Amsterdam
Tel: 575 5309
US Embassy
Lange Vorhout 102
2514 EJ Den Haag
Tel: 070-310 9209

These offices are generally open 8.30am–4pm and are closed on public holidays of their country.

Tel: 212-370 7360
Fax: 212-370 9507
E-mail: info@goholland.com
www.goholland.com
Netherlands Board of Tourism UK
PO Box 30783,
London WC2B 6DH
Tel: 0906-871 7777
Fax: 020 7828-7941
E-mail: hollandinfo-uk@nbt.org.uk
www.goholland.com

Travel Agents

American Express
Damrak 66
Tel: 504 8780
**Amsterdam Travel Service
and Tours**
(specialists for British travellers)
Dam 10
Tel: 627 6236;
UK office: Bridge House,
55–59 High Road, Broxbourne,
Herts EN10 7DT
Tel: 01992 456 056
Holland International
Prins Hendrikkade 33a
Tel: 625 3035
Lindbergh Excursions
Damrak 26
Tel: 622 2766

Religious Services

There are places to worship for
most denominations in Amsterdam
and they are held in a variety of
historic and unique venues.

Catholic Services
St Nicolaaskerk
73 Prins Hendrikkade
High Mass, Sundays 10.30am
Obrechtkerk
28 Jacob Obrechtstraat
High Mass, Sundays 9.30 and 11am
De Papegaai
58 Kalverstraat
Sundays 10.30am and 12.15pm

Reformed Services
The Anglican Church
42 Groenburgwal
Sundays 10.30am
**English Reformed Church/
Presbyterian/Church of Scotland**
48 Begijnhof
Sundays 10.30am

Jewish Services
Portugees-Israëlitische Synagoge
(Orthodox) 1 Mr Visserplein
Saturdays 9am

Business Hours

Normal shopping hours are 8.30am
or 9am–6pm. Late-night shopping is
usually Thursday and Friday until
9pm. Most shops close at 5pm on
Saturday. All shops close for one
half-day a week, usually Monday
morning, when they open at 1pm.
Many grocery stores, such as the
Albert Heijn chain, are open most
evenings until either 7pm or 9pm.
Some shops have Sunday hours of
1–7pm. Many department stores
and speciality shops in the city
centre are also open on Sunday
from noon–5pm.

Most banks and government
offices are open 9am–5pm Monday
to Friday. For general information on
government hours, call City Hall,
tel: 624 1111.

Doing Business
Amsterdam ranks fifth in the world
as a congress centre, hosting more
than 300 international congresses
every year as well as hundreds
of trade shows and exhibitions.
The Dutch tend to be efficient
and civilised when it comes to
doing business and the wide
knowledge of English is obviously
an enormous advantage. For
further information, contact the
Amsterdam Congress Bureau,
Postbus 3901, 1001 AS
Amsterdam, the Netherlands; tel:
551 2570, fax: 551 2575. E-mail:
acb@amsterdamcongress.nl;
www.amsterdamcongress.nl

Medical Services

The most central hospital in
Amsterdam is the Onze Lieve
Vrouwe Gasthuis, le (first)
Oosterparkstraat 279, tel: 599
9111. The main hospital is the
Academisch Medisch Centrum
(AMC), Meibergdreef 9, tel: 566
3333. Both hospitals have an out-
patients department and an
emergency casualty ward.

Emergency Numbers

● **Police, Fire, Ambulance**
tel: 112
● **General Doctors' and Dental
Service:** tel: 592 3434.
(For urgent medical or dental
treatment; open 24 hours.)

The medical services in the
Netherlands are good. People with
middle-to-high incomes usually have
private (or *particuliere*) insurance
while the rest of the population falls
under the National Health or
Ziekenfonds. People go to a general
practitioner *(huisarts)* for check-ups
and general ailments. Visitors who
require medical treatment can ask at
their hotel for the name of a local GP.

For emergency services, the two
hospitals *(ziekenhuizen)* listed above
provide excellent care. As long as
one is medically insured, services
are rendered and are billed at a
later date to your home address.

Chemists
Chemists *(Apotheken)* are normally
open Monday–Friday 9am–5.30pm
or 6pm. Weekend and late-night
chemists operate on a rotating
basis. If you have a general
question about your state of health,
a pharmacist will generally suggest
an over-the-counter remedy. A list of
out-of-hours pharmacies is posted
on the front of every *apotheek*
(pharmacy).

Lost Property

You should report loss or theft of
valuables to the police immediately
as most insurance policies insist on
a police report. The main police
station is at Elandsgracht 117,
tel: 559 9111. For items lost on
public transport, contact the GVB
Head Office, Prins Hendrikkade
108–114, tel: 551 4911. Loss of
passports should be reported
immediately to the police and your
consulate *(see page 263)*.

The Lost Property Office is at
Stephensonstraat 18, tel: 559
3005 or you can also contact the
main police station.

Getting Around

From the Airport

Shuttle trains leave every 15 minutes for Amsterdam Centraal Station throughout the day, and in late evenings around once an hour. Travel time is 15 minutes. Trains also run to the RAI station and to Amsterdam Zuid for the World Trade Centre, both in the south of the city. KLM operates a coach service to the city every half an hour, but it's more than twice the price of the train.

Orientation

Thanks to its size and layout, the centre of Amsterdam is easily covered on foot. Main streets radiate out from Centraal Station, crossing a more or less regular pattern of concentric canals. It all looks very simple on paper but the canal system can be tricky to negotiate if you are a first-time visitor. It is worth spending some time studying a map and mastering the relative positions of the main squares, streets and canals, bearing in mind that *plein* means square, *straat* street and *gracht* canal. *Dwaars straatjes* are side streets, and *steegs* are alleys.

The most prominent landmarks are the three main squares, the Dam, Rembrandtplein and Leidseplein. The best way to get your bearings is to take the Circle trams 20a and 20b, which start and end at Centraal Station and pass by almost all the tourist attractions on two different routes. These trams set off every 10 minutes from 9am–7pm. The last tram leaves at 6pm. Then take to the streets on foot – the best way of getting around.

Maps

The GVB office in front of Centraal Station provides free public transport route maps. The Insight *Fleximap* to Amsterdam is detailed and easy-to-use, and its laminated finish means that getting wet in the frequent Amsterdam rain is not a problem.

Public Transport

Amsterdam's public transport network consists of tram and bus routes and four Metro/light rail lines. All operate from 6am until midnight, after which a night bus network is in operation.

One-day or multiple-day tickets are valid on all public transport lines within the city and can save you time and money. Otherwise use the *strippenkaarten* – strip tickets; the more strips you buy, the cheaper they come. These are valid for one hour's travel and the amount you use depends on the number of public transport zones you cover. The city is divided into public transport zones and you cancel one strip more than the number of zones you will be travelling within – two strips for one zone, three strips for two zones, and so on.

Tickets are available from the GVB office next to Centraal Station as well as at tourist offices, post offices, some tobacconists and at major hotels. Tickets purchased on trams and buses cost more than those bought in advance.

Trams

Within the city centre the prominent yellow trams are easily the best means of getting around. Tickets must be stamped in the machines that are usually located next to the doors of the tram. If you have no ticket enter through the front door (doors open automatically if you press the "*Deur Open*" button), state your destination and buy a ticket from the driver. If the tram has a conductor, enter at the rear, where there will be a small counter.

Do not give in to temptation and try to ride without a ticket ("riding black"). Tram controllers make random checks, and failure to purchase or punch the tickets can result in a substantial fine – around €30. Be aware that on heavily travelled trams, such as Nos. 2 and 5 to the Museum Quarter, teams of *zakenrollers* (pickpockets) "work" the trams, especially in summer months and holiday periods. Be aware of your personal property at all times.

Buses and Trains

You are unlikely to use buses or the Metro system unless you are travelling outside the city centre. Networks are clean and efficient. On the Metro you must stamp your ticket in the machines provided – these are usually found close to the steps leading to the platforms.

Overground rail lines connect Amsterdam with nearby attractions such as Volendam, Alkmaar and Haarlem, as well as Schipol airport.

Boats

The Canal Buses are modern, glass-topped launches which pick up passengers at 11 major points along three different routes. They take you through some of the loveliest parts of Amsterdam en route to various museums and tourist attractions. Day passes, which enable you to hop on and off at your whim, are available, but be prepared to queue in summer.

The **Museum Boat** service stops at nine major museums at 75-minute intervals – well worth considering if you intend doing a lot of sightseeing. You can buy a day ticket from the VVV office opposite Centraal Station, where the boat service starts. The Canal Bus 52-seat cruiser provides a regular service between Centraal Station and the Rijksmuseum, with three stops on the way. For further information, tel: 623 9886.

The traditional *Rondvaart*, or canal boat tour, is a delightful way to discover the city from a watery perspective and gives a duck's-eye view of the 17th-century houses which grace the canals. There are several companies in front of Centraal Station, along the Dam and Rokin, by the Rijksmuseum and Heineken Brewery which offer a basic hour to hour-and-a-half tour.

Lovers operates canal boat cruises as well as the popular Water Taxis, when money is no object. These custom-made voyages can last from an hour to a full evening and offer a more intimate approach to exploring the city's waterscape.

It is also possible to hire small motorboats and navigate the canals yourself. But be aware that there are safety rules and that canal boats and flocks of swans always have the right of way! Electric-powered boats can be rented from **Duba**.

Lovers: tel: 622 2181.
Canal Motorboats: by the Jaren Café opposite Kloveniersburgwal 141, tel: 422 7007.
Sesa Rent a Boat: on the Nieuwmarkt opposite Kloveniersburgwal 23. (Open May–Oct; identity and a deposit of €300 is required.)
Duba: Prinseneiland 34, tel: 624 6424.

Waterbikes

Canal pedaloes for two or four are fun for exploring the canals. Detailed maps and suggested routes are provided by the hire companies, located opposite the Centraal Station, Anne Frank's House, by the American Hotel and opposite the Rijksmuseum.

Amsterdam Pass

This Amsterdam Pass gives free entry or substantial discounts to all the most important museums in the city and various tourist attractions such as the Museum Boat and Canal Bus *(see page 265)*. The Pass costs around €20 and represents a total value of more than €90. It can be purchased at any of the VVV offices in Amsterdam and at many of the hotels in the city. It is an alternative for visitors to the Museum Year Card, which is used mainly by local residents.

Private Transport

On Foot

The centre of Amsterdam is well suited to walking provided you don't object to cobbled streets, chaotic cyclists and an inordinate amount of dog dirt. The major museums and galleries are conveniently located in the same area (Museumplein) to the southwest of the centre *(see page 200)*. From here it is about 30 minutes' walk to Dam Square and Centraal Station. Most of the hotels are within walking distance of the centre – notable exceptions are those in the south and southeast, and the business hotels near the World Trade Centre and RAI Congress Centre. There are several walking tours to be enjoyed.

By Bicycle

Being a city of cyclists, Amsterdam has numerous bike lanes. Cycling is a fun way of getting around but bear in mind that there are 600,000 other cyclists in the city, and a lot of chaotic traffic with which to contend. Locals run the red lights, taxis drive on tram tracks. Be careful of tram tracks – they should only be crossed at right angles!

Two of the main places for renting cycles are **Damstraat Rent-a-bike** and **MacBike**. Bicycle theft is rife (hence high deposits on rentals), so lock up at all times – wherever possible attaching your bike to railings or some other immovable object. If you prefer safety in numbers, why not take a **Yellow Bike** tour of the city? For tours outside of the city try **Let's Go** or **Mike Bike Tours.**

Damstraat Rent-a-bike
Pieter Jacobsz Dwarsstraat 11
Tel: 625 5029.
MacBike:
Mr Visserplein 2
Tel: 620 0985.
Yellow Bike:
Nieuwezijds Kolk 29
Tel: 620 6940.
Let's Go
Tel: 600 1809.
Mike Bike Tours
Tel: 622 7970.

By Taxi

Cabs cannot be flagged down. They can be hired from ranks at key locations throughout the city (Rembrandtplein, Leidseplein, Museumplein, Dam Square) and in front of Centraal Station or by dialling (0900) 677 7777 (50 cents per minute). Meters are used and the cost is calculated according to the zone and the time of day. On longer journeys it is always wise to establish the cost before you set off. You can also make use of the water taxi in front of Centraal Station (tel: 622 2181).

Driving

Driving within the city is best avoided. Parking is prohibitively expensive, spaces are hard to find, and the aggressive meter brigade clamps wheels and issues tickets with a vengeance. Always be on the lookout for cyclists (who travel at speed and seem to appear from nowhere) and take particular care on the narrow canal streets (often blocked by delivery vans). Other hazards are the complex one-way systems, and trams which always have right of way.

If you arrive by car, the best thing to do is leave it in a car park and either walk or use public transport. There is a large underground car park in front of Centraal Station by the Lovers Excursion Boat office, as well as the underground car park by the Museumplein. Just outside the centre is the multi-storey Euro-parking at Marnixstraat 250, which usually has space and is within walking distance of the centre.

The **Dutch National Automobile Club (ANWB)** has maps and other travel information. They also offer a breakdown service.
Dutch National Automobile Club (ANWB): Museumplein 5, Osdorpplein 885 or Bijlmerplein 1001.

Car Hire

Renting a car is worth considering if you want to explore cities and regions beyond Amsterdam. Roads are good and signposting is clear. Try the following agencies:

Avis
380 Nassaukade
Tel: 683 6061
Budget
121 Overtoom
Tel: 612 6066
Europcar
197 Overtoom
Tel: 683 2123
Hertz
333 Overtoom
Tel: 612 2441
Kuperus BV
175 Middenweg
Tel: 693 8790

Day Trips

Amsterdam makes a good base for day trips. Distances to towns of interest are short and easily covered: The Hague 52 km (33 miles), Utrecht 43 km (27 miles), Delft 62 km (39 miles).

A wide and very efficient network of rail services operates throughout the country. Fast electric trains link Amsterdam with most Dutch towns on an hourly or half-hourly basis. It is well worth finding out about excursion fares, which include entrance fees to museums and other attractions as well as the return rail fare.

Coach excursions are organised by **Lindbergh Excursions**. Most popular are the bulb fields at Keukenhof *(see page 246)*, the traditional eel-fishing villages of Volendam and Marken *(see page 241)*, the cheese market at Alkmaar, the cheese-making centre of Edam *(see page 241)*, the pretty town of Delft *(see page 252)* and the city of Den Haag (The Hague), seat of the Dutch government *(see page 249)*.
Lindbergh Excursions
Damrak 26
Tel: 622 2766

Where to Stay

Choosing a Hotel

For most visitors, the favourite overall location is southwest of the centre, close to the major museums and art galleries, to the large, green Vondelpark and to the popular square of Leidseplein. There are plenty of hotels to choose from in this area and most of them are quieter than those in the central Dam/Damrak area.

Roughly half the total number of beds in Amsterdam are in de luxe or first-class hotels but tourists tend to go for the small, family-run hotels, which are not only cheaper and more charming but are often more centrally located. Many of these lower category hotels are converted from narrow old town houses overlooking canals, but the disadvantages are very small rooms and steep stairs – many hotels don't have a lift.

Prices in all categories are rather steep but bear in mind that, unlike in most other European cities, breakfast is normally included in the price of the room and the choice of cheeses, cold meats, cakes and rolls is usually ample to keep you going for a good part of the day.

The busiest times of year, when you need to book well in advance, are the flower season (April and May), Easter, the summer months and Christmas. Low season, when packages and hotel prices are at their cheapest, is from October to March. The VVV publishes a useful guide called *Amsterdam Accommodation Guide* available from their offices locally and abroad.

Reservations can be made via a travel agency or through the **Amsterdam Reservation Centre**. For reservations outside of

Amsterdam, contact **The Netherlands Reservation Centre** website. The centre offers special winter packages known as "Amsterdam, the Amsterdam Way", a deal which includes lower rate accommodation (from budget to luxury hotels) plus, for example, free entrance to the Rijksmuseum, free drinks in certain bars and a free canal cruise.

Amsterdam House provides moderately priced housing in 30 apartments and eight houseboats for short or long rentals. Rooms are comfortable and fully equipped, with many overlooking the canals.

Bed & Breakfast Holland offers good-value accommodation at locations throughout the city, though not necessarily in the centre. Besides bed & breakfast rooms, they also offer studios with kitchens for those who want self-catering. They work only via fax and email and take no last-minute bookings as they are generally full, especially in holiday periods and summer months.

If you do arrive in the city on spec there is a free telephone reservation service at the airport, or you can ask the VVV office at Centraal Station to make a reservation for you – a small booking fee will be charged. If you want to stay with a family in a private house – which works out a lot cheaper than opting for a hotel – the VVV will also be able to help.

Immediately around Centraal Station you will find many so-called "Hotels" and "Youth Hostels" offering accommodation at rock-bottom prices and in summer you may be approached by touts as you arrive at the station. Cheap they may be, but they are also fleapits, often located above a noisy all-night disco or café, and you will be expected to share rooms as well as bathrooms. They are best avoided, but if you use them, never leave any of your valuables unattended.

Amsterdam Reservation Centre
De Ruyterkade 5, 1013 AA
Tel/fax: 020 201 8800; E-mail:
reservations@amsterdamtourist.nl;
www.amsterdamtourist.nl

The Netherlands Reservation Centre:
PO Box 404
2260 AK Leidschendam
Tel: (0)70-419 5500
Fax: (0)70-419 5519
www.hotelres.nl

Amsterdam House
Wilhelmina Visser, Amstel 176A
1017 AE Amsterdam
Tel: 626 2577
Fax: 626 2987

Bed & Breakfast Holland
Tel: 615 7527
Fax: 669 1573
E-mail: bbrholland@hetnet.nl

Price Guide

The following price categories indicate the cost of a double room in high season:
€€€€ **De Luxe:** €250–500
€€€ **Expensive:** €150–250
€€ **Moderate:** €75–150
€ **Inexpensive:** under €75

Hotel Listings

De Luxe

Amstel Inter Continental
1 Professor Tulpplein
Tel: 622 6060
Fax: 622 5808
E-mail: amstel@interconti.com
www.intercontinenti.com
Lavishly furnished 19th-century hotel (20 minutes' walk from the centre) which is popular among visiting celebrities. High-class cuisine in 2-Michelin star La Rive restaurant. Plush bedrooms and suites, efficient service, delightful terrace in summer.

Blakes
384 Keizersgracht
Tel: 530 2010
Fax: 530 20 30
E-mail: hotel@blakes.nl
www.slh.com
This former theatre (later it was an almshouse) is now an exclusive hotel (and restaurant) under the same stylish management as its London counterpart. There are currently 26 uniquely furnished rooms with all the chic accoutrements, and another 14 due in the future.

Grand Amsterdam
197 Oudezijds Voorburgwal
Tel: 555 3111
Fax: 555 3222
E-mail: hotel@thegrand.nl
www.thegrand.nl
This unique property has a history going back to 1400 when it was a convent and eventually a royal hostelry and a town hall. The rooms are comfortable and feature all amenities. The popular Café Roux is under the culinary direction of Master Chef Albert Roux.

Hotel De L'Europe
2–8 Nieuwe Doelenstraat
Tel: 531 1777
Fax: 531 1778
E-mail: hotel@leurope.nl
www.leurope.nl
Grand late-19th-century hotel overlooking the River Amstel and the Mint Tower. Facilities include swimming pool, open-air terrace, meeting rooms, fitness centre and two restaurants.

Okura Amsterdam
3 Ferdinand Bolstraat
Tel: 678 7111
Fax: 671 2344
E-mail: reservations@okura.nl
www.okura.nl
Essentially a hotel for business travellers, not far from the RAI building and with car parking space for guests and their visitors. Facilities include swimming pool and fitness centre, congress facilities and several excellent restaurants. The Ciel Bleu restaurant and bar on the 23rd floor offers a panoramic view of the city.

Expensive

Ambassade
Herengracht 341
Tel: 626 2333
Fax: 624 5321
E-mail: info@ambassade-hotel.nl
www.ambassade-hotel.nl
A hospitable, exclusive hotel created from a series of 17th- and 18th-century canalside houses. Lots of antiques, paintings, steep steps and spiral staircases. Popular with visiting authors.

American
97 Leidsekade
Tel: 556 3000

Fax: 556 3001
E-mail: american@intercontinenti.com
www.intercontinenti.com
Outstanding Art Nouveau building on the lively Leidseplein. Comfortable well-equipped bedrooms, popular café famous for Tiffany-style decor and colourful clientele, Night Watch cocktail bar with converted terrace (see page 171).

Grand Hotel Krasnapolsky
9 Dam
Tel: 554 9111
Fax: 554 7010
E-mail: reservations@
krasnapolsky.nl
www.krasnapolsky.nl
This historic hotel boasts comfortable rooms on Dam Square facing the Royal Palace. Breakfasts are served in a glass-roofed winter garden. Congress centre and short-term apartments are some of the extras (see page 171).

Golden Tulip Barbizon Palace
59–72 Prins Hendrikkade
Tel: 556 4564
Fax: 624 3353
E-mail: reservations@gtbpalace.
goldentulip.nl
www.goldentuliphotels.nl
Nineteen old houses converted into a luxury hotel overlooking Centraal Station. The interior is a combination of Old Dutch, French and Postmodern styles. Facilities include fitness centre and congress hall. Fine restaurant with Michelin star.

Pulitzer
315–331 Prinsengracht
Tel: 523 5235
Fax: 627 6753
E-mail:
res100_amsterdam@sheraton.com
www.sheraton.com
Terrace of 17th- and 18th-century canalside residences and warehouses, converted into a hotel of considerable charm and character. Exposed brick, beams, antiques and beautiful furnishings. Sophisticated bedrooms overlooking canals or gardens.

Swissôtel Amsterdam Ascot
Damrak 95–98
Tel: 626 0066
Fax: 627 0982
www.swissotel.com

Efficient, ultra-modern Swiss-run hotel in city centre, very close to the Royal Palace and Dam Square. Sound-proofed rooms and suites and excellent in-house restaurant. www.swissotel.com

Moderate

AMS Hotel Terdam
Tesselschadestraat 23
Tel: 6126876
Fax: 683 8313
E-mail: info@ams.nl
www.ams.nl
Friendly, with small, pleasant rooms and basic amenities, quietly located by the Vondelpark. A multi-storey car park is just 100 metres (110 yards) away. Bar on premises.

Amsterdam Wiechmann
Prinsengracht 328–330
Tel: 626 3321
Fax: 626 8962
www.hotelwiechmann.nl
Attractively located canalside hotel in two 17th- and 18th-century houses, north of Leidseplein. Antique furnishings.

Canal House
Keizersgracht 148
Tel: 622 5182
Fax: 624 1317
Email: info@canalhouse.nl
www.canalhouse.nl
American-owned hotel, expertly converted from two 17th-century merchant houses on a quiet canal. Lots of antiques and a charming breakfast room and cosy bar. Lift.

De Gerstekorrel
Damstraat 22–24
Tel: 624 1367
Fax: 623 2640
E-mail: gersteko@euronet.nl
Located just off Dam Square on the edge of the Red Light District, this bright, clean and cheerful hotel is operated by a Finnish family. Rooms are comfortably furnished. 24-hour reception desk to assure security.

De Filosoof
Tel: 683 3013
Fax: 685 3750
E-mail: reservations@hotelfilosoof.nl
www.hotelfilosoof.nl
Situated at the Vondelpark within walking distance of Leidseplein and the museums. The individually furnished rooms are inspired by the

great philosophers, as is the owner, a philosopher herself.

Estheréa
Singel 303–309
Tel: 624 5146
Fax: 623 9001
E-mail: info@estherea.nl
www.estherea.nl
A 17th-century canal house two minutes from Dam Square. Steep stairs but there is a lift. Ask the friendly management for a room with a view.

Jan Luyken Hotel & Residence
Jan Luykenstraat 58
Tel: 573 0730
Fax: 676 3841
E-mail: info@janluyken.nl
www.janluyken.nl
Late 19th-century building close to the Museumplein. The personalised service attracts returning guests. Quiet rooms and apartments. Motorists can reserve parking in the garage.

Mercure Amsterdam Arthur Frommer
Noorderstraat 46
Tel: 622 0328
Fax: 620 3208
E-mail: frommer@mercure-hotels.com
Popular hotel in quiet location not far from art museums and Rembrandtplein. Comfortable rooms built round private courtyard (where you can park free of charge).

Prinsen
Vondelstraat 36–38
Tel: 616 2323
Fax: 616 6112
E-mail: manager@prinsenhotel.demon.nl
www.prinsenhotel.demon.nl
Converted 19th-century houses form this recently renovated hotel on a quiet street near the Vondelpark and Leidseplein.

Toren
Keizersgracht 164
Tel: 622 6352
Fax: 626 9705
E-mail: hotel@toren.nl
www.toren.nl
Cosy canalside hotel located in two 17th-century buildings close to the Jordaan and Anne Frank's House. In-house bar and lovely garden. Ask

for a room with a view. A recent renovation installed a lift.

Tulip Inn Dam Square
Gravenstraat 12–16
Tel: 623 3716
Fax: 638 1156
www.tulipinndamsquare.com
Housed in a converted distillery behind the Nieuwe Kerk by Dam Square, this unique hotel is on a charming street with cafés and wine and liqueur tasting rooms.

Inexpensive

Acro
Jan Luykenstraat 44
Tel: 662 5538
Fax: 675 0811
One of the better-value budget hotels close to the art museums and the Vondelpark. Pleasant furnishings, in good condition.

AMS Hotel Holland
P.C. Hooftstraat 162
Tel: 676 4253
Fax: 676 5956
E-mail: info@ams.nl
www.ams.nl
Quiet location on Amsterdam's chic shopping street in the Museum Quarter close to the Vondelpark and the Concertgebouw.

AMS Hotel Trianon
J.W. Brouwersstraat 3–7
Tel: 673 2073
Fax: 673 8868
E-mail: info@ams.nl
www.ams.nl
Charming hotel behind the Concertgebouw near the museum and shopping quarters. The rooms are comfortable and well equipped. Bar and Italian restaurant.

Amstel Botel
Oosterdokskade 2–4
Tel: 626 4247
Fax: 639 1952
This boat hotel is moored between Centraal Station and the Maritime Museum. Rooms are comfortably furnished with a view over the water. Late at night the location can be dicey, so it is better for couples rather than single women.

Arena
's-Gravesandestraat 51
Tel: 694 7444
Fax: 663 2649
www.hotelarena.nl

This unusual establishment in a monument building near the Tropenmuseum *(see page 235)* began as a youth hostel many years ago and has evolved into a "cultural centre"/budget hotel with a popular disco, terrace and restaurant. It offers rooms for two to four people as well as larger rooms for groups.

Concert Inn
De Lairessestraat 11
Tel: 305 7272
Fax: 305 7271
A friendly, family-run hotel opposite the Concertgebouw that has clean and cosy rooms with basic amenities.

Hans Brinker
Kerkstraat 136
Tel: 622 0687
Fax: 638 2060
This no-frills establishment in the city centre on a quiet street near Leidseplein calls itself the "most exclusive budget hotel".

Hotel Fita
Jan Luykenstraat 37
Tel: 679 0976
Fax: 664 3969
E-mail: info@fita.nl
www.fita.nl
This renovated hotel in the Museum Quarter is quiet and comfortably furnished with large bathrooms. Management is friendly but slow.

Sint-Nicolaas
1a Spuistraat
Tel: 626 1384
Fax: 623 0979
E-mail: info@hotelnicolaas.nl
www.hotelnicolaas.nl
A friendly and comfortable establishment in a converted rope factory near Centraal Station.

Van Ostade Bicycle Hotel
123 Van Ostadestraat
Tel: 679 3452
Fax: 671 5213
www.etrade.nl/bicyclehotel
In a way it's surprising that nobody in this bike-mad city thought of this before, but great ideas are often hidden in plain sight. Anyway, the youthful proprietors translate a commitment to environmentally friendly transport – you can rent bikes cheaply – into a comfortable hotel for cyclists.

Wijnnobel
Vossiusstraat 9
Tel: 662 2298
Cheap and cheerful, with views of the Vondelpark. No private bathrooms. Near public transport, shopping quarter and museums.

Winston
Warmoesstraat 125–129
Tel: 623 1380
Fax: 639 2308
E-mail: winston@winston.nl
www.winston.nl
This has been described as similar to New York's Chelsea Hotel, attracting artists and musicians. Some rooms are basic and low-priced while others have been decorated by artists and are more expensive.

Youth Hostels

Amsterdam has a good choice of hostels open to people of all ages. Most offer dormitory accommodation only but some have private rooms and family facilities such as children's menus. If you are not a member, a card can usually be issued on the spot. For a list of hostels throughout the Netherlands, contact **NJHC**, 2 Prof Tulpstraat, Amsterdam, tel: 551 3133, fax: 623 4986, www.njhc.org. The official YHA hostels in Amsterdam are:

City Hostel Vondelpark
5 Zandpad, Vondelpark
Tel: 589 8996
Fax: 589 8955

Camping

Camping is permitted only on official camp-sites. The VVV office can provide a list of sites near the city but cannot make reservations. Most sites are easily accessible by bus from Centraal Station.

Amsterdamse Bos: Kleine Noorddijk 1, Amstelveen, tel: 641 6868, fax: 640 2378, is a quiet site and suitable for families. One of the closest to the city.

Vliegenbos: Meeuwenlaan 138, tel: 636 8855, fax: 632 2723; a short ride from the city centre,

Quiet, well-equipped hostel in the Vondelpark. All rooms with shower and toilet; recreation rooms, meals and snacks, bar and family rooms.

Hostel Stadsdoelen
97 Kloveniersburgwal
Tel: 624 6832
Fax: 639 1035
On a canal, 10 minutes' walk from Dam Square and close to the Red Light District. Bar and snacks, recreation room.

Staying Out of Town

DELFT

Best Western Delft Museum Hotel
189 Oude Delft,
2611 HD Delft.
Tel: 015-214 0930
Fax: 015-214 0935
E-mail: dmh@bestwestern.nl
www.museumhotel.nl
Located in the picturesque old quarter along the canal. €€€

Juliana
33 Maerten Trompstraat,
2628 RC Delft
Tel: 015-256 7612
Fax: 015 256 5707
A family-run hotel with a garden, located just outside the centre. €€€

De Plataan
10 Doelenplein, 2611 BP Delft
Tel: 015-212 6046
Fax: 015-215 7327
A family-run hotel in the heart of the old historic centre which is within walking distance of the

located in the middle of 25 hectares (60 acres) of woods with cabins as well as tent and shower accommodation.

The following three campsites are not so easy to get to, but the site's management can fax directions:

Zeeburg: Zuiderzeeweg 44, tel: 694 4430, fax: 694 6238.

De Badhoeve: Uitdammerdijk 10; tel/fax: 490 4294;

Gaspercamping: Loosdrechtdreef 7, tel: 696 7326; fax: 696 9369.

museums and market. Comfortable rooms, friendly staff, excellent breakfast and a pantry for tea and coffee. €€€

EDAM

Hotel De Fortuna
Spuisstraat 3, 1135 AV Edam
Tel: 0299 371 671
Fax: 0299 371 469
www.fortuna/edam.nl
This hotel consists of six restored 17th-century houses. Most rooms are fully equipped. In-house restaurant and garden with a terrace on the canal's edge. Accessible to Amsterdam in 20 minutes by bus. €€

HAARLEM

Carillon
27 Grote Markt, 2011 RC Haarlem
Tel: 023-531 0591
Fax: 023-531 4909
E-mail: info@hotelcarillon.com
www.hotelcarillon.com
Simple, well-located lodgings across from the Grote Markt in the heart of the old city. €€

Golden Tulip Lion d'Or
34–36 Kruisweg
2011 LC Haarlem
Tel: 023-532 1750
Fax: 023-532 9543
E-mail: reservations@hoteliondor.nl
www.goldentulip.nl
Just across from the train station, this hotel dates from 1820 and is now operated by a reputable Dutch chain. The 34 rooms are modern and well equipped and there is 24-hour reception and a lift. Bar/lounge and à la carte restaurant. €€€€

THE HAGUE (DEN HAAG)

Carlton Ambassador
2 Sophialaan
2514 JP Den Haag
Tel: 070-363 0363
Fax: 070-360 0535
E-mail: ambassador@carlton.nl
www.carlton.nl/ambassador

Located in the quiet, historic Mesdag quarter near the museums, Peace Palace and main shopping streets. The 80 rooms are decorated in Old Dutch and English styles and are tastefully furnished. Friendly staff. €€€

Price Guide

The following price categories indicate the cost of a double room in high season:
€€€€ **De Luxe:** €250–500
€€€ **Expensive:** €150–250
€€ **Moderate:** €75–150
€ **Inexpensive:** under €75

Esquire
65 Van Aerssenstraat
2582 JG Den Haag
Tel: 070-352 2341
Fax: 070 306 3366
www.esquire-hotel.com
This comfortable, friendly hotel is in the charming Statenkwartier with many shops and restaurants. It is accessible with tram Nos 7 and 10 from the Centraal Train Station and just minutes from Scheveningen if you want to smell the sea air. €€€

Corona
39–42 Buitenhof
2513 AH Den Haag
Tel: 070-363 7930
Fax: 070-361 5785
E-mail: info@corona.nl
www.corona.nl
Luxurious hotel on a central square across from the Binnenhof and the shopping quarter, with a highly regarded restaurant. €€€€

Inter-Continental Des Indes
54–56 Lange Voorhout
2514 EG Den Haag
Tel: 070 361-2345
Fax: 070 345-1721
E-mail: hotel_desindes@desindes.com
www.desindes.com
Former palace built in the 1850s, once the haunt of Mata Hari and Pavlova, now used by diplomats and well-heeled travellers who rely on the attentive service and luxurious rooms. Even if you are not a hotel guest, it is a great spot for afternoon tea. €€€€

Steigenberger Kurhaus
30 Gev. Deynootplein
2586 CK Scheveningen
Tel: 070-416 2636
Fax: 070-416 2646
E-mail: info@kurhaus.nl
www.kurhaus.nl
Architecturally splendid with marvellous views and elegant rooms, located in Scheveningen, the seaside resort town on the outskirts of The Hague. The Kandinsky restaurant is the hotel's pride. €€€€

LEIDEN

Golden Tulip Leiden
3 Schipholweg, 2316 XB Leiden
Tel: 071-522 1121
Fax: 071-522 6675
E-mail: reservations@golden-tulip-leiden.nl
www.goldentulip.nl
Just opposite the train station, this dependable hotel has all the usual amenities. €€

Nieuw Minerva
23 Boommarkt
2311 EA Leiden
Tel: 071-512 6358
Fax: 071-514 2674
E-mail: hotel@nieuwminerva.nl
www.nieuwminerva.nl
Homely hotel furnished with antiques, located in a group of historic buildings on a quiet tributary of the River Rhine. €€

ROTTERDAM

Best Western Pax Hotel
658 Schiekade
3032 AK Rotterdam
Tel: 010-466 3344
Fax: 010-467 5278
E-mail: info@paxhotel.nl
www.paxhotel.nl
This small hotel is known for its friendly atmosphere and personalised service. Centrally located, just 10 minutes by foot from downtown shopping, the Doelen concert hall and the World Trade Centre. The 53 rooms are comfortably furnished and there are also apartments with self-contained kitchens. €€€

Bilderberg Park Hotel
70 Westersingel
3015 LB Rotterdam
Tel: 010-436 3611
Fax: 010-436 4212
E-mail: parkhotel@bilderberg.nl
www.parkhotelrotterdam.nl
Well-located hotel along a canal in the heart of the city bordering Museum Park and near the shopping and entertainment centre. The Empress restaurant is recommended and the fitness centre offers facilities to work out as well as to relax. Within walking distance of the train station, accessible by tram and also has a car park. €€€€

Price Guide

The following price categories indicate the cost of a double room in high season:
€€€€ **De Luxe:** €250–500
€€€ **Expensive:** €150–250
€€ **Moderate:** €75–150
€ **Inexpensive:** under €75

Golden Tulip Rotterdam
Coolsingel/4 Aert von Nesstraat
3012 CA Rotterdam
Tel: 010-206 7800
Fax: 010-413 5320
E-mail:
reservations@goldentuliphotels.nl
www.goldentuliphotels.nl
Housed in an historic building in the heart of the city, this large hotel is geared to the business traveller. Rooms are fully equipped and you can enjoy breakfast with a view on the roof terrace. €€€€

Hotel New York
1 Koninginnenhoofd
3072 AD Rotterdam
Tel: 010-439 0500
Fax: 010-484 2701
E-mail: info@hotelnewyork.nl
www.hotelnewyork.nl
Located across the River Maas in the former headquarters of the Holland America Line, this is a splendid, very popular hotel with uniquely furnished rooms and waterfront views. Try to book the room in the Clock Tower, which has a waiting list of many months. The bar/restaurant is popular. €€€€

UTRECHT

Grand Hotel Karel V
1 Geertebolwerk
3511 XA Utrecht
Tel: 030-233 7555
Fax: 030-233 7500
E-mail: info@karelv.nl
www.karelv.nl
This luxury hotel in the historic city centre opened partially in autumn 1999 and was fully completed in winter 2000. On the site of a former military hospital with an illustrious history dating from the 14th century, this is Utrecht's first 5-star hotel. Worth a visit if only for lunch or tea. €€€€

Holiday Inn
24 Jaarbeursplein
3521 AR Utrecht
Tel: 030-297 7977
Fax: 030-297 7999
E-mail: reservations@nhutrecht.com
www.nh-hotels.com
Caters for business visitors to the next-door Exhibition Centre, with a panoramic restaurant and a bar on the 20th floor. €€€€

NH Centre
10 Janskerkhof
3512 BL Utrecht
Tel: 030-231 3169
Fax: 030-231 0148
E-mail: dirnhcentre.utrecht@nh-hotels.nl
www.nh-hotels.com
Charming hotel and restaurant in the heart of the old quarter opposite St Janskerk and local shops. €€€

Where to Eat

What to Eat

Although the heavy, calorie-loaded typical national dishes have gradually given way to the demands of diet-conscious Dutch, you can still find plenty of vegetable hotchpotches, thick pea soups, wholesome stews, apple pies and pancakes with lashings of cream. Dutch food may not be very exciting, but most of the time it is good and filling.

Typical Dutch breakfasts – consisting of a variety of cheeses, cold meats, sausages, breads and rolls along with coffee, tea or chocolate – are enough to keep you going for most of the day.

Amsterdam also excels in delicious snacks: salted herrings served from street stalls (and traditionally swallowed whole on the spot), smoked eel, meat croquettes, sausages, French fries with mayonnaise, sweet and savoury pancakes, waffles and *poffertjes* (mini-pancakes with sugar). Even the *automatieken*, the food-dispensing machines, provide some surprisingly appetising snacks such as meat and cheese croquettes and *loempia* (egg-roll). The local equivalent to sandwiches are *broodjes*, soft rolls loaded with cheese, roast beef, ham, prawns, herring, and an infinite variety of other fillings.

A lunch in a café might consist of an *Uitsmijter*, an open sandwich, with roast beef, meatballs, ham or cheese on bread topped with fried egg, a basic omelette or something more modern such as *ciabatta* with mozzarella and tomato, smoked salmon, or pickled beef. On a brisk winter day, a bowl of hearty *bruinenbonen* (brown bean soup) or

Erwtensoep, a thick soup with peas and pork, is guaranteed to keep out the cold.

Dinner is the main meal of the day, and although the Dutch usually dine at home around 6pm, most restaurants are filled around 8pm.

Where to Eat

When it comes to dining in Amsterdam, remember that it is possible to do it in almost any language – Turkish, Italian, Ethiopian, Tibetan, Polish, Vietnamese, and everything in between. But, as far as most visitors are concerned, the city's gastronomic forte is Indonesian cuisine, a legacy of Dutch colonialism. The *pièce de résistance* is the *rijsttafel*, an exotic variety of meat, fish and vegetable dishes such as satay, spicy meatballs and *loempia*, all served with steamed rice.

The neighbourhood "eetcafés" offer a dish of the day and some à la carte items which are quite reasonably priced.

Bear in mind that a 15 percent service charge and VAT are invariably included in bills, both for restaurants and bars, and there is no compulsion to tip. In cafés, you usually leave the leftover change. In better restaurants, an extra 10 percent gratuity is expected.

Restaurant Listings

Dutch
d'Vijff Vlieghen (Five Flies)
Spuistraat 294–302
Tel: 624 8369
The "New Dutch" cuisine is featured in this pricey but very picturesque setting with seven separate rooms in a monumental building, complete with beams, tiles, candles and original Rembrandt drawings. Closed lunch. €€€
De Blauwe Hollander
Leidsekruisstraat 28
Tel: 623 3014
Straightforward wholesome Dutch food in cosy, unpretentious setting. This is the place to try all those hearty dishes such as *hutspot*,

boerenkool and *erwtensoep*, especially in cooler weather. Closed lunch. €
Dorrius
Nieuwezijds Voorburgwal 5
Tel: 420 2224
This landmark restaurant moved, with all its antique furnishings, to a site adjoining the Crowne Plaza Hotel a few years ago. The kitchen is authentic as well as the ambience. Closed lunch. €€
The Pancake Bakery
Prinsengracht 191
Tel: 625 1333
Housed in a 17th-century canal house, this place serves up sweet and savoury pancakes daily. €
Spanjer en Van Twist
Leliegracht 60
Tel: 639 0109
This cosy restaurant has a popular terrace in summer months. Terrific for lunch and very busy for dinner. €

Price Guide

The following price categories are for a three-course meal for one, without drinks:
€€€ **Expensive:** €50–€100
€€ **Moderate:** €20–€50
€ **Inexpensive:** under €20.

Fish/Seafood
Al's Plaice
Nieuwendijk 10
Tel: 427 4192
If you want some good, straightforward fish and chips, kidney pies or pickled eggs, this is the place. Closed Tuesday. No credit cards. €
Lucius
Spuistraat 247
Tel: 624 1831
A bistro-style restaurant with a loyal crowd who come for the shellfish platters and fresh fish prepared in various ways. Closed lunch and Sunday. €
Werkendam
Sint Nicolaasstraat 43
Tel: 428 7744
This intimate restaurant features all kinds of fresh fish, baked, broiled, fried or steamed. There are oyster platters and an excellent bouillabaise. Closed lunch. €€

French
Christophe
Leliegracht 46
Tel: 625 0807
The owner and chef (from Toulouse) shows how he earned his Michelin star with imaginative cooking using traditional Mediterranean ingredients. Open 6:30pm. Closed Sunday and Monday. €€€
D'Theeboom
Singel 210
Tel: 623 8420
Another French chef with an imaginative menu but less imposing prices than some addresses in town. Closed lunch. €€
La Rive
Amstel Hotel
Professor Tulpplein 1
Tel: 622 6060
French cuisine in an intimate and elegant hotel restaurant with two Michelin stars. Faultless service. Closed Sunday. €€€

Indonesian
Bojo
Lange Leidsedwarsstraat 51
Tel: 622 7434
Good-value Indonesian food just off the Leidseplein. Open until 4am and thus attracts the night crowd. Closed lunch. €
Poentjak Pas
Nassaukade 366
Tel: 618 0906
Fine home cooking and reasonably priced *rijsttaffels*, which can be adapted for vegetarians. Closed lunch. €
Sama Sebo
27 Pieter Cornelisz Hooftstraat
Tel: 662 8146
Sama Sebo serves classic Indonesian fare, the authenticity of which is complemented by a profusion of mats made from rushes and *batik*. €€
Srikandi
Stadhouderskade 31
Tel: 664 0408
Just minutes from the Rijksmuseum and Leidseplein, this intimate restaurant offers diverse and delicious cooking from the Java, Bali, Madoera and Sumatra regions of Indonesia. Closed lunch. €€

Price Guide

The following price categories are for a three-course meal for one, without drinks:

€€€ Expensive: €50–€100
€€ Moderate: €20–€50
€ Inexpensive: under €20.

Mediterranean
The Supper Club
Jonge Roelensteeg 21
Tel: 344 6400
This unique dining establishment was started by a few artists who liked performance art and good food. Instead of dining at tables, one reclines on extravagant mattresses and no night is ever the same. Closed lunch. Book weeks in advance for weekends. **€€€**
Grekas Traiterie
Singel 311
Tel: 620 3590
This Greek takeaway also has tables where one can enjoy dinner in an unpretentious atmosphere. Vegetarian *mezes* and hearty meat stews. Closed lunch. **€**
Porto Carrara
Lange Leidsedwaarstraat 138
Tel: 623 5672
This delicious, unpretentious pizzeria/pasta house serves great food at great prices. Just off the Leidseplein in a sea of fast-food places, but worth the visit. **€**
Vertigo
Film Museum, 3 Vondelpark
Tel: 612 3021
Putting a restaurant with a name like this in a basement might seem odd, until you realise that this is film-buff central. The food is Mediterranean-inspired and in good weather you can dine outdoors on one of the finest terraces in town. **€€**

Vegetarian
De Bolhoed
Prinsengracht 60–62
Tel: 626 1803
Popular vegetarian restaurant for lunch and dinner in the Jordaan district. Soups, salads and interesting hot meals. Small terrace by the canal in summer. **€**

Golden Temple
Utrechtsestraat 126
Tel: 626 8560
Small local spot in Utrechtsestraat shopping street serving excellent vegetarian food with many ethnic specialities The salad buffet is very popular. Closed lunch. **€**

Chic Dining
Pier 10
De Ruyterkade, Steiger (Pier) 10
Tel: 624 8276
On a pier just behind Centraal Station, this harbourside restaurant is both small and popular enough to make reservations essential. The menu changes seasonally and places a strong, though not exclusive, emphasis on fish. **€€**
Wildschut
1–3 Roelof Hartplein
Tel: 676 8220
Permanently trendy, this cafe-restaurant stands on a curving street corner that catches enough rays from the late-afternoon sun to make its pavement terrace hallowed ground in good weather for recently liberated office workers. The food ranges from bar snacks to well-prepared international dishes. **€–€€**

Other Cuisines
Café Bern
Nieuwmarkt 9
Tel: 622 0034
This popular Swiss café serves the best fondue in town. Other specialities include steak served on a table grill with pesto sauce. Reservations a must or you can eat at the bar. Closed lunch. **€**
OLa Brasa
Haarlemmerdijk 16
Tel: 625 4438
If you like steaks cooked on a charcoal grill with a jacket potato, steamed veggies and a salad, then this is the place. The grilled lamb is another mouth-watering option. Non red meat-eaters can get a half chicken or salmon steak. Closed lunch and Wednesday. **€€**
Sherpa
Korte Leidsedwaarstraat 58
Tel: 623 9495
This cosy restaurant offers authentic Tibetan cuisine in the

spirit of Marco Polo. The appetisers and main courses are all worth trying. The house aperitif must also be experienced. Closed lunch. **€**
Yamazato
Okura Hotel
Ferdinand Bolstraat 333
Tel: 678 7111
Best Japanese food in the country (forming part of a Japanese hotel). Open daily, lunch and dinner. **€€**

Drinking Notes

The most popular drinks are fresh coffee and pilsner beer. The Netherlands is the world's number one producer of beer and the local pilsner is served in cafés and restaurants throughout the city, usually in 25cl (half-pint) measures. Heineken is the most popular. Foreign brands are available at much higher prices.

The native gin is jenever, drunk neat (and traditionally knocked back in one) or with a beer chaser. Varieties include *oude* (old), which is the sweeter, and *jonge* (young), the more powerful. The place to try out the local spirits and liqueurs is a *proeflokaal* or tasting house, the best known being Wijnand Fockink (*see page 277*).

Cafés and Bars

There are numerous cafés, traditional and modern, throughout the city, serving good coffee – often with apple tart or spicy biscuits.

There is also a plethora of New Wave bars, with cool, whitewashed and mirrored walls, an abundance of greenery and a long list of cocktails. Some bars have live music, often jazz or blues. These establishments are not to be confused with the city's infamous "coffee shops" which sell soft drugs as well as coffee and display a green and white licence in the window and usually feature Jamaican-style decor and Pink Floyd soundtracks (*see page 102*).

American
American Hotel
Leidseplein 28
Splendid Art Nouveau café

overlooking Leidseplein, very popular among fashionable locals *(see page 171)*. Mata Hari had her wedding reception here.
Eylders
Korte Leidsedwarsstraat 47
Former haunt of the literati, just by Leidseplein. Occasional modern art exhibitions.
Het Hok
Lange Leidsedwarsstraat 134
Specialises in chess, backgammon and draughts.
Hoppe
Spui 20
Smoke-filled and crowded bar, unremarkable except for the fact that the locals all love it. Crowds usually spill out on to the street.
De Jaren
Nieuwe Doelenstraat 20–22
Spacious grand café with a wonderful view over the Amstel; mixed clientele of students and prosperous locals.

De Leidse Bocht and Max Grand
Adjoining each other on Max Euweplein (close to Leidseplein), with terraces on the square and on the Singelgracht, opposite to the canal boat landing stages.
Metz
Keizersgracht 455
Café on top of a luxury store *(see page 169)*. Splendid views.
De Prins
Prinsengracht 124
Charming 18th-century canal house where you can linger over a drink or have a full breakfast, lunch or dinner.
Schiller
Rembrandtplein 26
Splendid Art Deco interior; otherwise uninspiring.
Vertigo
Vondelpark 3
Café-restaurant with big terrace on the Vondelpark; good for people-watching.

Wijnand Fockink
Pijlsteeg 31
Picturesque, famous old bar and tasting house off Dam Square where you can try out the local spirits and liqueurs.

Gay Cafés

Argos
Warmoesstraat 95
Tel: 622 6595
Open until 4am Friday and Saturday, special parties organised (ask at the bar).
The Cuckoo's Nest
Nieuwezijds Kolk 6
Tel: 627 1752
Open until 3am at weekends, reputed to have the largest play/darkroom in Europe.
Mankind
Weteringstraat 60
Tel: 638 4755
Bar/café in Museum Quarter,

Brown Cafés

A typical brown café is an intimate, semi-Bohemian bar with nicotine-stained walls (hence the name), rugs on tables, sawdust on the floor and newspapers to peruse. These are usually frequented by the locals (as well as tourists) and are places where you can often get good-quality food at reasonable prices or linger over a drink and a book on a rainy afternoon *(see page 102)*.
Café Oosterling
Utrechtsestraat
Tel: 623 4140.
A charming café with very low stools and a beautiful floor, once a distillery (easy to see in the fixtures and fittings). One of the very few cafés with off-sales.
Joop Heuvel
Prinsengracht 568
Traditional brown café close to the Rijksmuseum.
Krom
Utrechtsestraat 76
Tel: 624 5343
The only extensive change in this café in the past 50 years is the removal of the carpet, revealing a

parquet floor, and the addition of a very good coffee machine. The decor reflects a period of rare elegance and the bar is unique.
Café Mulder
Weteringschans 163
Tel: 623 7874
A rather downbeat café, but nevertheless worth a visit. The staff still wear the traditional black and white attire and visitors could be forgiven for thinking they are sitting in pre-war Amsterdam. Drinks are cheap and there is a terrace in warm weather.
Papeneiland
Prinsengracht 2
Tel: 624 1989.
This café, reputed to be the oldest in Amsterdam, is an institution with its thick low-hung oak beams, dark walls adorned with etchings and prints and the tables bedecked with tiny carpets from the East. The view from the small terrace affords the chance to look out over a canal intersection and a few old spritsail barges. Saturday afternoons are busy to the point of overflowing; however, this is the

ideal location for an intimate chat in the evening.
Prinsesse-Bar Café
Haarlemmerstraat 105
Tel: 624 0106
This little gem on the edge of the Jordaan has all the charms of a "local pub". It is one of the few bars that still has a traditional billiards table (minus pockets) and boasts two teams. The bar consists of a highly polished, long copper tray; the mosaic floor was laid by hand in 1928 and cost the then astronomical sum of 1,100 guilders. The atmosphere is friendly and informal and welcoming to tourists. The soup is highly recommended.
Other brown cafés worth mentioning are:
Pieper
Prinsengracht 424
Tel: 626 4775
Karpershoek
Martelaarsgracht 2
Tel: 624 7886
't Smalle
Egelantiersgracht 12
Tel: 623 9617

lunches and dinners. One of the tamer establishments.

Soho
Reguliersdwarsstraat 36
Tel: 330 4400
The newest gay pub in town.

Spyker Cafe
Kerkstraat 4
Tel: 620 5919
Popular and busy café with a pool table, also cruisy with darkroom. Happy hour every day 5–7pm.

The Web
Sint Jacobstraat 6
Tel: 623 6758
Large, dark café with numerous attractions including a darkroom – very cruisy and leather-based.

Vive La Vie
Amstelstraat 7
Tel: 624 0114
Friendly lesbian bar, intimate atmosphere. Mostly women, although men are welcome.

Pavement Cafés

Sitting and watching the world go by is one of the most entertaining ways of getting to know the city. Everything goes here so, from the vantage point of a pavement café, you will see plenty of way-out get-ups as well as all the street entertainment, including barrel organs, buskers and fire-eaters. The best spots for people-watching are Leidseplein, Rembrandtplein, Spui, Vondelpark, and at many of the canal terraces on the outskirts of the Jordaan.

Culture

Museums and Art Galleries

Amsterdam has more than 40 museums, ranging from some of Europe's finest art collections to a host of small, specialist museums reflecting the diversity of the city's culture. The top three attractions, the Rijksmuseum and the Van Gogh and Stedelijk museums, are all conveniently located round Museumplein, which underwent an extensive renewal project in 1999 and is now a popular meeting place once again (see page 200).

If you intend spending a large proportion of your time visiting museums, buy an Amsterdam Pass (see page 266) which gives free entry or substantial discounts to all the most important museums, a free canal cruise and discounts to tourist attractions. This is a viable alternative to the Museum Card (available at main museums and the VVV), valid for a year and entitling you to free entry to approximately 350 museums in the Netherlands, 16 of them in Amsterdam. The price of the Museum Card is such that you need to visit at least 10 museums before you make a saving, therefore making it more attractive to locals.

Most museums are closed all day Monday. They are generally open Tues–Fri 10am–5pm, Sat–Sun 11am–5pm.

Theatre, Music, Opera and Ballet

For the majority of theatre, music, ballet and opera performances, seats can be booked in advance at the Amsterdam Uitburo on Leidseplein or from the VVV (see page 263). For information on what's on, consult the English guide *What's On in Amsterdam*, available from the tourist office and main hotels (see page 263), or the monthly Uitburo publication, *Uitkrant*, published in Dutch, but easy to comprehend in terms of dates and events.

The chief venue for classical music is the **Concertgebouw** (see page 198) which holds special Sunday morning concerts, as well as other events. Chamber music is often performed in the city's historic churches and there are student performances at the Music Conservatory (Conservatorium) at 27 Van Baerlestraat. The IJsbreker café/concert hall at 23 Weesperzijde is a popular venue for contemporary music played by many international and local artists.

The impressive 1,600-seat **Muziektheater**, overlooking the River Amstel by Waterlooplein, is home of the National Ballet and Netherlands Opera (see page 206). The ballet, under the direction of Wayne Eagling, offers a varied repertoire of classics as well as modern work by today's top choreographers. As artistic director of the opera for more than a decade, Pierre Audi has helped it achieve worldwide renown with its mixed repertoire of classic and modern productions, from Monteverdi to Robert Wilson.

The **Vondelpark** is the venue in summer for free concerts, dance and more, afternoons and evenings in the amphitheatre (see page 232). The Holland Festival is an annual event each June, featuring international opera, theatre, music and dance (see page 92). The main venue is the Stadsschouwburg theatre at the Leidseplein.

Cinema

Amsterdam has many cinemas throughout the city. The large cinemas are located around Leidseplein, Rembrandtplein and Haarlemmerplein. Due to the popularity of the large multiplex cinemas, small art house cinemas are becoming more scarce, but fortunately there are still some thriving, notably The Movies, Kriterion, Rialto, Desmet and Uitkijk.

All films are shown in their original language with Dutch subtitles. In the larger cinemas, many films are stopped halfway to encourage custom at the snack bar. Listings of screening times and venues are posted in most cafés and in front of cinemas.

Literary Events

Amsterdam has many bookshops and many people who are still reading books and appreciating literature. There are occasional book signings for a foreign author at local stores such as Athenaeum or Scheltema and that often means the author might be giving a reading somewhere *(see page 280)*.

The **John Adams Institute for American Literature** offers a reading series throughout the year at various venues in the city. Authors have included John Irving, Paul Theroux, Peter Matthiessen and Carole Shields. For information, call: 624 7280. **Winston Kingdom**, a cultural centre/hotel holds poetry evenings on Monday around 10pm *(see page 279)*.

Diamond Factories

Amsterdam is a major diamond centre with dozens of workshops where you can watch the cutting and polishing of the gems. Entrance is free and there is absolutely no obligation to buy. If you are tempted, bear in mind the import tax you might have to pay.
The following factories operate free guided tours:
Amsterdam Diamond Centre
Rokin 1–5
Bonebakker & Zn
88/90 Rokin
Coster Diamonds
Paulus Potterstraat 2–6
Gassan Diamonds
Nieuwe Uilenburgerstraat 173–5

Stoeltie
Wagenstraat 13–17
Van Moppes Diamonds
Albert Cuypstraat 2–6

Brewery Tours

Brouwerij 't IJ
Funenkade 7
Tel: 622 8325
Located in an old public bath house and next to a prominent windmill. Open to visitors Wed–Sun 3–8pm. Brewery tours: Fri, Sat, Sun after 4pm by arrangement only, cost €2 including a drink. Real beer devotees may enjoy free tours on Fridays.
Amsterdams Brouwhuis Maximiliaan
Kloveniersburgwal 6–8
(near Nieuwmarkt)
Tel: 624 2778
Reservations: 626 6280
Situated in an old convent where the reverend ladies used to brew beer themselves. The fact that you can drink a beer in the brewing hall next to the copper kettles makes it all the more appealing *(see page 148)*. There is a very reasonable restaurant located in the old refectory. Open Tues–Thur noon–1am, Fri & Sat noon–2am and Sun noon–midnight. Brewery tours: by appointment only (phone or ask at the bar), cost €5 including drink, groups of up to 15.
Heineken Experience
Stadhouderskade 78
Tel: 523 9239
The former brewery building opened its doors as a brewing museum in 2001, and their guided tours involve a certain amount of beer consumption. Of course Heineken is still brewing, but has relocated its operation outside Amsterdam *(see page 180)*.

"Proeflokalen" (Tasting Rooms)
These are usually associated with spirits and distilleries and are, generally speaking, of the brown café genre and make excellent watering holes. Their original function was to serve as a tasting room before customers made their purchases – alas, no more.

Wijnand Fockink Proeflokaal
Pijlsteeg 31, 1012 HH
(next to the Krasnapolsky Hotel)
Tel: 639 2695.
The current owner has lovingly restored this distillery to its former glory and it may be visited from 3–9pm daily. Inside you may expect to drink the numerous varieties and qualities of jenevers (Dutch gins) which vary from a light jenever to beautifully cask-matured nectar comparable to the finest single malt whiskies. In addition to the fine display of jenever bottles there is a magnificent collection of homemade liqueurs. The interior decor reflects its 17th-century splendour including the traditional sand on the massively thick floorboards. Guided tours round the distillery by arrangement only.

City Walks

Brochures are available from the VVV and the Amsterdam Historical Museum detailing walks around the city and covering the Jordaan, Maritime Quarter, Jewish Amsterdam, famous shopping streets and Amsterdam School architecture, among other themes.

Excursions

Travel agents organise city bus tours, canal cruises and excursions further afield *(see page 264)*. Within the city the most popular excursions are daytime and evening *rondvaart* canal cruises in modern glass-covered motor-launches *(see page 157)*. You can also take an organised tram ride around the city, starting from Centraal Station. City tours by coach take in the Royal Palace, the Rijksmuseum, a diamond-cutting factory and other sights. It is cheaper to visit these yourself, but a tour is worth considering if time is limited and you don't know the city. For excursions outside Amsterdam, the main operators are Holland International and Lindbergh Excursions *(see page 267)*.

For those interested in personal guides who specialise in art, architecture, antiques, and even the Red Light District, get the Amsterdam Information booklet at VVV offices. The booklet also includes information about special building tours of such landmarks as the Tuschinski Cinema, Arena football stadium, Beurs van Berlage, Concertgebouw and the ING Bank Headquarters in Amsterdam Southeast.

The following are some of the most popular excursions:

Volendam and Marken: Traditional fishing villages with wooden houses and locals in traditional colourful costumes. Quaint but very touristy. The excursion also takes in a visit to a cheesemaker and perhaps a clogmaker too *(see page 241).*

Aalsmeer: Venue of the world's biggest flower auctions. The flower festival is also held here on the first Saturday of September *(see page 255).*

Alkmaar: On Fridays from April to September Alkmaar is the scene of a lively and very picturesque cheese market, with barrel organs, buskers and streets packed with stalls selling cheeses.

Delft: A picturesque little town of canals and white bridges, where you can watch craftsmen making Delft pottery *(see page 252).*

The Hague: Seat of the Dutch Parliament and home of Dutch royalty, less than an hour's journey from Amsterdam. A prosperous, somewhat sedate city of

embassies, parks and palaces, well worth visiting for good museums and art galleries. The Mauritshuis has a collection of Dutch masterpieces *(see page 250).*

Haarlem: A well-preserved 17th-century city whose chief attractions are the Frans Hals and Teylers Museums *(see page 245).*

Utrecht: Historic religious centre which still preserves Gothic churches and old patrician houses. Also an international business/industrial centre. Most impressive of all is the Dom tower, the highest cathedral tower in the Netherlands *(see page 244).*

Grand Holland Tour: A day's excursion taking in Aalsmeer, The Hague, the miniature town of

Annual Festivals

The following are the main events of the city:

January–March:

1 January: New Year's Day.

25 February: Commemoration of the "February Strike", led by the dockers in 1941 against the Nazis' treatment of the Jews, held on J.D. Meijerplein *(see page 210).*

February and March: Amsterdam Carnival.

March: On the Sunday closest to 15 March there is a silent procession through the city – the Stille Omgang – which celebrates the "Amsterdam Miracle", a 14th-century communion wafer which was supposedly impossible to destroy in fire *(see page 25).*

April–June:

30 April: Koninginnedag (Queen's Day). Street markets, street parties, fireworks and festivities throughout the entire city until the early evening *(see page 91).*

Late April: Keukenhof Floral Parade at Keukenhof Gardens, 30 km (19 miles) southwest of Amsterdam *(see page 246).*

4 May: Dodenherdenking (National Remembrance Day)

5 May: Bevrijdingsdag (Liberation Day) is celebrated by a smaller version of Queen's Day, held

primarily in the Vondelpark.

June: The Netherlands feast of culture, the Holland Festival, is held throughout most of the month at the Stadsschouwburg and other nearby venues. It features major theatrical, operatic, dance and musical events, many for an English-speaking audience *(see page 92).*

July–September:

Free concerts and theatre are held on summer afternoons and evenings at the open-air pavilion in the Vondelpark, while classical music is performed by internationally renowned musicians on a barge in front of the Pulitzer Hotel.

Late August: On the last weekend of the month, the annual Uitmarkt takes place in Museumplein. This popular event, which attracts thousands, celebrates the opening of the cultural season in the Netherlands. There are mini-performances from dance, theatre and musical groups as well as hundreds of stalls which provide information on the various events.

Early September: The annual Bloemencorso (Flower Parade) winds its way from Aalsmeer to

Amsterdam in the first week of the month.

Mid-September: Jordaan Festival. Weekend in the Jordaan district devoted to a number of events, including brass bands and *smartlap* (tearjerker music) choirs, and more *(see page 158).*

October–December:

Mid-November: The parade of St Nicolaas is held on a Saturday in the middle of the month. St Nicolaas (the Dutch version of Santa Claus) arrives by steamer at Centraal Station, together with his Moorish helpers (the *Zwarte Pieten*), who distribute *pepernoten* (spice biscuits) to the city's children along the parade site *(see page 92).*

5 December: Shops close early so that families can celebrate *Sinterklaas* or *Pakjesavond* (gift evening) exchanging presents and poems in honour of Saint Nicholas' birthday on 6 December.

31 December: Fireworks around the harbour and around the Nieuwmarkt in Chinatown at midnight. Try some *oliebollen* (doughnuts without the hole) which is an *Oudejaars* (New Year) tradition.

Madurodam, Rotterdam and Delft.
VIP Tours: This offers more exclusive excursions by day and night in a minibus with a personal guide. Tel: 0900 543 23300

Parks

The Vondelpark, close to Leidseplein, provides a welcome retreat from the narrow, traffic-filled streets of the city. Extensive lawns, flowerbeds, free concerts in summer, Sunday afternoon pop groups, fire-eaters and jugglers and teas by the lakeside are all part of the attraction. Café Vertigo at the Film Museum is a great spot for lunch, dinner or a drink on the terrace in the warm summer months *(see page 232).*

For outdoor activities, there's nothing to beat the Amsterdamse Bos – an 890-hectare (2,200-acre) public park southwest of Amsterdam, with miles of walking and biking paths, and places for boating, riding and swimming. Drop in at the Meerzicht farmhouse restaurant for a traditional Dutch pancake, located in the middle of the park to the right of the rowing lake. Take Bus 170, 171 or 172 from Centraal Station *(see page 135).*

Nightlife

Nightspots

After dark, entertainment focuses on three main areas: Leidseplein, for lively discos and nightclubs; Rembrandtplein for clubs, discos, cabarets and strip shows pandering to older tastes; and the Red Light District, notorious for scantily dressed females sitting in windows *(see page 151).*

Strip shows, porn videos and sex shops centre on the main canals of Oudezijde Voorburgwal and Oudezijde Achterburgwal. The smaller, sleazier streets leading off these two canals are best avoided – and don't take photographs.

On a different note, you could take a candlelit canal cruise, with wine and cheese or full dinner provided *(see page 157),* or try a brown café, some of which have live music *(see page 102).*

Music Venues

Akhnaton
Nieuwezijds Voorburgwal 161
Hosts salsa, tango and world music-themed evenings. Performances as well as dance nights.
Bamboo Bar
Lange Leidsedwarsstraat 66
Live jazz and blues in exotic setting.
Bimhuis
Oudeschans 73
The in-place for jazz music, featuring top international players as well as locals.
Bourbon Street
Leidsekruisstraat 6
Blues, rock, and Latin bands perform during the week.
Café Alto
Korte Leidsedwaarstraat 115
Live jazz from 9pm. No admission fee but buying drinks is essential.

Gambling

The main venue for gambling in Amsterdam is **Holland Casino Amsterdam,** Max Euweplein 62, close to Leidseplein. Passport or ID card necessary for entry.

Cotton Club
Nieuwmarkt 5
Live jazz at weekends in this local landmark.
De IJsbreker
23 Weesperzijde
Tel: 668 1805
This café-venue beside the River Amstel is the place to go for the latest in pioneering musical sounds.
Last Waterhole
Oudezijds Armsteeg 12
Live music of all kinds is offered nightly.
Melkweg
Lijnbaansgracht 234a
Long-standing off-beat arts centre-cum–club, with concert hall, disco, experimental plays (some in English) and art exhibitions. Dope and space cakes for sale.
Paradiso
Weteringschans 6–8, just off Leidseplein
The hot spot for rock, reggae and pop concerts, attracting top international headliners as well as new talent from all around Europe.
Winston Kingdom
Warmoesstraat 123
The essence of cool with art, live music, poetry happenings being offered during the week.

Nightclubs

Casablanca
Zeedijk 26
Some nights they have a disco with top local DJs and other nights live jazz, blues and more.
Club Arena
's-Gravesandestraat 51
A popular disco out of the city centre that attracts a mixed crowd according to age and trendiness.
Dansen Bij Jansen
11 Handboogstraat
A popular student disco that also attracts non-students.

Escape
Rembrandtplein 11
Big disco with variety of music and
theme nights and a mixed crowd.

Havana
Reguliersdwarsstraat 17
Club for gay clientele and people
who like to party hard.

House of Soul
Amstelstraat 32A
This place tries to live up to its
name with various DJs on hand
keeping things swinging and soulful.

Ministry
Reguliersdwarsstraat 12
Offers something for everyone from
Groove to Soul, Hip Hop and beyond.

Odeon
Singel 460
Elegant 17th-century house
converted into disco and café, with
a mixed, suitably smart clientele as
well as students.

Sinners in Heaven
3 Wagenstraat
This attracts a more "up-market"
crowd who come to see and be
seen and dance the night away.

Trance Buddha
Oudezijds Voorburgwal 216
Stylish and relaxed club.

Vakzuid
Olympisch Stadion 35
In the southern part of the city, this
new spot is *the* place to lounge,
attracting a mix of creative and city
types. The Quincy Lounge on
Sunday afternoon is where people
begin dancing early.

Comedy Cafés

Comedy has become popular in
Amsterdam in recent years. There
are places to go offering English-
speaking entertainment, from
stand-up comedy at two local clubs
to the improvisational techniques of
the Boom Chicago comedy troupe.

Boom Chicago Theater
Leidseplein 12
Tel: 423 0101 for reservations.
Restaurant on the premises.

Comedy Café
Max Euweplein 43
Tel: 638 3971
Many comedians from the US, UK
and Canada, and an occasional
"open mike" evening.

Shopping

What to Buy

Bargains are a rarity in Amsterdam
but browsing is fun, particularly in the
markets and specialist shops. Avoid
the tourist areas and high streets,
where you won't find anything you
can't find at home. Instead, go where
the locals shop: on the nine small
streets which run adjacent to
Prinsengracht and Herengracht
canals, between Leidsestraat and
Raadhuisstraat. There are boutiques
specialising in buttons, candles,
custom-made handbags and wallets,
erotic lingerie, kites and much more.

Most museums have interesting
gift shops, especially the Jewish
Historical Museum, Amsterdams
Historisch Museum, Maritime
Museum, NEMO and the Nieuwe
Kerk. The Rijksmuseum and Van
Gogh Museum have a shared gift
shop on Museumplein that has a
broad selection of items.

Where to Buy

Antiques
Nieuwe Spiegelstraat is lined with
small and immaculate antiques
shops selling a fascinating range of
items: old Dutch tiles, copper and
brass, glass, pewter, Russian icons,
prints and paintings, Delftware,
period jewellery, Asian *objets d'art*,
Art Deco, medical instruments,
snuff boxes, clocks and dolls. The
dealers have a lot of expertise as
well as international reputations and
welcome interested browsers (*see
page 169*). In markets, beware of
imitation antique copper and brass.

Art and Reproductions
The major museums and art
galleries sell excellent reproductions
of their paintings, particularly the

Rijksmuseum, Van Gogh Museum
and Stedelijk (*see page 200*).

Numerous small commercial
galleries sell original oil paintings,
watercolours, drawings, engravings
and sculpture. For old prints and
engravings, try the **Antiekmarkt de
Looier**, Elandsgracht 109.

Books
The city has an exceptionally large
choice of books, both new and
second-hand. For second-hand
English-language books, try the **Book
Exchange**, Kloveniersburgwal 58 or
Book Traffic at Leliegracht 50. For
new English-language books try **The
American Book Center**, Kalverstraat
185 or **Waterstone's**, Kalverstraat
152. **Scheltema** in Koningsplein
boasts six storeys of books,
including an antiquarian section and
a café. The **Athenaeum Boekhandel
& Nieuwscentrum**, Spui 14–16, has
a superb selection of literature in a
splendid Art Nouveau setting and a
competent staff. **Architectura &
Natura** specialises in books on
architecture, nature and gardens.
Premsela (at 78 Van Baerlestraat)
and **Art Book** (126 Van Baerlestraat)
both specialise in art and artists.

There are many antiquarian
booksellers in the streets around
the Spui, where it is possible to get
a list of the city's antiquarian shops.
Every Friday on the Spui square, an
Antiquarian Book Market is held
from 10am–6pm. In summer there
are book markets held one Sunday
a month at either Dam Square or in
front of the Muziektheater.

For gay and lesbian books, go to
Boekhandel Vrolijk, Paleisstraat
135, the largest gay and lesbian
bookshop in Europe, or **Vrowen in
Druk**, Westermarkt 5, which sells
second-hand and antiquarian books
about and by women. Try also
Intermale, Spuistraat 251.

Clothing
Amsterdam has several department
stores, the most prestigious of which
is **De Bijenkorf** at Damrak 90. It has
several restaurants and cafés and is
a good place to relax between
shopping and museum visits. Rokin,
which extends from Damrak, is the

location for other fine shops and department stores, including Maison de Bonneterie and Vroom & Dreesman. For designer labels, try P.C. Hooftstraat, Leidsestraat, Rokin and Van Baerlestraat; for high street shops, go along Kalverstraat and into the Kalvertoren complex; just up the road is a Marks & Spencer.

Behind the Royal Palace is the elegant Magna Plaza shopping centre. For less conventional boutiques and speciality shops, try the side streets between the canals (Runstraat, Reestraat, Wolvenstraat), the streets around the Jordaan (Prinsenstraat), Damstraat and St Antoniesbreestraat.

Jewellery

Jewellery shops all over town have eyecatching displays of modern and traditional pieces, some original and designed on the spot. But the fact that Amsterdam is a major diamond-cutting centre doesn't mean you'll get them cheap *(see page 277)*.

For hand-made costume jewellery that is elegant and exotic, visit **Christopher Clark** (Molsteeg 4), and for sculptural designs in gold and silver drop by **Anneke Schat**, Spiegelgracht 20 or **Hans Appenzeller**, Grimburgwal 1.

Porcelain and Pottery

Cheap imitations of the familiar blue Delftware are sold all over town. The genuine article, always with a capital "D", is sold at Royal Delft's official retail branch, **Holland Gallery De Munt**, Muntplein 12 and on Spiegelgracht.

Focke & Meltzer, with branches at Gelderlandplein 149 and the Okura Hotel *(see page 268)*, have a good choice of porcelain, pottery and glass, and some attractive reproduction Delft tiles. For a huge range of antique tiles, try **Eduard Kramer**, Nieuwe Spiegelstraat 64.

Gifts

Tulips and bulbs are always popular. If you fail to get them at the flower market, you can buy them at higher prices at the airport. Other things typically Dutch are cigars (the best-known shop is **Hajenius**, Rokin 92)

Sex Shops

Almost everybody who visits Amsterdam is curious about the city's many sex shops, but the ones that you see in the Red Light District are so sleazy on the outside that even the most curious and daring tourist is likely to hesitate. Yet once you are inside the atmosphere is low-key with friendly, sensitive and knowledgeable staff.

Female & Partners at Spuistraat 100 sells erotic clothing and articles for women in a small shop just minutes from Dam Square. They carry the Marlies Dekkers line of lingerie, among others, which

and chocolates. For the latter, try **Pompadour** at Huidenstraat 12, **Jordino** at Haarlemmerdijk 25 and **Bonbon Jeannette** in Centraal Station, which has a superb selection; Droste and Van Houten are popular brand names.

In terms of cheese, Edam and Gouda are household names but they come in a variety of types depending on their age, fat content and flavouring – *jonge* (young), *belegen* (medium) and *oude* (old). *Leidsekaas* is cheese made with cumin. For those who like to garden, a pair of clogs makes a practical souvenir.

Schiphol Airport

There is an enormous range of goods at Schiphol Airport. Apart from duty-free goods, there is an excellent food section, selling smoked Dutch eel and cheeses, and shops specialising in bulbs and seeds, flowers, Delftware, clothes and souvenirs. Although quite pricey, you can also find some unusual and affordable gifts here.

Tax Refunds

Non-EU residents are entitled to a refund of most of the 17.5 percent sales tax (VAT) levied on individual items costing in excess of €137. The leaflet *Tax Free for Tourists*,

includes bras and panties creatively designed to put a little spice in your life, in basic black, white or red. There are also a variety of sex toys for sale. No need to feel embarrassed. The clientele is made up mainly of women or couples.

The next stop is usually the **Condomerie** (Warmoesstraat 141) which sells hundreds of condoms in a wide variety of colours, shapes and scents. Again, it is operated by a friendly, female staff. Other options are: **Mail & Female** (Prinsengracht 489) and the **Christine le Duc** shops around the city.

available at Schiphol Airport and the VVV office, explains the procedure and shopkeepers are always happy to help. For information, call **Global Refund:** 023-524 1909.

Markets

All markets are held Monday to Saturday unless otherwise stated:
"Floating" Flower Market: Singel. Dazzling flower displays, many sold from barges. Some stalls will pack and export bulbs. Reasonable prices and worth seeing, even if you don't intend to buy.
Albert Cuypstraat: Large bustling general market with a wide choice of food, household goods, clothes, etc *(see page 230)*.
Boerenmarkt (Farmers' Market): Held Saturdays at Noorderkerkplein, with organic fruits, vegetables, fresh herbs, baked goods, cheeses, juices, and related wares from massage oil to ceramic pots.
Book Market: 10am–6pm Fridays on the Spui Square.
Oudemanhuispoort: Passageway with stalls selling antique books and prints.
Stamp Market: N.Z. Voorburgwal. Stamps and coins, held on Wednesday and Saturday.
Waterlooplein: Extensive flea market with a lot of junk and occasional bargains; clothes, books, records and antiques.

Sport

Spectator Sports

Football

Amsterdam's Ajax is one of the top European clubs. Home matches are played at the Amsterdam ArenA, Bijlmermeer, in the southeastern part of the city (take the Metro to the Strandvliet exit). Tickets can be bought at the gate or booked in advance from the vvv or by writing to Ajax Travel, p/a Packages, PO Box 12522, 1100 AM Amsterdam (fax: 311-1945; e-mail: tickets@ ajax.nl).

Groups of 10 or more can take a 2-hour tour of the Amsterdam ArenA, which includes an audio-visual presentation and coffee (tel: 311-1336 for reservations). The Ajax Museum (tel: 311-1444) is also worth visiting, though it is closed on match days.

Athletics

In May 2000, the Olympic Stadium reopened and will host various athletic events once again.

Participant Sports

Cycling

The Dutch are a nation of cyclists and the country is crisscrossed with cycle paths and routes. You can either hire a bike *(see page 266)* and set off independently, or opt for a bike excursion, which will include bike hire, a cheese farm visit and boat rides. Information from vvv.

The Amsterdamse Bos, southwest of Amsterdam, offers several bike trails *(see page 229)*.

Golf

The greens closest to the city centre are at the Golf & Conference

Centre Amstelborgh, 6 Borchlandweg, tel: 697 5000. Open year-round.

Ice Skating

If it's cold enough, you can skate on the canals or at a new skating rink at the Museumplein, and there is also year-round skating at the Jaap Edenbaan ice-skating rink, 64 Radioweg, tel: 694 9894.

Squash

Squash City, Ketelmakerstraat 6, has squash courts, aerobics classes, showers and sauna. Tel: 626 7883 for information.

Swimming

De Mirandabad, De Mirandalaan 9, has both indoor and outdoor pools and the Marnixbad, Marnixplein 9, is an indoor pool with slides.

Watersports

Canoes, rowing boats and windsurfing boards can be hired in the Amsterdamse Bos. Canal bikes (similar to pedaloes) can be hired at various points in the city.

Language

Useful Words

Almost every Dutch person speaks English, but it is useful to be able to recognise some words and phrases in timetables and menus. You will also gain respect if you try to speak the language, however hesitantly.

Days of the Week
Monday *Maandag*
Tuesday *Dinsdag*
Wednesday *Woensdag*
Thursday *Donderdag*
Friday *Vrijdag*
Saturday *Zaterdag*
Sunday *Zondag*

Numbers
One *Een*
Two *Twee*
Three *Drie*
Four *Vier*
Five *Vijf*
Six *Zes*
Seven *Zeven*
Eight *Acht*
Nine *Negen*
Ten *Tien*
Twenty *Twintig*
Thirty *Dertig*
Forty *Veertig*
Fifty *Vijftig*
Sixty *Zestig*
Seventy *Zeventig*
Eighty *Tachtig*
Ninety *Negentig*
Hundred *Honderd*

Greetings and Pleasantries
hello/goodbye *dag (pronounced "dach")*
good morning *goedenmorgen*
good afternoon *goedenmiddag*
good evening *goedenavond*
goodbye *tot ziens*

Dutch Pronunciation

Eavesdropping on any Dutch conversation, one could be forgiven for thinking that Dutch people constantly need to clear their throat! This is, of course, not the case; they are merely speaking their native language which regularly uses a guttural consonant similar to the "ch" in the Scottish word loch. In Dutch terms this is known as the "soft g", although the "hard g" sounds almost the same – if you look at Dutch words that begin with a "g", then you can reasonably assume the word starts with that infamous "ch". This is important if, for example, you wish to greet someone with a "goedemorgen" (good morning);

pronouncing the first or second "g" without the "ch" will almost certainly identify you as German. Don't worry about being wrongly identified though; any attempt you may make at speaking Dutch will be received as a compliment.

To this end, here are a few tips on Dutch pronunciation:

Consonants

As a rule, the "hard consonants" such as t, k, s and p are pronounced almost the same as in English, but sometimes a little softer. For example, the Dutch would refer to little as "liddle". j is pronounced as a y (*ja* meaning yes is pronounced ya)

v is pronounced as f (*vis* meaning fish is pronounced fiss)
je is pronounced as yer
tje is pronounced as ch (*botje* meaning little bone is pronounced botchyer)

Vowels

ee is pronounced as ay (*nee* meaning no is pronounced nay)
oo is pronounced as o (*hoop* meaning hope is also pronounced as hope)
ij is pronounced as eay (*ijs* meaning ice cream is pronounced ace)
a is pronounced as u (*bank* also meaning bank is pronounced as bunk)

see you later *tot straks*
thank you very much *dank u wel*
please *als't u blieft*
I am sorry, pardon *neemt u mij niet kwalijk* (but these days most people just use the English "sorry")
yes *ja*
no *nee*

Out and About
open *open*
closed *gesloten*
entrance *ingang*
exit *uitgang*
admission free *vrije toegang*
left *links*
right *rechts*
church *kerk*
theatre *theater*
cinema *bioscoop*

Street Signs
no entry *verboden toegang*
through traffic *doorgaand verkeer*
no parking *niet parkeren*
hospital *ziekenhuis*
police *politie*
fire brigade *brandweer*

Bars and Cafés
bottle *fles*
glass *glas*
cup *kop*
lager *bier*
Dutch gin *jenever*
coffee *koffie*

wine *wijn*
liqueur *likeur*
no smoking *verboden te roken*

Restaurants
restaurant *restaurant*
voorgerecht *starter*
hoofdgerecht *main course*
nagerecht *dessert*
soep *soup*
vis *fish*
kabeljauw *cod*
tong *sole*
haring *herring*
zalm *salmon*
forel *trout*
paling *eel*
schol *plaice*
vlees *meat*
varkensvlees *pork*
varkenshaas *pork tenderloin*
varkenskotelet *pork chop*
varkenslapje *pork cutlet*
varkenslever *pork liver*
rundvlees *beef*
biefstuk *beefsteak*
lendebiefstuk *rump steak*
sirloin *sirloin*
lamsvlees *lamb*
lamsbout *leg of lamb*
lamskarbonade *lamb chop*
lamskotelet *lamb cutlet*
kip *chicken*
eend *duck*
wilde *game*
groenten *vegetables*

Newsagents and Post Offices
newspaper *krant*
magazines *tijdschriften*
how much does it cost? *wat kost dit?*
airmail *luchtpost*
ordinary mail *gewone post*
registered *aangetekend*
stamp *postzegel*

Further Reading

There are surprisingly few books on Amsterdam that go beyond the practicalities of staying in the city. But there's plenty of choice for those who want to steep themselves in specific themes such as history, art and architecture.

History

Amsterdam: A Brief Life of the City by Geert Mak (Harvill Press 1999). **A Short History of Amsterdam** by Richter Roegholt (Amsterdam Historical Museum) is packed with historical information on the city and is available from the Amsterdam Historical Museum (see page 131).
The Guide to the Jewish Historical Museum by Judith Belinfante, Julie-Marthe Cohen and Edward van Voolen, provides comprehensive coverage of the history of Amsterdam's Jews, the Jewish community, walking tours of the areas, and the shops and restaurants that are still the centre of Jewish daily life. No real competition, however, for the world-famous *Diary of Anne Frank*, still one of the most compelling reads of its time.

Art and Architecture

Amsterdam Architecture: A Guide edited by Guus Kemme (Uitgeverij Thoth). The most comprehensive guide to the city's buildings, old and new, describing more than 250 in detail, with lots of illustrations.
The Amsterdam School of Architecture by Maristella Casciato (010 Publishers 1996).
Dutch Painting by R.H. Fuch (Thames and Hudson). One of the numerous books written on Dutch art, this volume (by the director of the Stedelijk Museum) is an invaluable introduction to a huge subject.

Dutch Art and Architecture 1600–1800 by Jakob Rosenberg, Seymour Slive and E.H. ter Kuile (The Pelican History of Art). An admirable and highly detailed study by three of the greatest authorities on Dutch art.

Other Insight Guides

Europe is comprehensively covered within the collection of more than 450 books that make up Apa Publications' three series of guides covering the world: **Insight Guides**, which provide a full cultural background and top-quality photography; **Insight Compact Guides**, which combine portability with encyclopedia-like attention to detail and are ideal for on-the-spot reference; and **Insight Pocket Guides**, which highlight recommendations from a local host and include a full-size fold-out map.
Titles which highlight destinations in this part of Europe include:

Insight Guide: The Netherlands, a companion to the present volume, captures the essence of the Netherlands with incisive text and memorable photography.

Insight Guide: Belgium surveys the entire country with insightful text and superb photography, and **Insight Guide: Brussels** focuses on the capital city. There's also a Pocket Guide and a Compact Guide to Brussels.

Compact Guides to the Netherlands and Amsterdam are the perfect on-the-spot companions. Text, photographs and maps are all carefully cross-referenced for maximum practicality in this superbly portable format.

Feedback

We do our best to ensure the information in our books is as accurate and up-to-date as possible. The books are updated on a regular basis, using local contacts, who painstakingly add, amend and correct as required. However, some mistakes and omissions are inevitable and we are ultimately reliant on our readers to put us in the picture.
We would welcome your feedback on any details related to your experiences using the book "on the road". Maybe we recommended a hotel that you liked (or another that you didn't), as well as interesting new attractions, or facts and figures you have found out about the country itself. The more details you can give us (particularly with regard to addresses, e-mails and telephone numbers), the better.
We will acknowledge all contributions, and we'll offer an Insight Guide to the best letters received.

Please write to us at:
**Insight Guides
PO Box 7910
London SE1 1WE
United Kingdom**
Or send e-mail to:
insight@apaguide.demon.co.uk

ART & PHOTO CREDITS

INSIGHT GUIDE
AMSTERDAM

Cartographic Editor **Zoë Goodwin**
Design Consultants
Carlotta Junger, Graham Mitchener
Picture Research
Hilary Genin, Britta Jaschinski

Map Production Laura Morris
© 2002 Apa Publications GmbH & Co.
Verlag KG (Singapore branch)

Index

*Numbers in italics refer to
photographs*

66 I was first drawn to the Insight Guides by the excellent "Nepal" volume. I can think of no book which so effectively captures the essence of a country. Out of these pages leaped the Nepal I know – the captivating charm of a people and their culture. I've since discovered and enjoyed the entire Insight Guide series. Each volume deals with a country in the same sensitive depth, which is nowhere more evident than in the superb photography. **99**

Sir Edmund Hillary

INSIGHT GUIDES

The classic series that puts you in the picture

Alaska
Amazon Wildlife
American Southwest
Amsterdam
Argentina
Arizona & Grand Canyon
Asia, East
Asia, Southeast
Australia
Austria
Bahamas
Bali
Baltic States
Bangkok
Barbados
Barcelona
Beijing
Belgium
Belize
Berlin
Bermuda
Boston
Brazil
Brittany
Brussels
Buenos Aires
Burgundy
Burma (Myanmar)
Cairo
California
California, Southern
Canada
Caribbean
Channel Islands
Chicago
Chile
China
Continental Europe
Corsica
Costa Rica
Crete
Cuba
Cyprus
Czech & Slovak Republics
Delhi, Jaipur & Agra
Denmark
Dominican Rep. & Haiti

Dublin
East African Wildlife
Eastern Europe
Ecuador
Edinburgh
Egypt
England
Finland
Florence
Florida
France
France, Southwest
French Riviera
Gambia & Senegal
Germany
Glasgow
Gran Canaria
Great Britain
Great Railway Journeys
  of Europe
Greece
Greek Islands
Guatemala, Belize
  & Yucatán
Hawaii
Hong Kong
Hungary
Iceland
India
India, South
Indonesia
Ireland
Israel
Istanbul
Italy
Italy, Northern
Italy, Southern
Jamaica
Japan
Jerusalem
Jordan
Kenya
Korea
Laos & Cambodia
Lisbon
London
Los Angeles

Madeira
Madrid
Malaysia
Mallorca & Ibiza
Malta
Mauritius, Réunion
  & Seychelles
Melbourne
Mexico
Miami
Montreal
Morocco
Moscow
Namibia
Nepal
Netherlands
New England
New Orleans
New York City
New York State
New Zealand
Nile
Normandy
Norway
Oman & The UAE
Oxford
Pacific Northwest
Pakistan
Paris
Peru
Philadelphia
Philippines
Poland
Portugal
Prague
Provence
Puerto Rico
Rajasthan
Rio de Janeiro

Rome
Russia
St Petersburg
San Francisco
Sardinia
Scandinavia
Scotland
Seattle
Sicily
Singapore
South Africa
South America
Spain
Spain, Northern
Spain, Southern
Sri Lanka
Sweden
Switzerland
Sydney
Syria & Lebanon
Taiwan
Tenerife
Texas
Thailand
Tokyo
Trinidad & Tobago
Tunisia
Turkey
Tuscany
Umbria
USA: On The Road
USA: Western States
US National Parks: West
Venezuela
Venice
Vienna
Vietnam
Wales

The world's largest collection of visual travel guides & maps

Amsterdam Transport